Chloe's THE High-end

IGCSE & MYP MATH
CORE AND EXTENDED

Chloe's The Highend IGCSE & MYP MATH

발 행	2022년 1월 28일 초판 1쇄
	2024년 8월 23일 초판 2쇄
저 자	김수민
발행인	최영민
발행처	헤르몬하우스
주 소	경기도 파주시 신촌로 16
전 화	031 - 8071 - 0088
팩 스	031 - 942 - 8688
전자우편	hermonh@naver.com
출판등록	2015년 3월 27일
등록번호	제406 - 2015 - 31호

ⓒ 김수민 2022. Printed in Korea.

ISBN   979-11-91188-71-4   (53410)

- 책 값은 뒤 표지에 있습니다.
- 헤르몬하우스는 피앤피북의 임프린트 출판사입니다.
- 이 책의 어느 부분도 저작권자나 발행인의 승인 없이 무단 복제하여 이용할 수 없습니다.
- 파본 및 낙장은 구입하신 서점에서 교환하여 드립니다.

Chloe's THE High-end

IGCSE & MYP MATH
CORE AND EXTENDED

김수민 (Chloe Kim) 지음

HERMONHOUSE

Preface

초중고 학창시절 중 고등학교까지 약 9년을 해외에서 공부하면서 가장 힘들었던 부분이 필요한 정보와 자료를 구하는 것이었습니다. 한국에서 중등 교육을 받으며 한국 학습서의 높은 질과 다양성에 익숙해져 있었고 이것이 얼마나 큰 축복인지는 해외생활을 하기 전에는 미쳐 알지 못했습니다. 해외에서 미국과 영국의 교육과정을 공부할 때는 교재의 다양성은 기대하기가 어려웠고 같은 맥락에서 학생들에게 맞는 교재가 거의 없어서 많은 어려움을 겪었습니다. 그래서 유학생들의 선택권이 제한적인 점이 아쉬워 강사생활을 시작하면서 아예 직접 교재 집필을 시작했습니다.

시중에 IGCSE/MYP Math를 공부하는 학생들을 위해 출간된 학습서가 따로 없어 더욱 책임감을 느끼고 집필에 임했습니다. 향후 성공적인 IB Diploma 혹은 A-Level 수료를 위해서 IGCSE, MYP 단계에서 탄탄하게 기본기를 다지는 것이 중요합니다. 단순히 내용을 이해하고 거기서 그치는 것이 아니라, 배운 내용을 확장하는 응용력을 기를 수 있도록 내용을 구성하려 노력한 만큼 학생들에게 많은 도움이 되었으면 좋겠습니다.

최근 영국 수학 교육과정에 큼직한 변화들이 있어 학생들을 당황시키기도 했습니다. 최근 변화 동향과 출제경향을 발빠르게 파악하여 학생들이 실전에 제대로 대비할 수 있도록 내용을 담았습니다. 그리고 지난 10년 이상을 다양한 학생들을 지도하면서 받은 피드백과 그동안 쌓아온 노하우를 이 교재에 빠짐없이 넣고자 노력했습니다.

이 교재를 출간할 수 있도록 물심양면으로 지원해주신 마스터프렙 권주근 대표님께 감사드리며 또한 유학전문 출판사의 역량을 보여주신 헤르몬하우스의 관계자 여러분들께도 감사드립니다. 저를 믿고 응원해주신 부모님께도 항상 감사합니다. 앞으로도 질 높은 강의와 교재로 학생들에게 좋은 영향력을 끼치는 강사로 찾아뵙겠습니다.

2021년 겨울의 길목에서 김수민 드림

이 책의 특징

✔ IGCSE 가이드라인과 기출문제를 완벽하게 분석하고 반영한 책

40페이지가 넘는 IGCSE 가이드라인을 빠짐없이 꼼꼼하게 읽고 최신 기출문제까지 전부 풀어보고 분석한 내용을 담은 체계적인 교재입니다. 개념을 이해하고 끝나는 것이 아니라, 실전까지 학생들이 확장하고 응용할 수 있도록 문제들을 구성했습니다.

✔ 학생들이 어려워하는, 그리고 가려운 부분을 콕콕 짚어 해결해주는 책

오랜 강의 경력으로 학생들이 공통적으로 어떤 부분에서 어려움을 느끼고 헷갈려 하는 지를 잘 파악하고 있기 때문에, 그런 학생들의 혼란을 미리 차단하고 명확하게 이해할 수 있도록 집필하려 노력했습니다.

✔ 기본에 충실한 책

IGCSE, MYP는 IB, A-Level 들어가기 전 기본기를 탄탄하게 다져야 하는 중요한 단계입니다. 이 과정을 제대로 공부하지 않고 IB 혹은 A-Level 과정으로 진학하여 고생하는 학생들을 정말 많이 봤습니다. 이 시점에서 학생들이 꼭 알고 넘어가야 할 부분들을 전부 담았습니다.

※ 저자직강 인터넷 강의는 SAT, AP No.1 인터넷 강의 사이트인 마스터프랩(www.masterprep.net)에서 보실 수 있습니다.

저자 소개

중고등학교 시절부터 이과 과목에 두각을 나타내며, 깊이 있는 이과 커리큘럼을 밟아온 강사이다. 고등학교 시절, 특히 수학분야에서 재미를 느끼고 Harvard-MIT Mathematics Tournament (HMMT), University of Michigan Math Competition 등 유명 대학에서 주최하는 수학경시대회에서 수상경력을 쌓으면서 미시간 한국 학부모들 사이에서 입소문을 탔다.

그로 인해 여러 한국 학부모들의 러브콜을 받았으며, 고등학교 시절부터 이미 다른 고등학생들을 가르치기 시작했으며 수업을 받은 학생들이 좋은 결과로 이어지다 보니 자연스럽게 전문강사의 길로 이어지게 되었다.

남아프리카공화국에서 5년, 한국에서 7년, 미국에서 4년을 교육받으면서 영국, 한국, 미국 교육과정을 모두 경험해본 특이한 이력을 가지고 있다. 이런 이력이 현재는 다양한 국제학교 학생에 대한 눈높이 교육을 할 수 있는 강점으로 작용하고 있다.

김수민 (Chloe Kim)
고등학교까지 약 9년을 해외 학교에서 공부
고려대학교 전기전자전파공학부 졸업
마스터프렙(www.masterprep.net) 수학, 물리강사

10년이 넘는 경력과 더해져 미국 및 영국의 수학, 물리 교육의 변화추이를 잘 파악하고 끊임없는 교재연구를 하고 이를 강의에 반영하고 있다. 그래서 유학전문 원장님들과 학부형들 사이에서 믿고 추천할 수 있는 수학 및 물리 강사로 인정받고 있다.

현재 유학 수학, 물리 강사로 활동 중이며, 이 교재를 시작으로 더 많은 유학 수학 및 물리 교재를 집필하고자 힘쓰고 있다.

Contents

Unit 1 Number   9

Ch.1	Numbers and Operations	10
Ch.2	Powers and Roots	30
Ch.3	Factors and Multiples	37
Ch.4	Accuracy	42
Ch.5	Ratio and Proportion	46
Ch.6	Percentage	52

Unit 2 Algebra   57

Ch.7	Algebraic Expression	58
Ch.8	Equations and Inequalities	69
Ch.9	Sequences	79
Ch.10	Variation	83
Ch.11	Functions	85

Unit 3 Graphs   89

Ch.12	Linear Functions	90
Ch.13	Quadratic and Cubic Functions	95
Ch.14	Differentiation	103
Ch.15	Inequality Graphs	109
Ch.16	Graphs in Practical Situations	113

Unit 4 Mensuration   117

Ch.17	Measures	118
Ch.18	Geometrical Terms	123
Ch.19	Two Dimensional Figures	129
Ch.20	Three Dimensional Figures	133

Unit 5 Geometry   139

Ch.21	Geometrical Constructions	140
Ch.22	Similarity	143
Ch.23	Congruent Triangles	148
Ch.24	Symmetry	152
Ch.25	Basic Angle Properties	159
Ch.26	Angles in Polygons	164
Ch.27	Angles in Circles	167

Unit 6 Trigonometry   173

Ch.28	Right Triangles	174
Ch.29	Trigonometric Functions	180
Ch.30	Non-right Triangles	186

Unit 7 Vectors and Transformations   193

Ch.31	Vectors	194
Ch.32	Transformations	201

Unit 8 Probability   215

Ch.33	Simple Probability	216
Ch.34	Further Probability	221

Unit 9 Statistics   229

Ch.35	Classifying and Organizing Data	230
Ch.36	Displaying Data with Charts	234
Ch.37	Central Tendency and Spread	239
Ch.38	Continuous Data Representation	244
Ch.39	Scatter Diagram	247

Answer   250

Unit 1
Number

- Ch.1 Numbers and Operations
- Ch.2 Powers and Roots
- Ch.3 Factors and Multiples
- Ch.4 Accuracy
- Ch.5 Ratio and Proportion
- Ch.6 Percentage

1 Number and Operations

1.1 Numbers

Types of Numbers

Natural Numbers: Whole numbers including positive numbers only

$$\mathbb{N} = \{1, 2, 3, ...\}$$

Integers: Whole numbers including positive, negative, and zero

$$\mathbb{Z} = \{..., -3, -2, -1, 0, 1, 2, 3, ...\}$$

Rational Numbers: A number that can be expressed as a fraction of two integers

$$\mathbb{Q} = \{n \mid n = \frac{p}{q}, \text{ where } p \text{ and } q \text{ are integers}, q \neq 0\}$$

Irrational Numbers: Real numbers that cannot be represented as a simple fraction of two integers

$$\mathbb{I} = \{\pi, e, \sqrt{2}, ...\}$$

Real Numbers: Existing numbers, which can be plotted on a number line

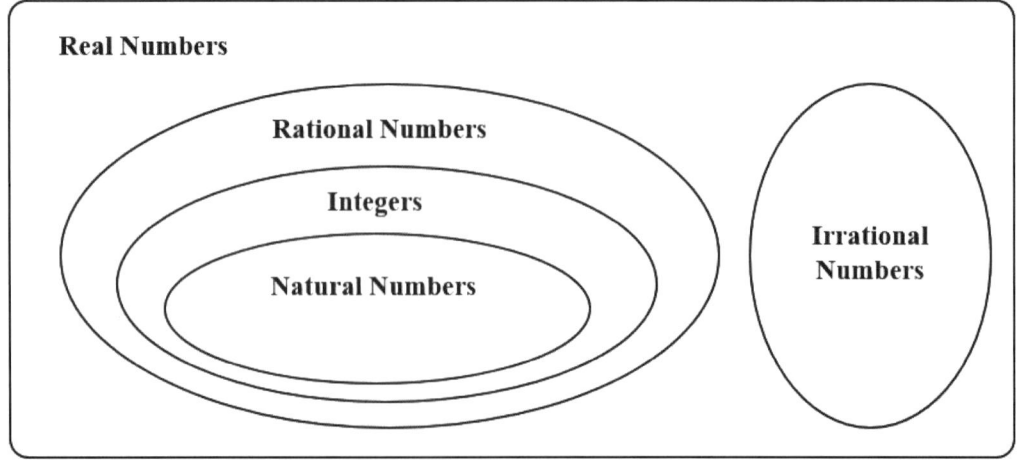

Example 1.1.1

$$\sqrt{3}+5 \quad 0.4\dot{5} \quad \frac{\pi}{5} \quad 0.67 \quad \frac{3\pi}{\pi} \quad -5 \quad \frac{20}{7}$$

(a) List all integers.

(b) List all rational numbers.

(c) List all irrational numbers.

(d) List all real numbers.

1.2 Directed Numbers

> **Directed Number**
>
> Numbers with magnitude and direction

Example 1.2.1

(a) After Daisy decided to make a cup of hot chocolate, she boiled tap water of 25°C. The temperature has risen by 55°C. What is the temperature of the water?

(b) After 12 minutes, it cooled by 34°C. What is the current temperature of the hot chocolate?

Example 1.2.2

A shark is at a depth of 130m. If the ocean floor is 746m below the surface, how far is the shark from the ocean floor?

1.3 Decimals

Decimal Addition and Subtraction

(1) Write the numbers in vertical column aligning the decimal points.
(2) Add placeholder zeros when needed.
(3) Add or subtract. Carry or borrow when needed.

Example 1.3.1

Evaluate the following without using a calculator.

(a) $23.74 + 1.6$ (b) $5 - 2.78$ (c) $3.1 - 8.59$

Decimal Multiplication

(1) Get rid of the decimal points and multiply the numbers as whole numbers.
(2) Count the digits after decimals in both numbers and find the sum.
(3) Shift the decimal point so that the number of digits to the right of the decimal point equals the sum obtained from step (2).

Example 1.3.2

Evaluate the following without using a calculator.

(a) 5.7×0.6 (b) 1.2×3.01

Decimal Division

(1) Move the decimal point of the divisor until it becomes a whole number.
(2) Move the decimal point of the dividend by the same number of hops from step (1).
(3) Place the decimal point in the quotient lined up with the decimal point of the dividend.
(4) Divide the numbers.

Example 1.3.3

Evaluate the following without using a calculator.

(a) $7.224 \div 0.08$

(b) $0.561 \div 0.06$

Mixed Operations with Decimals

(1) Brackets or parentheses
(2) Exponents
(3) Multiplication or division
(4) Addition or subtraction

Example 1.3.4

Evaluate the following and check your answers with a calculator.

(a) $(0.15 + 0.1) \times 0.04$

(b) $0.15 + 0.1 \times 0.04$

1.4 Fractions

Fraction Addition and Subtraction

(1) If there is a mixed number, change it to an improper fraction.
(2) If the fractions have different denominators, change them to an equivalent form with a common denominator.
(3) Add or subtract the numerators and leave the denominator. Simplify if possible.

Example 1.4.1

Evaluate the following without using a calculator.

(a) $\dfrac{2}{7} + \dfrac{1}{3}$

(b) $3\dfrac{7}{8} - 1\dfrac{5}{12}$

Fraction Multiplication

(1) If there is a mixed number, change it to an improper fraction.
(2) Multiply the numerators and multiply the denominators separately.
(3) Simplify if possible.

Example 1.4.2

Evaluate the following without using a calculator.

(a) $\dfrac{5}{6} \times \dfrac{3}{4}$

(b) $2\dfrac{2}{3} \times 3\dfrac{1}{2}$

Fraction Division

(1) If there is a mixed number, change it to an improper fraction.
(2) Take the reciprocal of the second fraction and multiply it with the first fraction.
(3) Simplify if possible.

Example 1.4.3

Evaluate the following without using a calculator.

(a) $\dfrac{12}{5} \div \dfrac{16}{3}$

(b) $5\dfrac{3}{5} \div 2\dfrac{1}{3}$

Mixed Operations with Fractions

(1) Brackets or parentheses
(2) Exponents
(3) Multiplication or division
(4) Addition or subtraction

Example 1.4.4

Evaluate the following and check your answers with a calculator.

(a) $1\dfrac{1}{2} \times \left(\dfrac{2}{3} - \dfrac{3}{10}\right)$

(b) $1\dfrac{2}{3} \div \left(\dfrac{2}{7} + \dfrac{1}{4}\right)$

1.5 Conversion Between Decimals and Fractions

Converting a Fraction to Decimal

Divide the numerator by the denominator.

Example 1.5.1

Change the following fractions to decimals.

(a) $\dfrac{3}{8}$
(b) $7\dfrac{23}{50}$
(c) $\dfrac{1}{3}$

Converting a Decimal to a Fraction

(1) Rewrite the decimal as a fraction with a denominator of 1.
(2) Multiply the numerator and denominator by 10^n, where n is the number of digits after the decimal point of the numerator.
(3) Simplify the fraction if possible.

Example 1.5.2

Convert the following decimals to fractions.

(a) 0.25
(b) 13.22

Converting a Recurring Decimal to a Fraction (EXTENDED ONLY)

(1) Let x be the recurring decimal and n be the number of recurring digits.

(2) Multiply the recurring decimal by 10^n.

(3) Subtract x and $x \times 10^n$ to eliminate the recurring part.

(4) Make x the subject.

Example 1.5.3 EXTEDNED ONLY

Convert the following recurring decimals to fractions.

(a) $0.\dot{5}$

(b) $0.\dot{1}\dot{2}$

(c) $2.1\dot{4}\dot{5}$

1.6 Using a Calculator

Difference between "Subtract" and "Negative"

Example: $-2 \times (-3 - 5)$

[(-)] [2] [×] [(] [(-)] [3] [−] [5] [)] [=]

```
-2×(-3-5)
              16
```

Operations with Fractions

Example: $1\frac{2}{3} \div \left(\frac{2}{7} + \frac{1}{4}\right)$

[(] [1] [+] [▤] [2] [▽] [3] [▶] [)] [÷] [(] [▤]
[2] [▽] [7] [▶] [+] [▤] [1] [▽] [4] [▶] [)] [=]

$$\left(1+\frac{2}{3}\right) \div \left(\frac{2}{7}+\frac{1}{4}\right)$$

$$\frac{28}{9}$$

Conversion Between Decimals and Fractions

Example 1: Convert $\frac{2}{3}$ to decimal

(1) [▭] [2] [▼] [3] [=]

(2) [S⇔D]

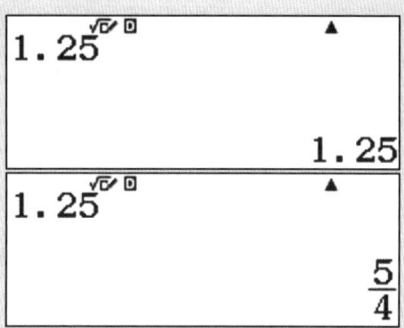

Example 2: Convert 1.25 to fraction

(1) [1] [.] [2] [5] [=]

(2) [S⇔D]

Example 3: Convert $1\frac{2}{3}$ to improper fraction

(1) [1] [+] [▭] [2] [▼] [3] [=]

(2) [SHIFT] [S⇔D]

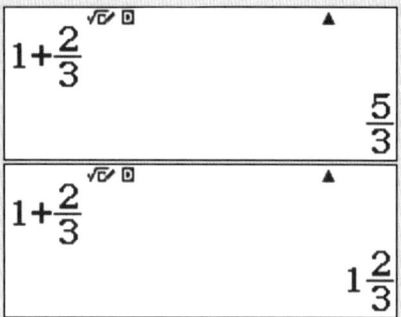

Powers and Roots

Example 1: $3^2 \times 4^{-1}$

[3] [x^2] [×] [4] [$x^\blacksquare$] [(−)] [1] [=]

Display:
$$3^2 \times 4^{-1}$$
$$\frac{9}{4}$$

Example 2: $\sqrt{2} \times \sqrt[3]{2}$

[√☐] [2] [▶] [×] [SHIFT] [√☐] [2] [=]

Display:
$$\sqrt{2} \times \sqrt[3]{2}$$
$$1.781797436$$

Operations with Standard Form

Example: $\dfrac{5 \times 10^{-4}}{2 \times 10^6}$

[▤] [5] [×10^x] [(−)] [4] [▽] [2] [×10^x] [6] [=]

Display:
$$\frac{5 \times 10^{-4}}{2 \times 10^6}$$
$$2.5 \times 10^{-10}$$

Operations with π

Example: $12^2 \times \pi$

[1] [2] [x^2] [×] [SHIFT] [×10^x] [=]

Display:
$$12^2 \times \pi$$
$$144\pi$$

Setting to Degree Mode

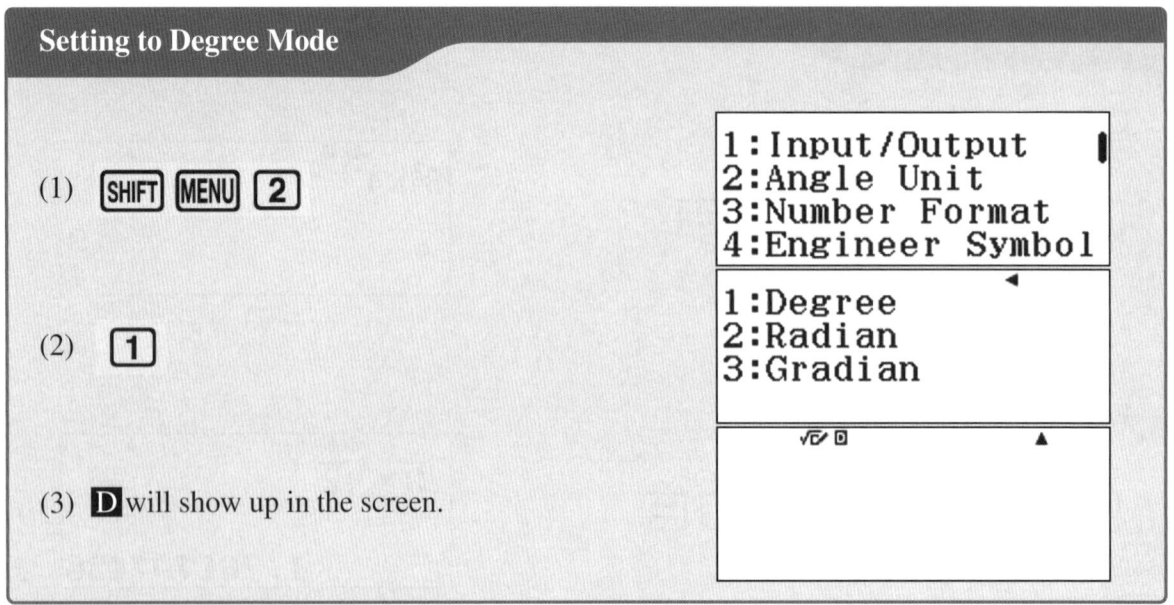

(1) [SHIFT] [MENU] [2]

(2) [1]

(3) **D** will show up in the screen.

Trigonometry

Example 1: sin(30°)

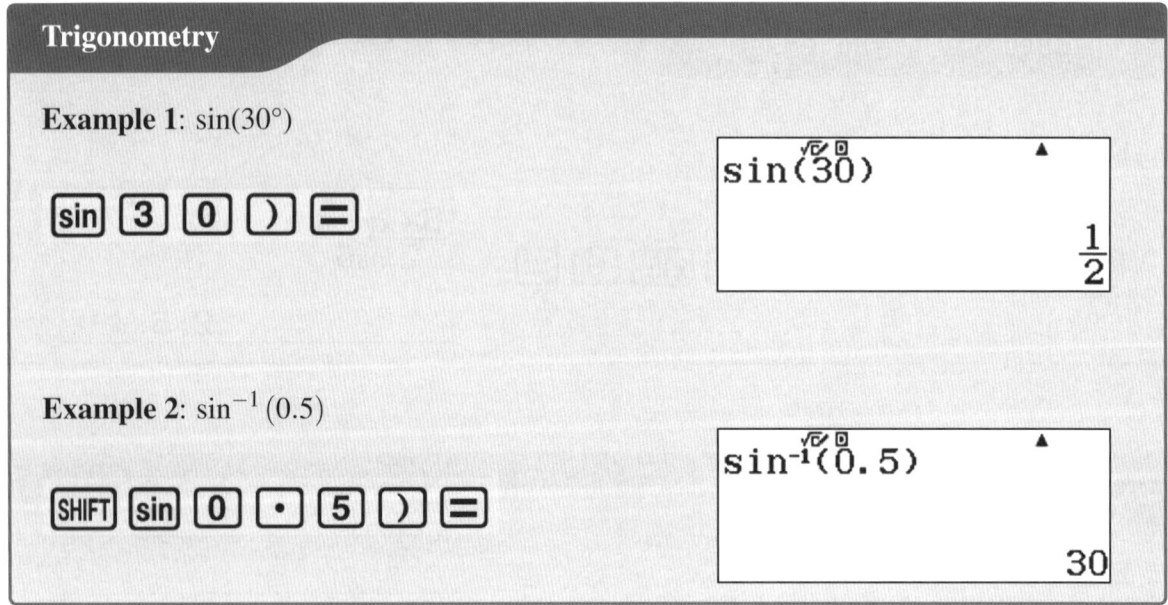

[sin] [3] [0] [)] [=]

Example 2: $\sin^{-1}(0.5)$

[SHIFT] [sin] [0] [.] [5] [)] [=]

Using ANS

Example: $\sqrt{\dfrac{5^2 - 4^2 - 6^2}{-2 \times 4 \times 6 \cos(30°)}}$

(1) [5] [x²] [−] [4] [x²] [−] [6] [x²] [=]

(2) [▭] [Ans] [▼] [(−)] [2] [×] [4] [×] [6] [cos] [3] [0] [)] [=]

(3) [√▭] [Ans] [=]

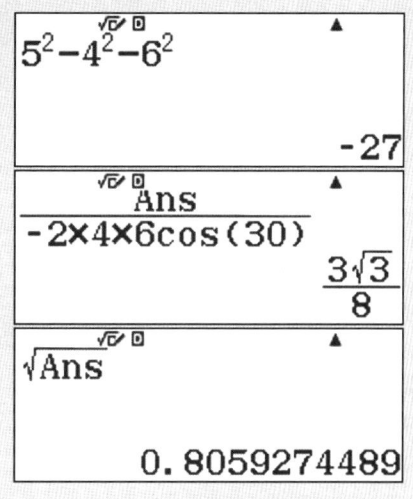

1.7 Calculations and Order

Symbols of Equality and Inequality

$x = y$ → x is equal to y
$x \neq y$ → x is not equal to y
$x > y$ → x is greater than y
$x < y$ → x is less than y
$x \geq y$ → x is greater than or equal to y
$x \leq y$ → x is less than or equal to y

Example 1.7.1

Insert the correct symbol, either =, > or < between each pair of numbers.

(a) -5.1 $\quad$ -5.095 $\qquad$ (b) $\dfrac{3}{8}$ $\quad$ 0.275 $\qquad$ (c) $\dfrac{11}{5}$ $\quad$ 2.201

Ordering

(1) Convert all values to decimals.
(2) Write the numbers in a column with the decimal points lined up.
(3) Compare the digits starting from the leftmost digit and order the numbers.
(4) Compare the next digit and order the numbers. Continue until you reach the rightmost digit.

Example 1.7.2

Write the following numbers in order of magnitude, starting with the smallest.

$$4^{-1} \qquad \sqrt{0.04} \qquad \frac{1}{3} \qquad 0.26 \qquad 0.55^2$$

1.8 Sets and Venn Diagrams

Sets and Elements

Set: A collection of objects.
$$A = \{a, b, c, \ldots\}$$
$$B = \{x : a \leq x \leq b\}$$
$$C = \{x : x \text{ is an integer}\}$$
$$D = \{(x, y) : y = mx + c\}$$

Element: Any one of the distinct objects.

Empty Set: A set with no elements, which is denoted as $\varnothing$

Example 1.8.1

Represent each of the following as a set notation.

(a) Set S contains odd numbers between 10 and 20.

(b) Set A from the Venn diagram on the right.

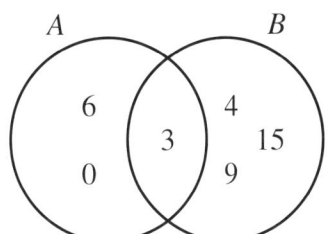

(c) Set B from the Venn diagram on the right.

Number of Elements in a Set

The number of elements in set A is denoted as n(A).

Example 1.8.2

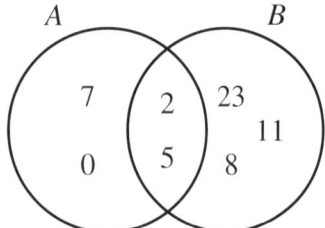

Find n(A) and n(B)

Inclusion in a Set (EXTENDED ONLY)

Symbol	Meaning	Example
$\in$	"… is an element of …"	$2 \in S$
$\notin$	"… is not an element of …"	$3 \notin S$

Example 1.8.3 EXTENDED ONLY

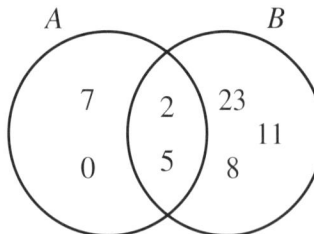

Fill in the black with either $\in$ or $\notin$.

(a) 7 _____ A   (c) 5 _____ A

(b) 2 _____ B   (d) 0 _____ B

Universal Set and Complement of a Set

Universal Set: The set which contains all elements of the other sets. It is denoted as $\mathscr{E}$.

Complement of a Set: Complement of set A is the set of all elements of the universal set with the elements of A excluded. It is denoted as A'.

Example 1.8.4

If $\mathscr{E} = \{1, 2, 3, 4, 5, 6, 7, 8\}$ and $S = \{3, 6, 8\}$,

(a) draw a Venn diagram that shows this information.

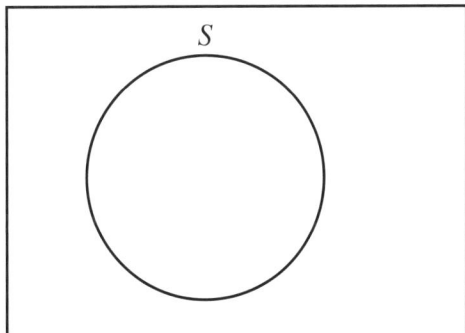

(b) list the set S'.

(c) find n(S) and n(S').

Subsets and Proper Subsets (EXTENDED ONLY)

A is a **subset** of B if every element of A is also contained in B.

A is a **proper subset** of B if every element of A is also contained in B, and $A \neq B$.

Symbol	Meaning	Example
$\subseteq$	A is a subset of B	$A \subseteq B$
$\not\subseteq$	A is not a subset of B	$A \not\subseteq B$
$\subset$	A is a proper subset of B	$A \subset B$
$\not\subset$	A is not a proper subset of B	$A \not\subset B$

Properties of Subsets

(1) Every set is a subset of itself. ($A \subseteq A$, but $A \not\subset A$)

(2) The empty set $\varnothing$ is a subset of every set. ($\varnothing \subseteq A$)

Example 1.8.5 EXTENDED ONLY

If $A = \{2, 5, 6\}$,

(a) list all subsets of A.

(b) list all proper subsets of A.

Example 1.8.6 EXTENDED ONLY

Fill in the blank with $\in, \subset$, or $\subseteq$ so that the statement becomes true. If more than one of them makes the statement true, write all of them.

(a) $\{3\}$ _____ $\{2, 3, 4\}$

(b) 3 _____ $\{2, 3, 4\}$

(c) $\{22, 23, 24, 25\}$ _____ $\{22, 23, 24, 25\}$

(d) $\{1, 2, 3\}$ _____ $\{1, 2, 3, 4\}$

(e) $\varnothing$ _____ 5

(f) $\varnothing$ _____ $\varnothing$

Intersection and Union

Intersection (AND)

The set of all elements that belong to both A and B.

$$A \cap B$$

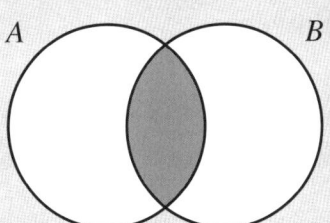

Union (OR)

The set of all elements that belong to either A or B, or both.

$$A \cup B$$

$$n(A \cup B) = n(A) + n(B) - n(A \cap B)$$

Example 1.8.7

If $A = \{2, 4, 7, 8, 9\}$, $B = \{1, 2, 5, 6, 7\}$, and $\mathcal{E} = \{x: x$ is an integer between 1 and 10 inclusive$\}$, draw a Venn diagram to show this information.

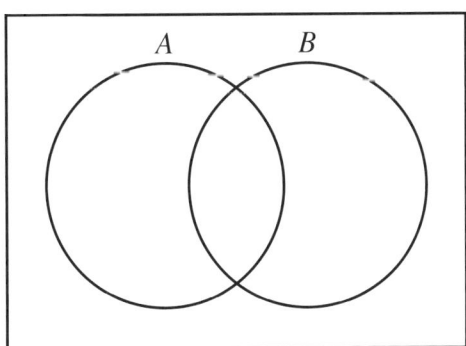

Hence find:

(a) $A \cap B$

(b) $A \cup B$

(c) $A' \cap B$

(d) $A \cup B'$

(e) $n(A' \cup B')$

(f) $n(A' \cap B')$

Unit 1. Number

2 Powers and Roots

2.1 Powers

Square Numbers and Cube Numbers

Square Numbers: A number that is a square of an integer

$$1 \cdot 1 = 1^2 = 1 \qquad 2 \cdot 2 = 2^2 = 4 \qquad 3 \cdot 3 = 3^2 = 9$$

Cube Numbers: A number that is a cube of an integer

$$1 \cdot 1 \cdot 1 = 1^3 = 1 \qquad 2 \cdot 2 \cdot 2 = 2^3 = 8 \qquad 3 \cdot 3 \cdot 3 = 3^3 = 27$$

Indices: A way to express repeated multiplication

$$2 \cdot 2 \cdot 2 \cdot 2 = 2^4 = 16 \rightarrow \text{2 to the power of 4}$$
$$2 \cdot 2 \cdot 2 \cdot 2 \cdot 2 = 2^5 = 32 \rightarrow \text{2 to the power of 5}$$

Example 2.1.1

Find the value of

(a) 5^2

(b) $(-6)^3$

(c) $3^2 \times 5^3$

Root (Fractional Indices)

The n-th root of a is defined as follows:

$$\sqrt[n]{a} = a^{\frac{1}{n}} = b \qquad \text{means} \qquad b^n = a$$

$$2^2 = 4 \;\to\; \sqrt{4} = 4^{\frac{1}{2}} = 2 \qquad \text{square root}$$

$$2^3 = 8 \;\to\; \sqrt[3]{8} = 8^{\frac{1}{3}} = 2 \qquad \text{cube root}$$

$$2^4 = 16 \;\to\; \sqrt[4]{16} = 16^{\frac{1}{4}} = 2 \qquad \text{4-th root}$$

$$2^5 = 32 \;\to\; \sqrt[5]{32} = 32^{\frac{1}{5}} = 2 \qquad \text{5-th root}$$

Example 2.1.2

Find the following:

(a) $\sqrt{25}$

(b) $\sqrt{\dfrac{1}{144}}$

(c) $169^{\frac{1}{2}}$

(d) $\sqrt[3]{\dfrac{8}{27}}$

(e) $(-125)^{\frac{1}{3}}$

(f) $\sqrt[3]{343}$

Reciprocal

A reciprocal of a number is 1 divided by that number $\quad n = \dfrac{1}{n} = n^{-1}$

Negative Indices

$$a^{-n} = \dfrac{1}{a^n}$$

Zero Indices

$$a^0 = 1$$

Example 2.1.3

Evaluate the following without using a calculator.

(a) 3^{-2}

(d) $\dfrac{1}{6^{-2}}$

(b) $\left(\dfrac{1}{5}\right)^{-3}$

(e) $8765^0 \times 7^{-2}$

(c) 965^0

(f) 4×4^{-2}

Properties of Exponents

$$x^a \times x^b = x^{a+b} \qquad \frac{x^a}{x^b} = x^{a-b} \qquad (x^a)^b = x^{a \cdot b}$$

Example 2.1.4

Evaluate the following without using a calculator.

(a) $\dfrac{8^{\frac{1}{3}}}{2^4}$

(b) $5^{\frac{1}{2}} \times 5^{\frac{1}{3}}$

(c) $\dfrac{(5^{\frac{3}{4}})^{\frac{1}{3}} \times 5^{\frac{3}{4}}}{2^{-2}}$

Unit 1. Number

2.2 Roots

Properties of Roots

Multiplication		$\sqrt{a} \times \sqrt{b} = \sqrt{ab}$
Division		$\dfrac{\sqrt{a}}{\sqrt{b}} = \sqrt{\dfrac{a}{b}}$
Addition		$a\sqrt{c} + b\sqrt{c} = (a+b)\sqrt{c}$
Subtraction		$a\sqrt{c} - b\sqrt{c} = (a-b)\sqrt{c}$

Example 2.2.1

Simplify the radical expressions.

(a) $\sqrt{12} \times \sqrt{3}$

(b) $\dfrac{\sqrt{60}}{\sqrt{5}}$

(c) $\sqrt{20} - \sqrt{45}$

34 IGCSE & MYP Math

2.3 Standard Form

Standard Form: Numbers that are too small or too large can be written in standard form $A \times 10^n$, where n is a positive or negative integer and $1 \leq A < 10$.

> **Changing a Number Into Standard Form**
>
> Moving the decimal point to the left $\rightarrow$ Exponent increases
> Moving the decimal point to the right $\rightarrow$ Exponent decreases

Example 2.3.1

Write the following numbers in standard form.

(a) 5600

(b) 948 000

(c) 0.000 726

(d) 0.0108

> **Changing a Number Out of Standard Form**
>
> Positive exponent $\rightarrow$ Move the decimal point to the right
> Negative exponent $\rightarrow$ Move the decimal point to the left

Example 2.3.2

Convert the following numbers to decimals.

(a) 9.82×10^5

(b) 7.01×10^2

(c) 1.23×10^{-6}

(d) 4.22×10^{-4}

Calculations with Standard Form

(1) Change all numbers into standard form.
(2) Work out the powers of 10.
(3) Work out the numbers.
(4) Shift the decimal point if needed.

Example 2.3.3

Calculate the following in standard form.

(a) 51000×6000

(b) $16000 \div 0.008$

3 Factors and Multiples

3.1 Prime

> **Prime Numbers and Prime Factorization**
>
> **Prime Numbers:** A number that has no factors other than itself and 1
>
> $$\mathbb{P} = \{2, 3, 5, 7, 11, 13, 15, 17, 19, 23, ...\}$$
>
> **Prime Factorization:** Breaking down a number into a product of prime numbers

Example 3.1.1

Prime factorize the following numbers.

(a) 24

(b) 20

(c) 60

3.2 Factors

Factors

Factor is a number that divides another number evenly

Example 3.2.1

Find all factors of the following numbers.

(a) 12

(b) 18

(c) 26

Common Factors and Highest Common Factors

Common Factor: A factor that divides two numbers

Highest Common Factor: The greatest factor that divides two numbers

Example 3.2.2

Find the common factors and the highest common factor of the two numbers.

(a) 12 and 30

(b) 15 and 24

(c) 28 and 42

Example 3.2.3

Find the common factors and the highest common factor of the three numbers.

(a) 60, 90, and 120

(b) 56, 42, and 98

(c) 33, 99, and 132

3.3 Multiples

Common Multiples and Least Common Multiples

Common Multiple: A number that is divisible by multiple of numbers

Least Common Multiple: The smallest number that is divisible by multiple of numbers numbers

Example 3.3.1

Find the common multiples and the least common multiple of the two numbers.

(a) 12 and 30

(b) 15 and 21

Example 3.3.2

Find the common multiples and the least common multiple of the three numbers.

(a) 14, 21, 28

(b) 9, 13, 26

(c) 9, 20, 22

4 Accuracy

4.1 Rounding

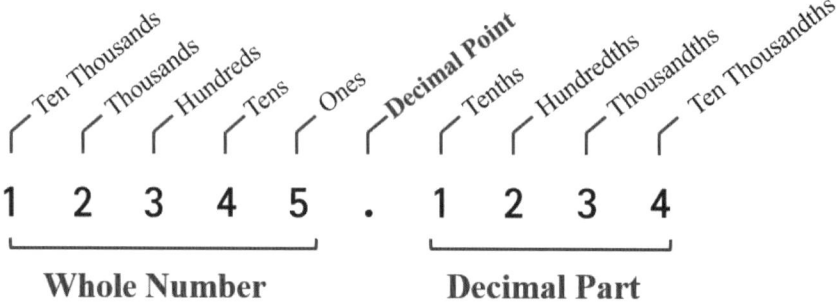

How to round

(1) Identify the digit to the right of the given place value
(2) If the digit is greater than or equal to 5, round up. If the digit is less than 5, round down.

Example 4.1.1

Round 423,991.7425 to the nearest

(a) thousand

(b) hundred

(c) ten

(d) thousandth

(e) hundredth

(f) tenth

Example 4.1.2

Round 12.35299 to

(a) 1 decimal place

(b) 2 decimal place

(c) 3 decimal place

(d) 4 decimal place

How to Count the Number of Significant Figure

(1) Identify the left-most non-zero digit

(2) Count the number of digits until you reach the digit that contains the uncertainty

Example 4.1.3

Identify all significant figures and count the number of significant figures.

(a) 23500000

(b) 0204900

(c) 0.00305890

(d) 10.0

Example 4.1.4

Round 7.6497 to

(a) 1 s.f

(b) 2 s.f

(c) 3 s.f

(d) 4 s.f

4.2 Lower and Upper Bound

Lower and Upper Bound

Lower Bound: Smallest value that would round to the approximated value

Upper Bound: Greatest value that would round to the approximated value

Example 4.2.1

Jim's height is measured as 176cm to the nearest cm. Find the lower bound and upper bound.

(a) Find the lower and upper bound.

(b) Express the range on a number line.

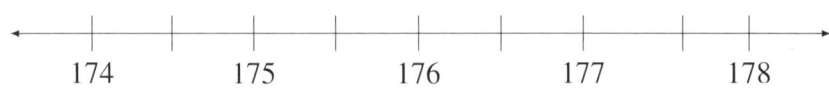

(c) Express the range in inequality.

Lower and Upper Bound of with Operations (EXTENDED ONLY)

Addition:	Lower Bound	=	Lower Bound	+	Lower Bound
	Upper Bound	=	Upper Bound	+	Upper Bound
Subtraction:	Lower Bound	=	Lower Bound	−	Upper Bound
	Upper Bound	=	Upper Bound	−	Lower Bound
Multiplication:	Lower Bound	=	Lower Bound	×	Lower Bound
	Upper Bound	=	Upper Bound	×	Upper Bound
Division:	Lower Bound	=	Lower Bound	÷	Upper Bound
	Upper Bound	=	Upper Bound	÷	Lower Bound

Example 4.2.2 EXTENDED ONLY

Find the upper and lower bounds for the following calculations, given that each number is accurate to 1 decimal place.

(a) $34.2 + 18.6$

(b) $34.2 - 18.6$

(c) 34.2×18.6

(d) $\dfrac{34.2}{18.6}$

5 Ratio and Proportion

5.1 Ratio

Ratio

Ratio: A comparison of two numbers.

(1) Word a to b

(2) Colon $a:b$

(3) Fraction $\dfrac{a}{b}$

Ratios in Simplest Form

$$a \times c : b \times c = a : b$$

Dividing both numbers by the highest common factor (HCF) gives the ratio in simplest form.

Example 5.1.1

Write the following ratios in simplest form.

(a) 24:60

(b) 15:30:105

Dividing a Quantity in the Ratio $a:b$

$$\text{Total} = a+b$$

$$\text{part } a = \text{Quantity} \times \frac{a}{a+b}$$

$$\text{part } b = \text{Quantity} \times \frac{b}{a+b}$$

Example 5.1.2

Divide the following quantities in the ratio given.

(a) Divide 24 in the ratio 1:3.

(b) Divide 400 in the ratio 1:2:5.

Increase and Decrease by a Given Ratio (EXTENDED ONLY)

$$\text{Increasing/Decreasing a quantity by the ratio } a:b = \text{Quantity} \times \frac{a}{b}$$

Example 5.1.3   EXTENDED ONLY

Increase or decrease the following numbers by the given ratios.

(a) Increase 120 by the ratio 6:5.

(b) Decrease 60 by the ratio 2:3.

5.2 Proportion

Direct Proportion

As a increases, b increases $\to$ a is in direct proportion to b

Example 5.2.1

A ribbon of length 50 cm costs $20.

(a) Find the cost of a ribbon of length 3 m.

(b) Find the length of a ribbon that you can purchase with $65.

Inverse Proportion

As a increases, b decreases $\to$ a is in inverse proportion to b

Example 5.2.2

5 students can finish a project in 16 hours. How long will it take 4 students to finish the same project?

5.3 Exchanging Currency

Example 5.3.1

The exchange rate for for US dollars is given as the table below.

Currency	Exchange Rate
Euro (Europe)	$1 = €0.86
Won (Korea)	$1 = ₩1200
Pounds (UK)	$1 = £0.74

Convert

(a) $2.5 to won.

(b) $120 to pounds.

(c) €200 to US dollars.

5.4 Rates

Rate

Rate: Ratio that compares two quantities of different unit
Unit Rate: Rate in which the second quantity is 1

Example 5.4.1

Find the following rates.

(a) 6 liters in 2.5 minutes in liters per minute

(b) 2500 meters in 2 hours in meters per second.

5.5 Distance, Speed, and Time

Example 5.5.1

Change the units of 16 m/s into kilometers per hour.

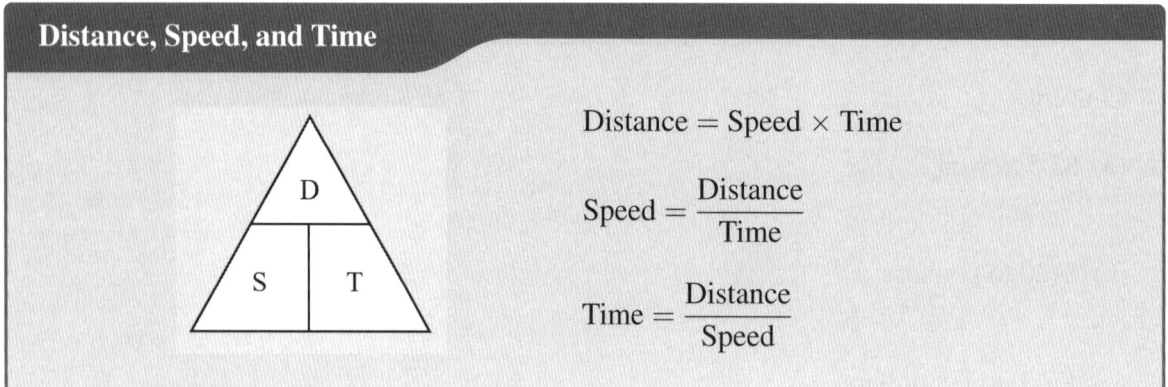

Example 5.5.2

Daisy runs at a constant speed of 5 km/h. She started the race at 17:34.

(a) If she ran 3200 meters, find the total time she ran in minutes.

(b) Find the time she ended the race.

(c) After she takes a 5 minute break, she continues running for an additional 12 minutes. Find the distance she ran in kilometers.

Average Speed

$$\text{Average Speed} = \frac{\text{Total distance}}{\text{Total time}} = \frac{d_1 + d_2}{t_1 + t_2}$$

Example 5.5.3

A cyclist travels 30 kilometers at 25 km/h on the first day and travels 65 kilometers at 20 km/h on the second day.

(a) Find the total travel time.

(b) Find the average speed of the cyclist.

6 Percentage

6.1 Basic Percentage

Percentage

Percentage: A ratio of a number to 100 (Per-cent means per 100)

$$x\% = \frac{x}{100} \quad \text{OR} \quad x\% = \frac{\text{Part}}{\text{Whole}}$$

Percent to Decimal/Fraction

Decimal Equivalent = Percentage $\div$ 100

Decimal/Fraction to Percent

Percentage = Decimal Equivalent $\times$ 100

Example 6.1.1

Convert the following.

(a) 0.73 to percentage (b) 65% to fraction (c) 26.3% to decimal

Percentage of a Quantity

$$x\% \text{ of } A = A \times \frac{x}{100}$$

Example 6.1.2

Find the percentage of the given quantity.

(a) 23% of 200 (b) 80% of 45

6.2 Percent Increase and Decrease

Increase and Decrease by x Percent

Increase by x Percent

New Value $= A + A \times \dfrac{x}{100} = A\left(1 + \dfrac{x}{100}\right)$

Decrease by x Percent

New Value $= A - A \times \dfrac{x}{100} = A\left(1 - \dfrac{x}{100}\right)$

Example 6.2.1

David bought stock worth $50.00.

(a) The price fell 10% in the first month. What is the current price?

(b) The price increased by 25% during the next month. What is the price now?

Percent Change

$$\text{Percent Change} = \dfrac{\text{New Value} - \text{Original Value}}{\text{Original Value}} \times 100$$

※ If the percent change is positive, the value increased.
   If the percent change is negative, the value decreased.

Example 6.2.2

Find the percentage profit or percentage loss.

(a) Cost Price: $20.00   Selling Price: $24.50

(b) Cost Price: $150.00   Selling Price: $120.00

Reverse Percentage (EXTENDED ONLY)

$$\text{New Value} = \text{Original Value} \times \left(1 \pm \frac{x}{100}\right) \quad \rightarrow \quad \text{Original Value} = \frac{\text{New Value}}{1 \pm \frac{x}{100}}$$

Example 6.2.3 EXTENDED ONLY

Find the cost price of each case.

(a) Selling Price: $2400   Loss of 30%

(b) Selling Price: $300   Profit of 45%

6.3 Simple and Compound Interest

Simple Interest

Simple Interest: Interest computed on principal only

$$I = \frac{P \times r \times t}{100}$$

$$A = P + I = P + \frac{Prt}{100} = P\left(1 + \frac{rt}{100}\right)$$

I = Interest
A = Total amount
P = Principal
r = Annual rate of interest
t = Time in years

Example 6.3.1

Jenny invests $400 for 3 years and 6 months at 6% simple interest each year.

(a) Find the interest.

(b) Find the total investment.

Compound Interest

Compound Interest: Interest computed on principal and interest earned previously

$$A = P\left(1 + \frac{r}{100}\right)^t$$

$$I = P\left(1 + \frac{r}{100}\right)^t - P = P\left[\left(1 + \frac{r}{100}\right)^t - 1\right]$$

I = Interest
A = Total amount
P = Principal
r = Annual rate of interest
t = Time in years

Example 6.3.2

Jessica puts $5,000 into a savings account that pays interest at a rate of 4% per year.

(a) How much money does Jessica have after 10 years?

(b) How much interest did she earn?

Unit 2
Algebra

- Ch.7 Algebraic Expression
- Ch.8 Equations and Inequalities
- Ch.9 Sequences
- Ch.10 Variation
- Ch.11 Functions

7 Algebraic Expression

7.1 Substitution

Example 7.1.1

Find the value of each of the following when $a = -2$, $b = -3$, and $c = 4$

(a) $2a - b$

(b) $\dfrac{b(a^2 - 3b)}{c}$

(c) $\sqrt{b^2 - 4ac}$

7.2 Expanding

> **Expanding Products of Monomial and a Bracket**
>
> $$a(b+c) = ab + ac$$

Example 7.2.1

Expand the following expressions.

(a) $3x(4y+5)$

(b) $-2p(5p-8q+3r)$

(c) $3x^2 \left(x+4-\dfrac{1}{3x} \right)$

> **Expanding Products of Two Brackets**
>
> $$(a+b)(c+d) = ac + ad + bc + bd$$

Example 7.2.2

Expand the following expressions.

(a) $(x-3)(x+4)$

(b) $(2x-5)(x+3)$

Expanding Products of More Than Two Brackets (EXTENDED ONLY)

(1) Expand the first two brackets

(2) Multiply the result from (1) and the third bracket

Example 7.2.3 EXTENDED ONLY

Expand the following expressions.

(a) $(x-2)(x+1)(x+3)$

(b) $(x+4)(2x-3)(x+5)$

7.3 Factoring

> **Factoring out the Highest Common Factor**
>
> $$ab + ac = a(b+c)$$

Example 7.3.1

Factor the following expressions.

(a) $-7p - 35p + 49$

(b) $a^2b - 8ab^2$

(c) $5x^3y^2 - 20x^2y + 30xy^2$

> **Differences of squares (EXTENDED ONLY)**
>
> $$a^2 - b^2 = (a+b)(a-b)$$

Example 7.3.2 EXTENDED ONLY

Factor the following expressions.

(a) $4x^2 - 25y^2$

(b) $a^2b^2c^2 - 16c^2$

(c) $16m^4 - 81n^4$

Factoring Perfect Square Trinomials (EXTENDED ONLY)

$$a^2 + 2ab + b^2 = (a+b)^2 \quad \text{OR} \quad a^2 - 2ab + b^2 = (a-b)^2$$

Example 7.3.3 EXTENDED ONLY

Factor the following expressions.

(a) $x^2 - 24x + 144$

(b) $4a^2 + 12ab + 9b^2$

Factoring Trinomials with Leading Coefficient of 1 (EXTENDED ONLY)

$$x^2 + (a+b)x + ab = (x+a)(x+b)$$

Example 7.3.4 EXTENDED ONLY

Factor the following expressions.

(a) $x^2 - 3x - 4$

(b) $x^2 - 5x + 6$

Factoring Trinomials (EXTENDED ONLY)

$$acx^2 + (ad+bc)x + bd = (ax+b)(cx+d)$$

Example 7.3.5 EXTENDED ONLY

Factor the following expressions.

(a) $2x^2 + 7x + 6$

(b) $16x^2 - 8x + 1$

Factor by Grouping (EXTENDED ONLY)

(1) Split into two groups of binomials.
(2) Factor the HCF of each group.
(3) Factor out the common binomial.

Example 7.3.6 EXTENDED ONLY

Factor the following expressions.

(a) $ab - 3a - 4b^2 + 12b$

(b) $xy^2 - 6y^2 - x + 6$

7.4 Transformation of a Formula

Simple Transformation

If we have to make x the subject, we need to rearrange the equation and isolate x on the left hand side.

Example 7.4.1

Make x the subject of the formula.

(a) $3a - bx = 5c$

(b) $x(a+b) = a-b$

(c) $a(3x-y) = b+c$

Transformation with Fractions

Example 7.4.2

Make x the subject of the formula.

(a) $\dfrac{mx+a}{n} = b$

(b) $a + \dfrac{b}{x} = c$

(c) $\dfrac{a+b}{x} = c$

Transformation with Factoring

Example 7.4.3 EXTENDED ONLY

Make x the subject of the formula.

(a) $mx + n = px - q$

(b) $2x + a = \dfrac{3x - b}{c}$

Transformation with Radical Expressions

Example 7.4.4 EXTENDED ONLY

Make x the subject of the formula.

(a) $\sqrt{x^2 - m} = n$

(c) $\sqrt{ab - 3x} = c$

(b) $(mx - n)^2 = p$

(d) $\sqrt{\dfrac{x - a}{x}} = b$

7.5 Algebraic Fractions (EXTENDED ONLY)

Simplifying Algebraic Fractions

(1) Factor the denominator and numerator
(2) Cancel out the highest common factor

Example 7.5.1 EXTENDED ONLY

Simplify the following algebraic fractions.

(a) $\dfrac{3x}{7x^2}$

(b) $\dfrac{x^2 - 4x}{6xy}$

Simplifying Rational Expressions with Trinomials

(1) Factor the denominator and numerator
(2) Cancel out the highest common factor

Example 7.5.2 EXTENDED ONLY

Simplify the following algebraic fractions.

(a) $\dfrac{x^2 - 2x}{x^2 - 5x + 6}$

(b) $\dfrac{x^2 + x - 20}{x^2 + 4x - 5}$

Multiplication and Division of Algebraic Fractions

Example 7.5.3 EXTENDED ONLY

Simplify the following algebraic fractions.

(a) $\dfrac{x}{y} \times \dfrac{a}{b}$

(b) $\dfrac{24x^2y}{z} \times \dfrac{z^2}{3xy^2}$

(c) $\dfrac{4a}{5} \div \dfrac{2a^2}{25}$

Addition and Subtraction of Algebraic Fractions

(1) Find the least common denominator of the two fractions.
(2) Express both fractions in the least common denominator form.
(3) Add or subtract the numerators.
(4) Simplify if possible.

Example 7.5.4 EXTENDED ONLY

Simplify the following algebraic fractions into a single fraction.

(a) $\dfrac{x}{2} + \dfrac{x-5}{3}$

(b) $\dfrac{3x}{4} - \dfrac{2(x-7)}{3}$

(c) $\dfrac{1}{x+2} - \dfrac{3}{x-4}$

7.6 Indices

Rules of Indices

(1) $x^a \times x^b = x^{a+b}$ (2) $x^a \div x^b = x^{a-b}$ (3) $x^0 = 1$

(4) $(x^a)^b = x^{ab}$ (5) $(xy)^a = x^a y^a$

Example 7.6.1

Simplify the following algebraic expressions.

(a) $3x^5 \times 12x^9$

(b) $\left(\dfrac{3}{5x^3}\right)^2$

(c) $\left(7x^{-2}\right)^3 \div x^{-8}$

Negative and Fractional Indices

(1) $x^{-a} = \dfrac{1}{x^a}$ (2) $x^{\frac{1}{a}} = \sqrt[a]{x}$ (3) $x^{\frac{m}{n}} = \sqrt[n]{x^m}$

(2) and (3): EXTENDED ONLY

Example 7.6.2   EXTENDED ONLY

Simplify the following algebraic expressions.

(a) $6x^{-3} \times \dfrac{5}{6}x^{\frac{1}{2}}$ (b) $\dfrac{2}{13}x^{\frac{1}{2}} \div 5x^{-2}$

8 Equations and Inequalities

8.1 Linear Equations

> **Solving Equations**
>
> To solve an equation, make the unknown variable the subject.

Simple Linear Equations

Example 8.1.1

Solve the following equations.

(a) $2x - 13 = 23 - 3x$

(b) $\dfrac{3x}{5} = 12$

More Complicated Linear Equations

Example 8.1.2

Solve the following equations.

(a) $x - 3(x - 2) = 6 - 2(x + 1)$

(b) $(x + 2)^2 = (x - 1)(x + 3) - 6$

Linear Equations with Fractional Expression

Example 8.1.3

Solve the following equations.

(a) $\dfrac{6}{5x} = 18$

(b) $\dfrac{x-3}{2} = \dfrac{4x+5}{3}$

(c) $\dfrac{3}{x-7} + 4 = 15$

Constructing Linear Equations

Example 8.1.4

The width of a rectangle is twice the length. Find the dimension of the rectangle if the perimeter of the rectangle is 66cm.

Example 8.1.5

A number is 5 times the sum of the number and 3. What is this number?

8.2 Linear Simultaneous Equations

Substitution Method

(a) Using the first equation, make x or y the subject.

(b) Substitute the result from part (1) into the second equation.

Example 8.2.1

Solve the following simultaneous equations with the substitution method.

$$2x+y=12 \qquad 6x+5y=40$$

Elimination Method

(a) Multiply an appropriate constant to either equation, or both, to match a coefficient.

(b) Add or subtract the two equations to eliminate one variable and find the value of the remaining variable.

(c) Plug in the result from (2) to either equation to find the other variable.

Example 8.2.2

Solve the following simultaneous equations with the elimination method.

$$3x+5y=19 \qquad 2x-y=4$$

Constructing Linear Simultaneous Equations

Example 8.2.3

It cost Chloe 34 dollars to buy 20 pens. If each blue pen cost 1.5 dollars and each red pen cost 2 dollars, find the number of blue pens Chloe bought.

8.3 Quadratic Equations (EXTENDED ONLY)

Solving Quadratic Equations by Factorising

(a) Rearrange the equation and make the right hand side zero.
(b) Factor the left hand side.
(c) Set the factors equal to zero and make x the subject.

Example 8.3.1   EXTENDED ONLY

Solve the following equations.

(a) $6x^2 - 13x - 5 = 0$

(c) $2x^2 = 5x$

(b) $9x^2 - 16 = 0$

Solving Quadratic Equations by Formula

$$ax^2 + bx + c = 0 \quad \Longrightarrow \quad x = \frac{-b \pm \sqrt{b^2 - 4ac}}{2a}$$

Example 8.3.2   EXTENDED ONLY

Solve the following equations.

(a) $2x^2 + x - 28 = 0$

(b) $x^2 - 3x + 1 = 0$

Solving Quadratic Equation by Completing the Square

(1) Write the quadratic equation in the form $ax^2 + bx = c$.

(2) Divide a on both sides.

(3) Add $\left(\dfrac{b}{2a}\right)^2$ to both sides of the equation.

(4) Factor the left side into a perfect square.

(5) Square root both sides and solve for x.

Example 8.3.3 EXTENDED ONLY

Solve the following equations.

(a) $x^2 - 8x - 3 = 0$

(b) $2x^2 + 6x - 5 = 0$

(c) $-2x^2 + 5x + 1 = 0$

8.4 Non-linear Simultaneous Equations (EXTENDED ONLY)

Non-linear Simultaneous Equations

(1) Solve for y on both equations.

(2) Let the results from (1) equal to each other.

(3) Find x and plug into one of the original equations to find y.

Example 8.4.1 EXTENDED ONLY

Solve the following simultaneous equations.

(a) $y = 7x + 5$
    $y = x^2 + 4x - 5$

(b) $3x - y = 1$
    $y = x^2 + 4x - 2$

8.5 Exponential Equations (EXTENDED ONLY)

Exponential Equations

If $b^x = b^y$, then $x = y$.

Example 8.5.1 EXTENDED ONLY

Solve the following equations.

(a) $9^x = 27$

(b) $64^{2x-1} = 2$

8.6 Linear Inequalities (EXTENDED ONLY)

Representing Inequalities on Number Lines

$x > 2 \implies x$ is greater than 2

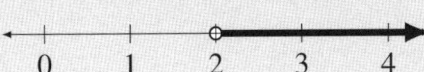

$x < 2 \implies x$ is less than 2

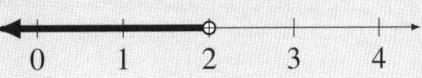

$x \geq 2 \implies x$ is greater than or equal to 2

$x \leq 2 \implies x$ is less than or equal to 2

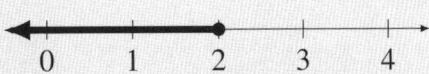

Solving Linear Inequalities

Addition: If $a < b$, then $a + c < b + c$

Subtraction: If $a < b$, then $a - c < b - c$

Multiplication: If $a < b$ and $c > 0$, then $ac < bc$

If $a < b$ and $c < 0$, then $ac > bc$

Division: If $a < b$ and $c > 0$, then $\dfrac{a}{c} < \dfrac{b}{c}$

If $a < b$ and $c < 0$, then $\dfrac{a}{c} > \dfrac{b}{c}$

Example 8.6.1 EXTENDED ONLY

Solve the following inequalities and represent the result on a number line.

(a) $3x - 5 < 16$

(b) $2 - 7x \leq -33$

Example 8.6.2 EXTENDED ONLY

Solve the following inequalities and represent the result on a number line.

(a) $25 < 3x - 2 \leq 43$

(b) $-8 \leq 12 - 5x < 67$

9 Sequences

Sequence $\{u_1, u_2, u_3, ..., u_n, ...\}$ is an ordered list of numbers, where u_n represents the n-th term of the sequence.

9.1 Arithmetic Sequence (Linear)

Arithmetic Sequence ($u_n = an + b$)

A sequence of numbers where the difference between each successive term is a constant.
$$2 \quad 5 \quad 8 \quad 11 \quad ... \quad 3n-1 \quad ...$$

Example 9.1.1

Find the next two terms and the n-th term of the following sequences.

(a) 7, 11, 15, ...

(b) 9, 2, −5, ...

9.2 Geometric Sequence (Exponential) (EXTENDED ONLY)

Geometric sequence ($u_n = a \times b^n$)

A sequence of numbers where the ratio of each successive term is a constant.
$$2 \quad 4 \quad 8 \quad 16 \quad \ldots \quad 2^n \quad \ldots$$

Example 9.2.1 EXTENDED ONLY

Find the next two terms and the n-th term of the following sequences.

(a) 4, 12, 36, ...

(b) 243, −81, 27, ...

9.3 Quadratic and Cubic Sequence (EXTENDED ONLY)

Quadratic Sequence

Quadratic sequences can be written as $u_n = an^2 + bn + c$

	$n = 1$		$n = 2$		$n = 3$
Term	$a + b + c$		$4a + 2b + c$		$9a + 3b + c$
1st Diff.		$3a + b$		$5a + b$	
2nd Diff.			$2a$		

Example 9.3.1 EXTENDED ONLY

Find the n-th term of the following sequence.

$$2, \quad 6, \quad 12, \quad 20, \quad 30, \quad 42, \quad \ldots$$

Cubic Sequence

Cubic sequences can be written as $u_n = an^3 + bn^2 + cn + d$

	$n=1$	$n=2$	$n=3$	$n=4$
Term	$a+b+c+d$	$8a+4b+2c+d$	$27a+9b+3c+d$	$64a+16b+4c+d$
1st Diff.		$7a+3b+c$	$19a+5b+c$	$37a+7b+c$
2nd Diff.			$12a+2b$	$18a+2b$
3rd Diff.			$6a$	

Example 9.3.2 — EXTENDED ONLY

Find the *n*-th term of the following sequence.

$$1, \quad 14, \quad 65, \quad 178, \quad 377, \quad \ldots$$

10 Variation (EXTENDED ONLY)

10.1 Direct Variation

Direct Variation

y varies as x
y varies directly as x $\implies$ $y \propto x$ or $y = kx$
y is proportional to x

Example 10.1.1 EXTENDED ONLY

a varies as b, and $a = 5$ when $b = 2$.

(a) Find the constant of proportionality.

(b) Find the value of b when $a = 9$

Example 10.1.2 EXTENDED ONLY

A stone is dropped from the top of a cliff. The vertical distance travelled is proportional to the square of the time travel. It took 2 seconds to fall a vertical height of 20 meters.

(a) Find the time it took to fall through a distance of 125 meters.

(b) Find the distance travelled during the first 6 seconds.

10.2 Inverse Variation

Inverse Variation

y varies inversely as x
y is inversely proportional to x $\implies$ $y \propto \dfrac{1}{x}$ or $y = \dfrac{k}{x}$

Example 10.2.1 EXTENDED ONLY

t varies inversely as $\sqrt{s}$, and $t = 6$ when $s = 144$.

(a) Find the constant of proportionality.

(b) Find the value of t when $s = 36$

(c) Find the value of s when $t = 9$

11 Functions (EXTENDED ONLY)

11.1 Function Notations

Function Notations

$$f : x \mapsto 3x - 2 \quad \text{or} \quad f(x) = 3x - 2$$

Example 11.1.1 EXTENDED ONLY

If $f(x) = x^2 - 5$ and $g : x \mapsto -2x + 6$, find:

(a) $f(-4)$

(b) $g(13)$

(c) $g(0)$

(d) x when $f(x) = 116$

11.2 Composite Functions

Composite Functions

A composite function is created by substituting a function into another function.

$$fg(x) = f(g(x))$$

Example 11.2.1 EXTENDED ONLY

If $f(x) = x - 3$ and $g(x) = -5x + 9$, find:

(a) $fg(x)$

(b) $gf(x)$

(c) $fg(15)$

11.3 Inverse Functions

Inverse Functions

An inverse function of $f(x)$ is written as $f^{-1}(x)$, and it "undoes" the operations of $f(x)$.

Composite of Inverse Functions

$$f(f^{-1}(x)) = x \quad \text{and} \quad f^{-1}(f(x)) = x$$

How to Find Inverse Functions

(1) Replace $f(x)$ with y
(2) Switch x and y
(3) Rearrange the equation and make y the subject.

Example 11.3.1   EXTENDED ONLY

Find the inverse of each of the following functions. Then, confirm by showing $ff^{-1}(x) = f^{-1}f(x) = x$

(a) $f(x) = -3x + 14$

(b) $g(x) = \dfrac{6x-5}{13}$

Unit 3
Graphs

Ch.12 Linear Functions
Ch.13 Quadratic and Cubic Functions
Ch.14 Differentiation
Ch.15 Inequality Graphs
Ch.16 Graphs in Practical Situations

12 Linear Functions

12.1 Gradient

Gradient

Gradient: Measure of steepness of a line

$$\text{Gradient} = \frac{\text{Rise}}{\text{Run}} = \frac{\text{Change in } y}{\text{change in } x} = \frac{y_2 - y_1}{x_2 - x_1}$$

Positive gradient: y increases as x increases

Negative gradient: y decreases as x increases

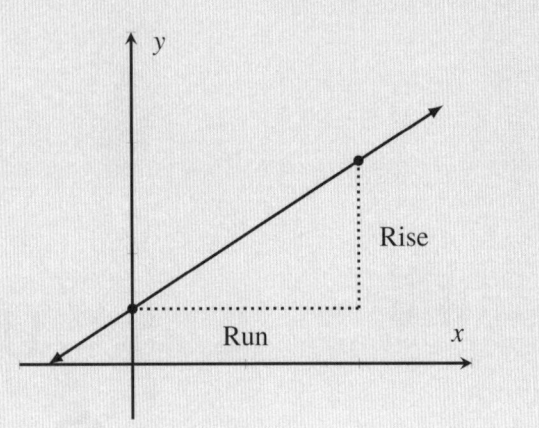

Example 12.1.1

Find the gradient of the given graphs.

(a)
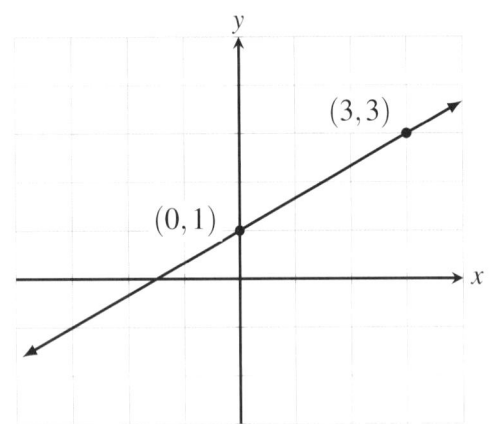

(b)
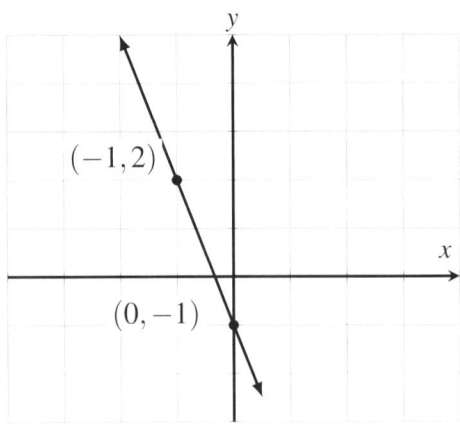

12.2 Midpoint and Distance Between Two Points (EXTENDED ONLY)

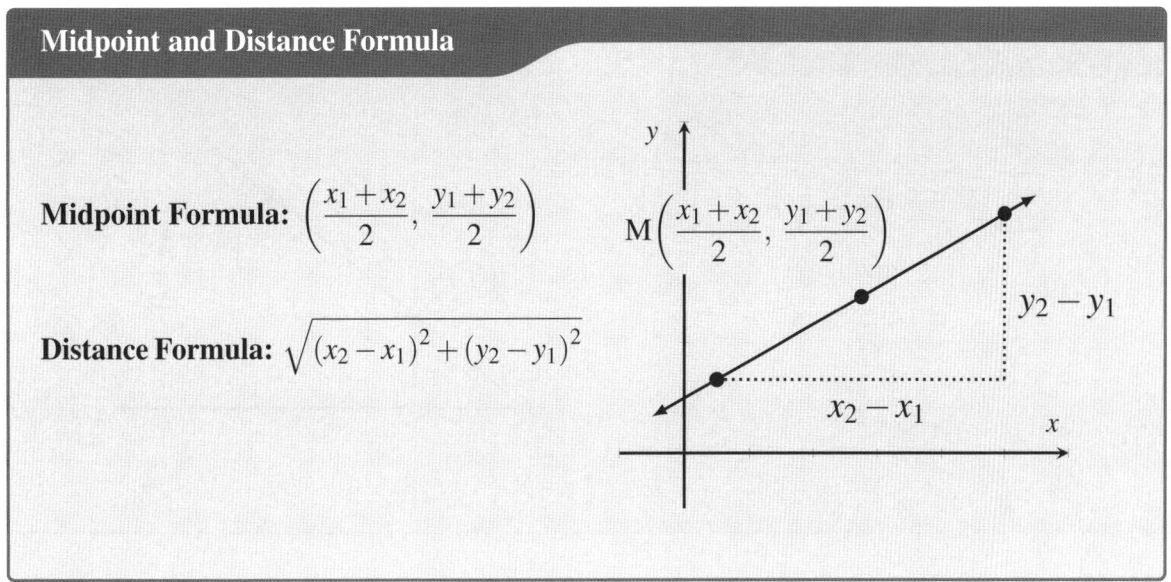

Midpoint and Distance Formula

Midpoint Formula: $\left(\dfrac{x_1+x_2}{2}, \dfrac{y_1+y_2}{2}\right)$

Distance Formula: $\sqrt{(x_2-x_1)^2+(y_2-y_1)^2}$

Example 12.2.1 — EXTENDED ONLY

Find the midpoint and distance between the two points $P(-2,5)$ and $Q(2,-1)$.

12.3 Gradient-intercept Form

Gradient-Intercept Form

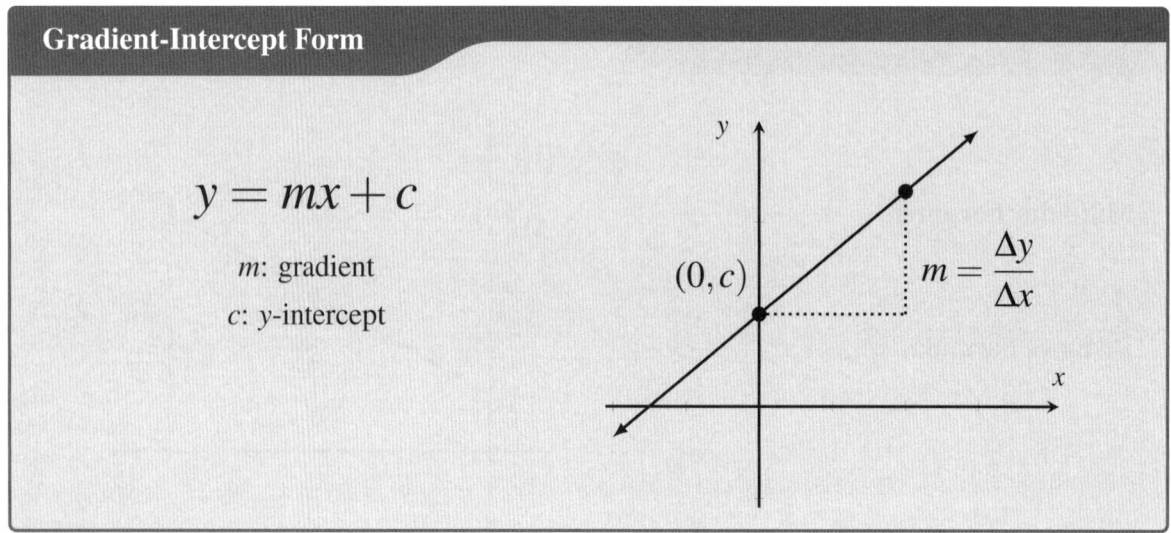

$$y = mx + c$$

m: gradient

c: y-intercept

Example 12.3.1

Identify the gradient and y-intercept of the following functions.

(a) $y = -2x + 3$

(b) $3x + 2y = 6$

Finding Linear Functions with a Point and Gradient

(1) Plug the gradient into m and write in the form $y = mx + c$

(2) Substitute the given point into the equation $y = mx + c$ and find c

Example 12.3.2

Find the equation of the straight line with the following properties.

(a) Passes through $(-1, 3)$ at a gradient of 4

(b) Passes through $(5, 2)$ at a gradient of -6

Finding Linear Functions with Two Points

(1) Find the gradient using the given two points $\left(m = \dfrac{y_2 - y_1}{x_2 - x_1} \right)$

(2) Substitute a point and gradient into the equation $y = mx + c$ to find c.

Example 12.3.3

Find the equation of the straight line with the following properties.

(a) Passes through $(1, -4)$ and $(5, 6)$

(b) Passes through $(3, 1)$ and $(5, -3)$

12.4 Parallel and Perpendicular Lines

Parallel and Perpendicular Lines

Two lines with gradient m_1 and m_2 are

$$\text{Parallel} \quad \text{if} \quad m_1 = m_2$$

$$\text{Perpendicular} \quad \text{if} \quad m_1 = -\frac{1}{m_2}$$

Perpendicular line gradient: EXTENDED ONLY

Example 12.4.1

Find the equation of the straight line which:

(a) Passes through $(7, 3)$ and is parallel to $y = -2x + 13$

(b) (EXTENDED ONLY)

Passes through $(-3, 1)$ and is perpendicular to $y = 5x - 24$

13 More Complicated Functions

13.1 Quadratic Function Graphs

Quadratic Function Graphs

Quadratic Functions of the form $y = ax^2 + bx + c$

If $a > 0$, the graph opens up.

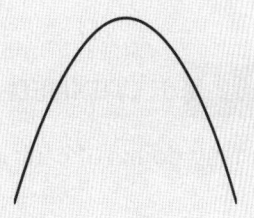

If $a < 0$, the graph opens down.

Example 13.1.1

(a) Complete the table for $y = x^2 - 4x + 3$

x	-1	0	1	2	3	4	5
y	8		0			3	

(b) Draw the graph of $y = x^2 - 4x + 3$.

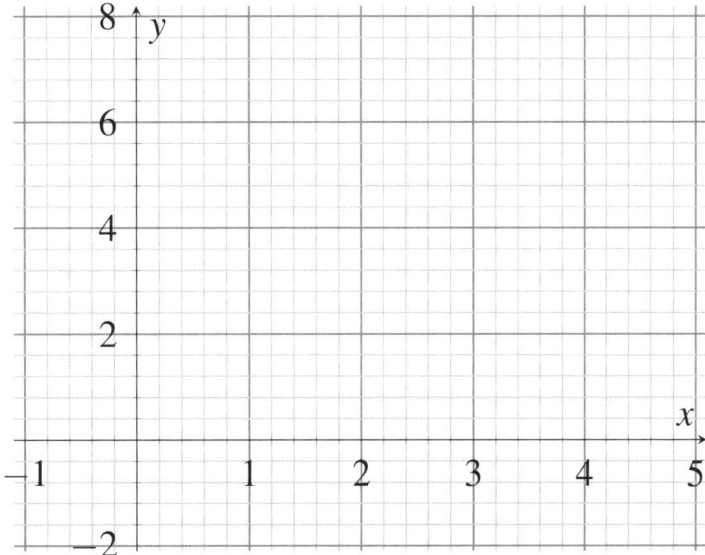

Turning Points of Quadratic Functions (EXTENDED ONLY)

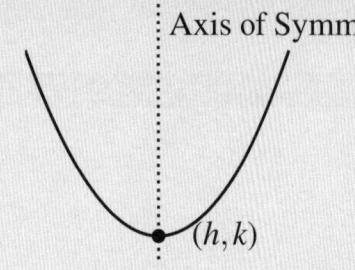

Axis of Symmetry

(h, k)

$y = ax^2 + bx + c \implies y = a(x-h)^2 + k$

(h, k) is the **vertex** or the **turning point**.

Example 13.1.2 EXTENDED ONLY

Find the turning points of each quadratic function.

(a) $y = 2x^2 - 3x + 4$

(b) $y = -x^2 + 6x - 11$

13.2 Cubic Function Graphs (EXTENDED ONLY)

Cubic Functions

Cubic Functions of the form $y = ax^3 + bx^2 + cx + d$

If $a > 0$, the right end goes up and the left end goes down.

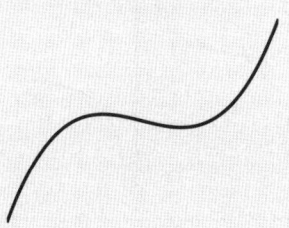

If $a < 0$, the right end goes down and the left end goes up.

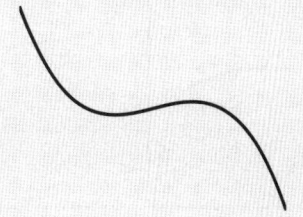

Example 13.2.1 EXTENDED ONLY

(a) Complete the table for $y = x^3 - 3x + 2$

x	−2.5	−2	−1.5	−1	−0.5	0	0.5	1	1.5	2
y	−6.125	0		4	3.375	2		0	0.875	

(b) Draw the graph of $y = x^3 - 3x + 2$.

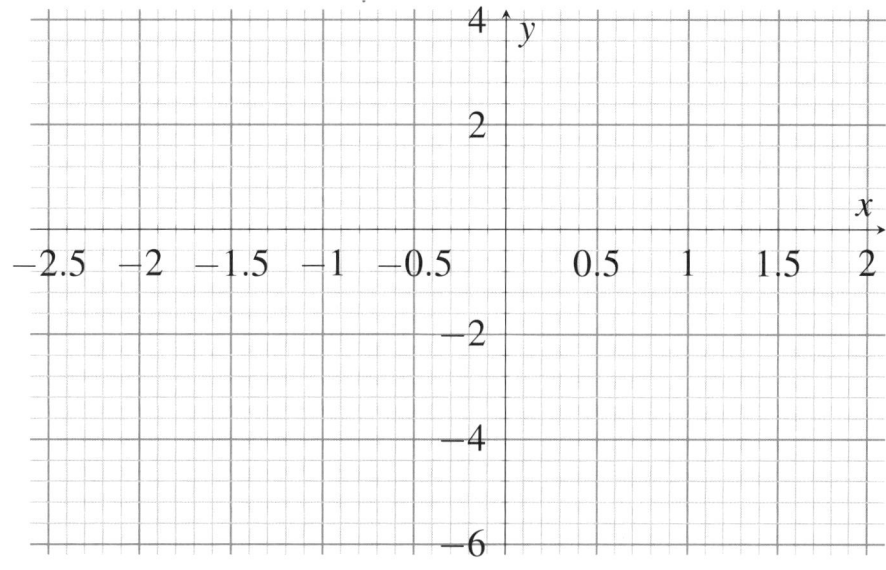

13.3 Rational Function Graphs

Rational Functions

Rational functions of the form $y = \dfrac{a}{x}$

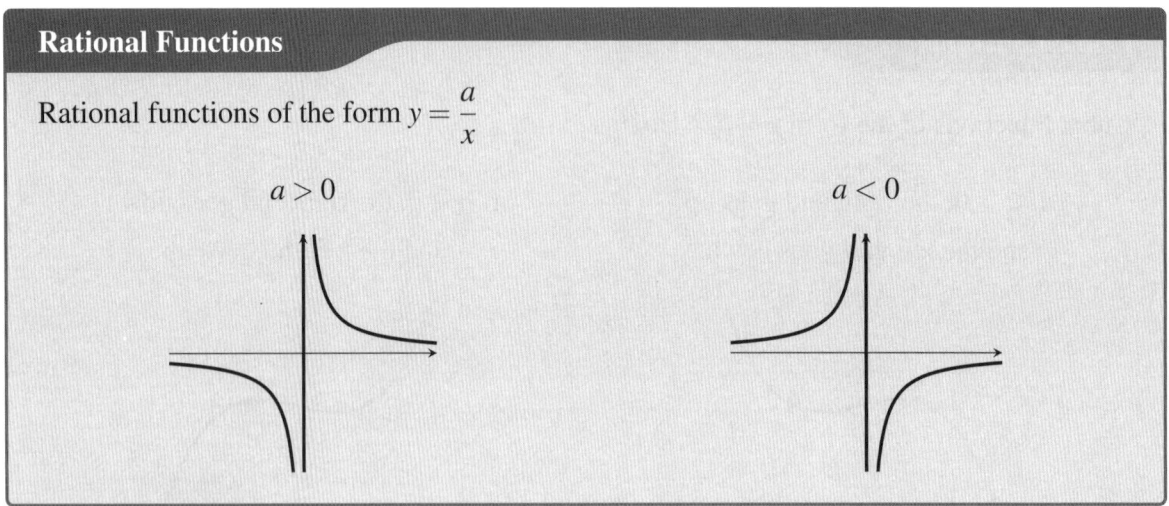

Example 13.3.1

(a) Complete the table for $y = \dfrac{1}{x}$

x	−2	−1	−0.4	−0.2	0.2	0.4	1	2
y	−0.5	−1		−5		2.5	1	

(b) Draw the graph of $y = \dfrac{1}{x}$.

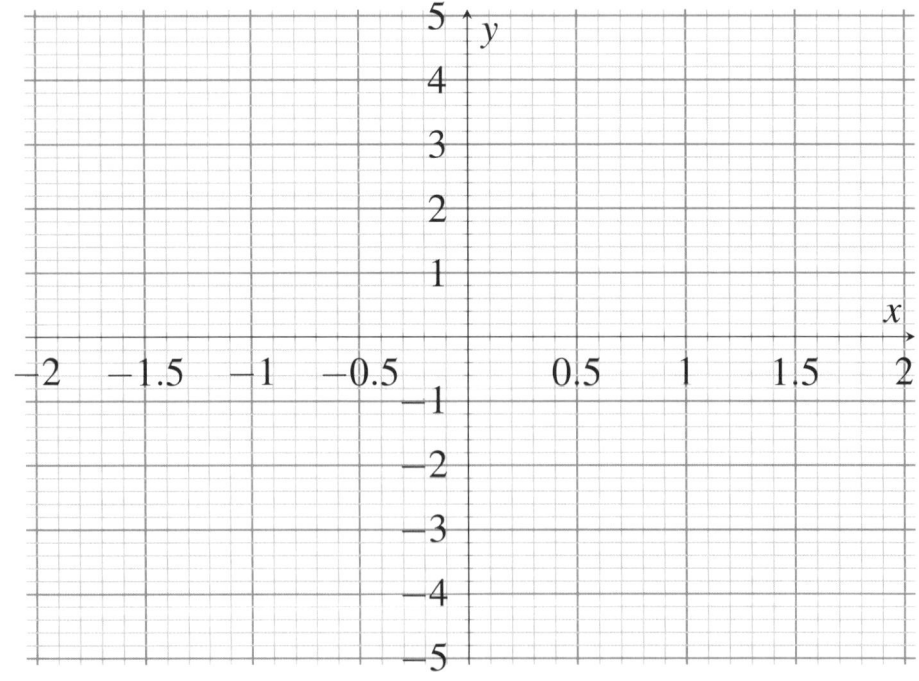

98 IGCSE & MYP Math

13.4 Exponential Function Graphs (EXTENDED ONLY)

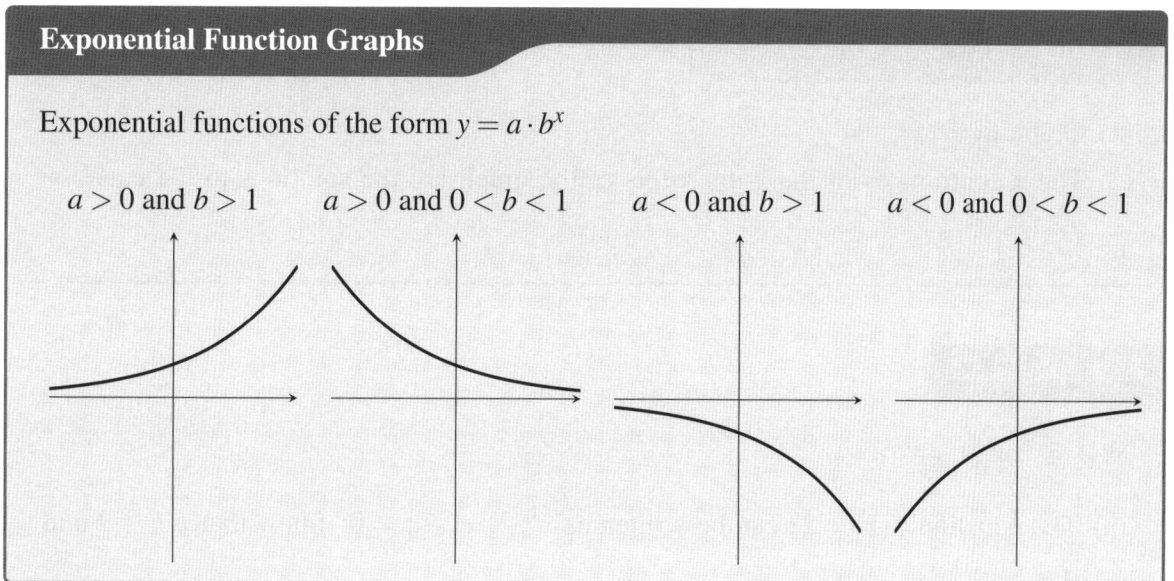

Example 13.4.1   EXTENDED ONLY

(a) Complete the table for $y = 2^x$

x	−3	−2	−1	0	1	2	3
y		0.25	0.5		2		8

(b) Draw the graph of $y = 2^x$.

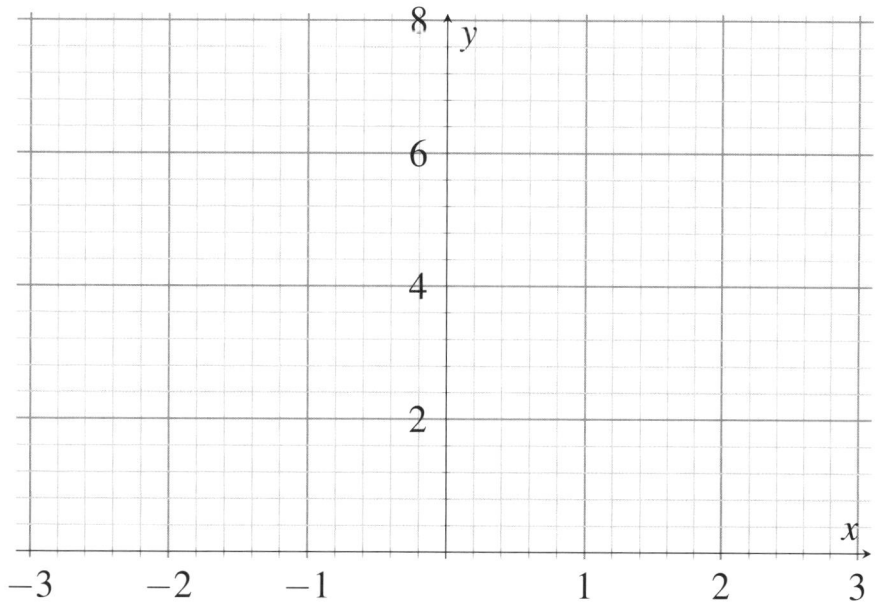

13.5 Solving Equations Graphically

Solving $f(x) = 0$ Graphically

(1) Graph $y = f(x)$.
(2) The x coordinates of the x-intercepts of the graph are the solutions to the equation $f(x) = 0$.

Example 13.5.1

$f(x) = \dfrac{5}{x} + x^2$, $x \neq 0$

(a) The equation $f(x) = 2x$ can be written as $x^3 + px^2 + q = 0$. Show that $p = -2$ and $q = 5$.

(b) The function $g(x) = x^3 - 2x^2 + 5$ is graphed below. Solve $x^3 - 2x^2 + 5 = 0$ using the graph.

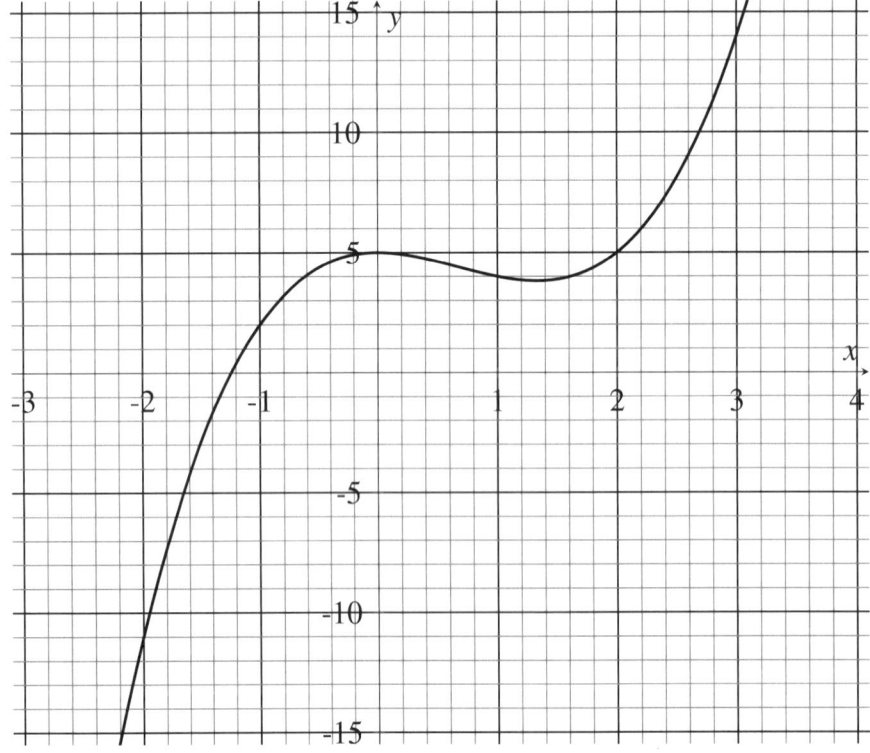

Solving $f(x) = c$ Graphically

(1) Graph $y = f(x)$ and $y = c$.
(2) The x coordinates of the intersection points are the solutions to the equation $f(x) = c$.

Example 13.5.2

A portion of the function $f(x) = 4x + \dfrac{1}{x}$ is graphed below.

(a) Using the graph below, solve the equation $f(x) = 10$.

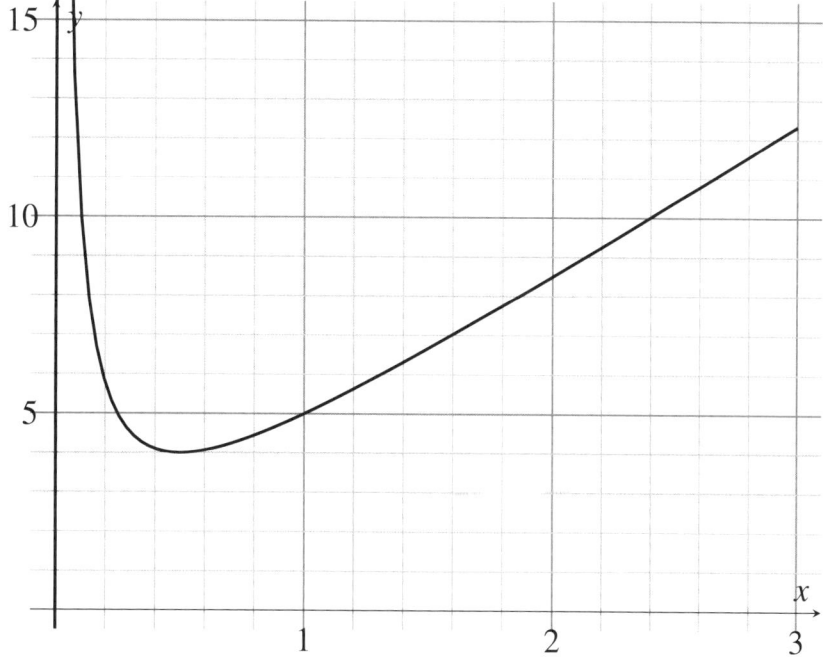

(b) k is a positive integer and $f(x) = k$ has no solutions. Find the possible values of k.

Solving $f(x) = g(x)$ Graphically

(1) Graph $y = f(x)$ and $y = g(x)$.

(2) The x coordinates of the intersection points are the solutions to the equation $f(x) = g(x)$.

Example 13.5.3

The function $f(x) = x + \dfrac{1}{x}$ is graphed below.

(a) Solve the equation $x - \dfrac{1}{x} = 0$ by drawing a suitable straight line on the same graph.

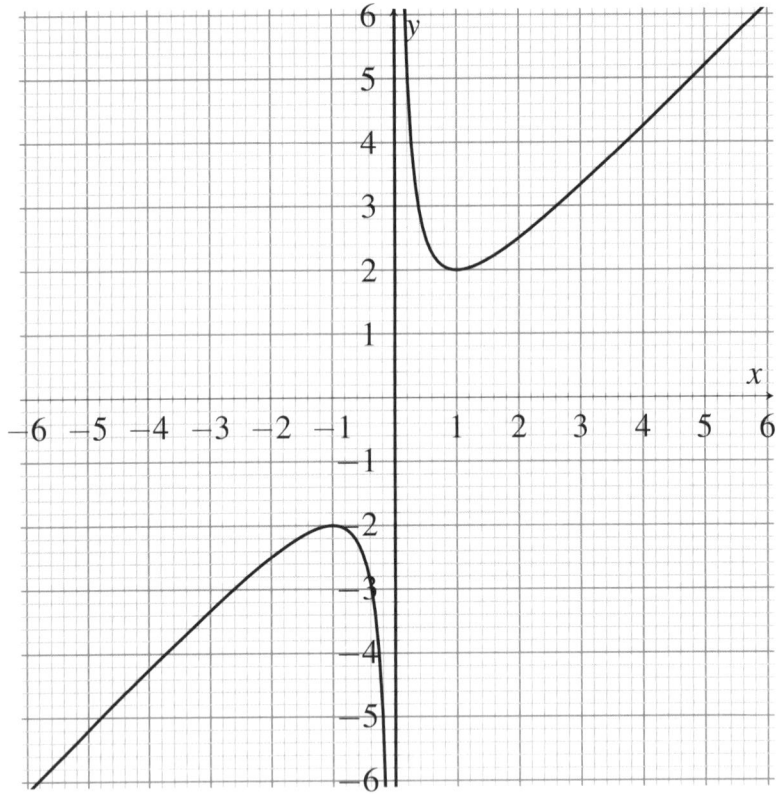

(b) (EXTENDED ONLY) Solve the same equation algebraically.

14 Differentiation (EXTENDED ONLY)

14.1 Derived Functions (EXTENDED ONLY)

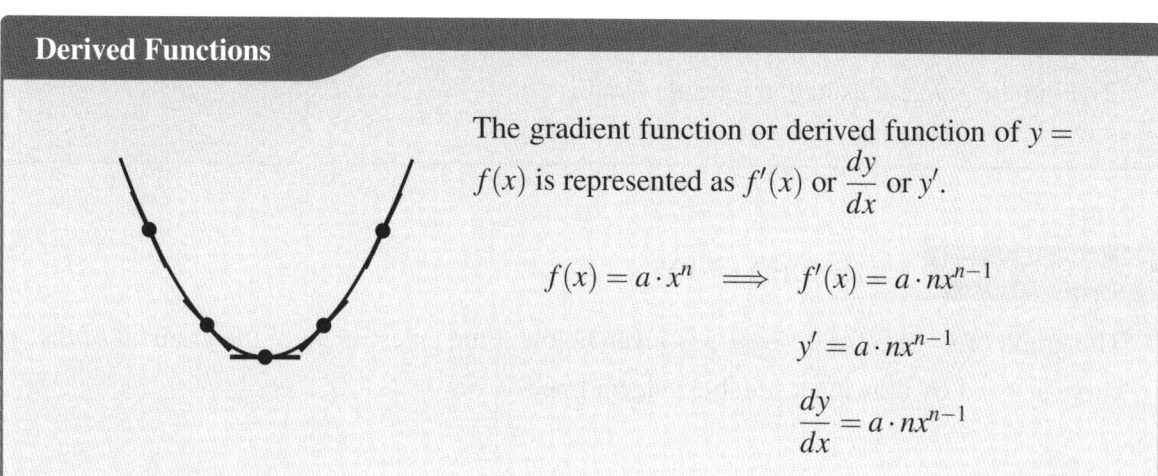

Derived Functions

The gradient function or derived function of $y = f(x)$ is represented as $f'(x)$ or $\dfrac{dy}{dx}$ or y'.

$$f(x) = a \cdot x^n \implies f'(x) = a \cdot nx^{n-1}$$

$$y' = a \cdot nx^{n-1}$$

$$\dfrac{dy}{dx} = a \cdot nx^{n-1}$$

Example 14.1.1 EXTENDED ONLY

Find $f'(x)$, the derived function of $f(x)$, for each function.

(a) $f(x) = 3x^2 - 5x + 8$

(b) $f(x) = -2x^4 + 12x^2 - 5$

14.2 Gradients at a Point (EXTENDED ONLY)

Estimating Gradients of Curves by Drawing Tangents

(1) Draw a line that passes through the given point on the graph.
(2) Find the gradient using the formula Gradient $= \dfrac{y_2 - y_1}{x_2 - x_1}$

Example 14.2.1 EXTENDED ONLY

The graph of $y = \sqrt{x}$ for $0 \leq x \leq 5$ is given below. Find an estimate of the gradient of the curve at $x = 1$ by drawing a suitable tangent line.

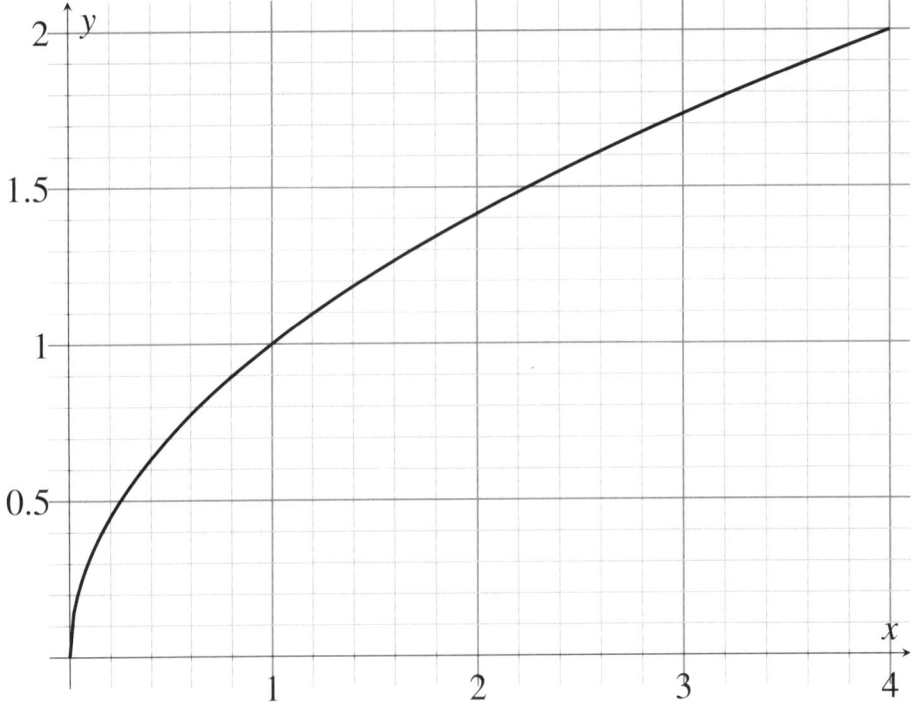

Calculating Gradients of Curves Using Differentiation

$$\text{Gradient of } f(x) \text{ at } x = c \implies f'(c)$$

Example 14.2.2 EXTENDED ONLY

Calculate the gradient of each curve at the given points.

(a) $y = 2x^3 - 5x^2 + 8$ at $x = -3$

(b) $y = -x^2 + 4x + 11$ at $x = 2$

14.3 Equations of Tangent Lines (EXTENDED ONLY)

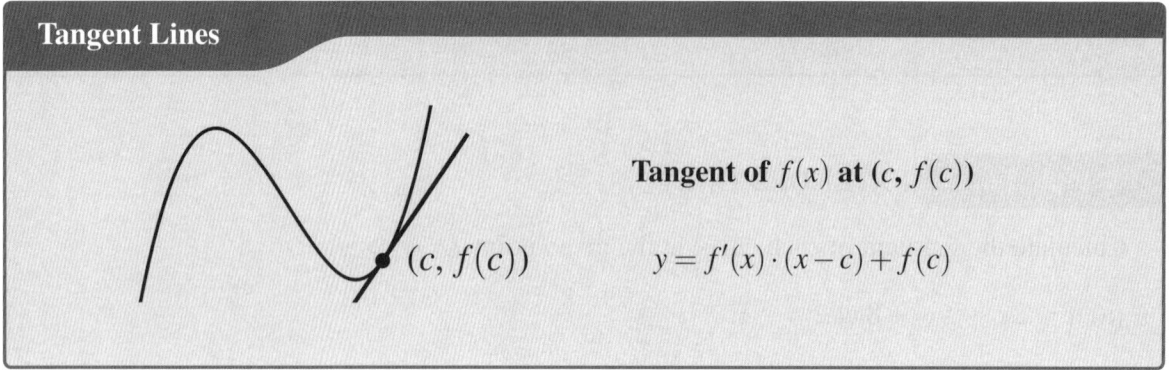

Tangent Lines

Tangent of $f(x)$ at $(c, f(c))$

$$y = f'(x) \cdot (x - c) + f(c)$$

Example 14.3.1 EXTENDED ONLY

Find the equation of tangent of the curve $y = 5x^2 - 3x + 4$ at $x = 2$.

14.4 Turning Points (EXTENDED ONLY)

> **Turning Point (Stationary Point)**
>
> **Turning Point (Stationary Point):** Point on a graph where the gradient is zero.
>
>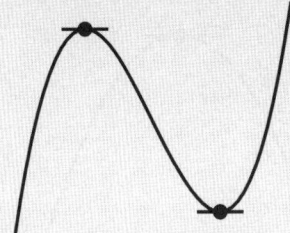
>
> $f'(c) = 0 \implies (c, f(c))$ is the turning point.

Example 14.4.1 EXTENDED ONLY

Find the coordinates of the turning points on the curve $y = 2x^3 - 3x^2 - 12x + 9$.

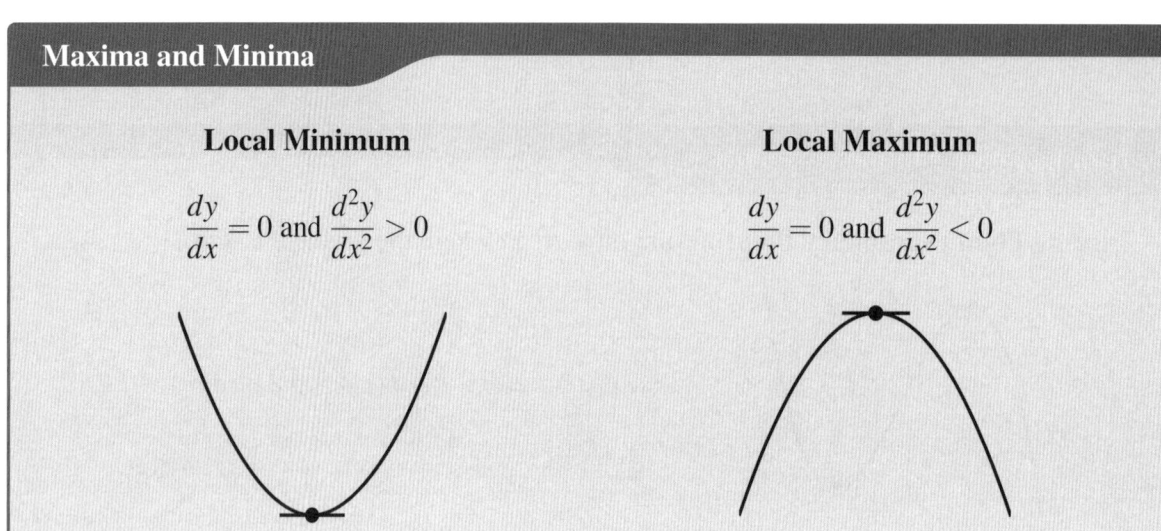

Example 14.4.2 EXTENDED ONLY

Find the stationary points of the curve $f(x) = x^3 - 3x^2 - 9x$. Then, state whether each stationary point is a maximum or a minimum.

15 Inequality Graphs (EXTENDED ONLY)

15.1 Vertical Boundary Lines (EXTENDED ONLY)

> **How to Graph Inequalities with Vertical Boundaries**
>
> (1) Draw a vertical line $x = c$.
>
> ※ If $x > c$ or $x < c$, draw a dotted line.
> If $x \geq c$ or $x \leq c$, draw a solid line.
>
> (2) Color the region where it makes the inequality statement false.

Example 15.1.1   EXTENDED ONLY

Represent the inequalities graphically by coloring the unwanted region.

(a) $x > 3$

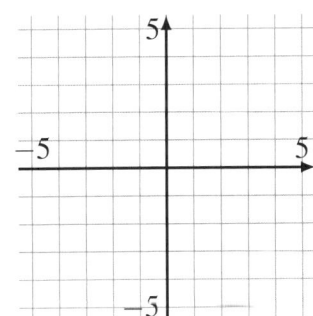

(b) $x \leq -2$

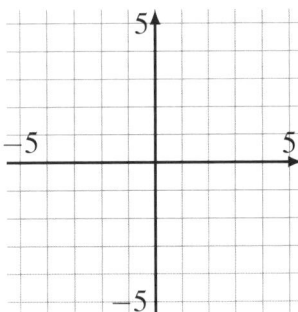

Example 15.1.2   EXTENDED ONLY

Describe the unshaded region.

(a)

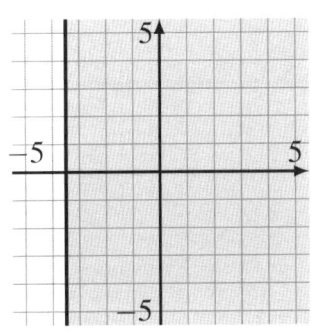

(b)

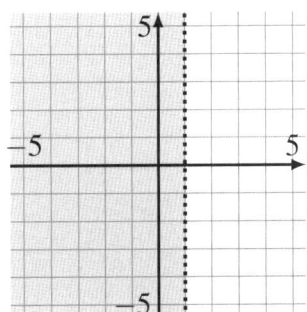

15.2 Horizontal Boundary Lines (EXTENDED ONLY)

How to Graph Inequalities with Horizontal Boundaries

(1) Draw a horizontal line $y = c$.
  * If $y > c$ or $y < c$, draw a dotted line.
    If $y \geq c$ or $y \leq c$, draw a solid line.
(2) Color the region where it makes the inequality statement false.

Example 15.2.1   EXTENDED ONLY

Represent the inequalities graphically by coloring the unwanted region.

(a) $y < -2$

(b) $y \geq 1.5$

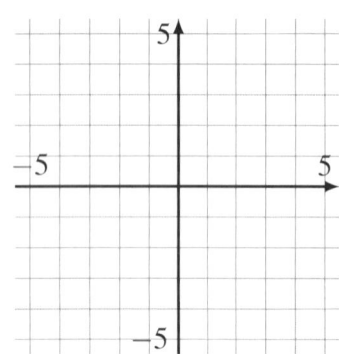
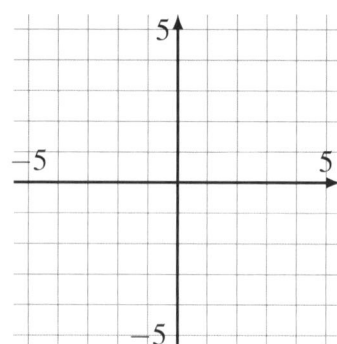

Example 15.2.2   EXTENDED ONLY

Describe the unshaded region.

(a)

(b)

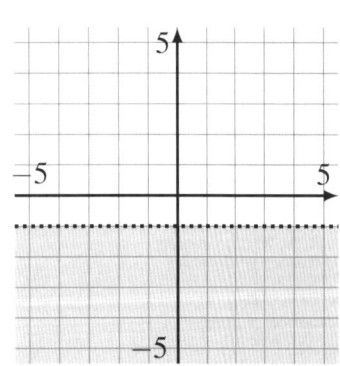
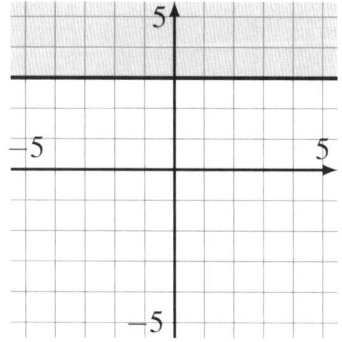

15.3 Linear Boundary (EXTENDED ONLY)

How to Graph Linear Ineqeualities

(1) Draw the boundary line.
   ※ If exclusive, draw a dotted line.
   If inclusive, draw a solid line.
(2) Color the region where the it makes the inequality statement false.

Example 15.3.1 EXTENDED ONLY

Represent the inequalities graphically.

(a) $y < 2x - 1$

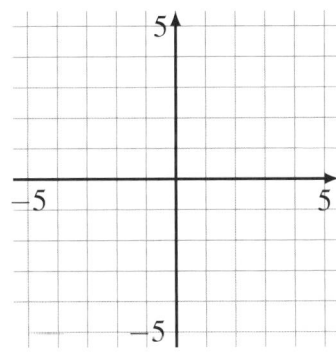

(b) $x + 2y \geq 4$

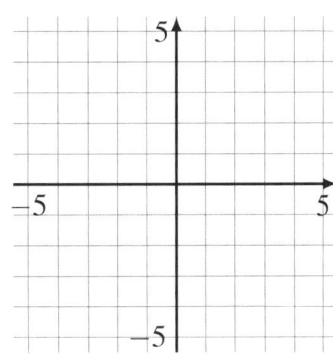

Example 15.3.2 EXTENDED ONLY

Describe the unshaded region.

(a)

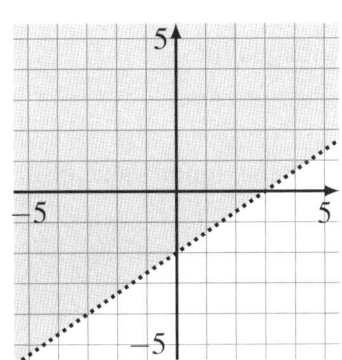

(b)

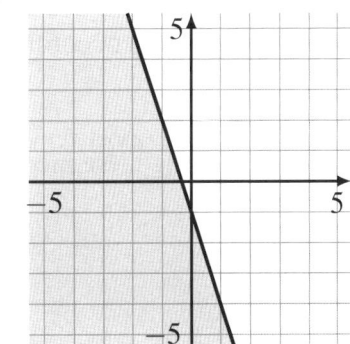

15.4 Linear Programming (EXTENDED ONLY)

Linear Programming

Linear Programming: A mathematical method to achieve the maximum or the minimum of a linear function that is subjected to various constraints.

Example 15.4.1 EXTENDED ONLY

Given the inequalities:
$$x > 3 \qquad y > x \qquad x + y \leq 12$$

(a) Graph the given inequalities and shade the unwanted region.

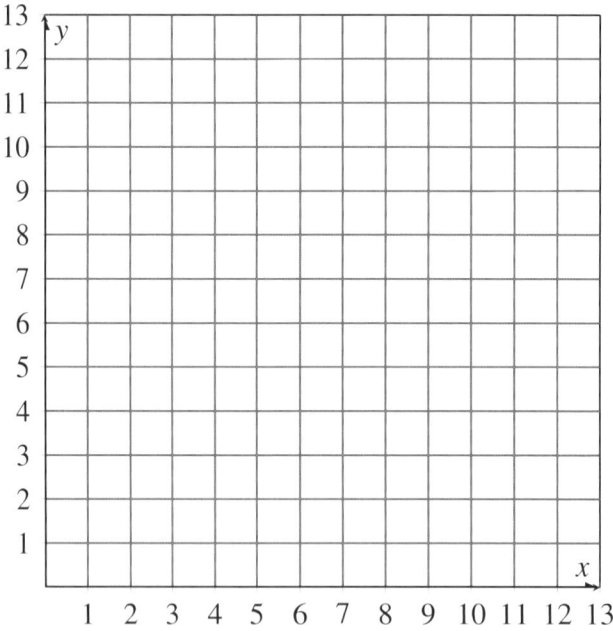

(b) Find the points with integer coordinates that satisfy the inequalities.

(c) Find the point satisfying these inequalities which gives the maximum value of $2x + 3y$.

16 Graphs in Practical Situations

16.1 Conversion Graphs

Conversion Graphs

Conversion graphs can be used to convert between two different units.

Example 16.1.1

The conversion graph below can be used to convert between meters and feet.

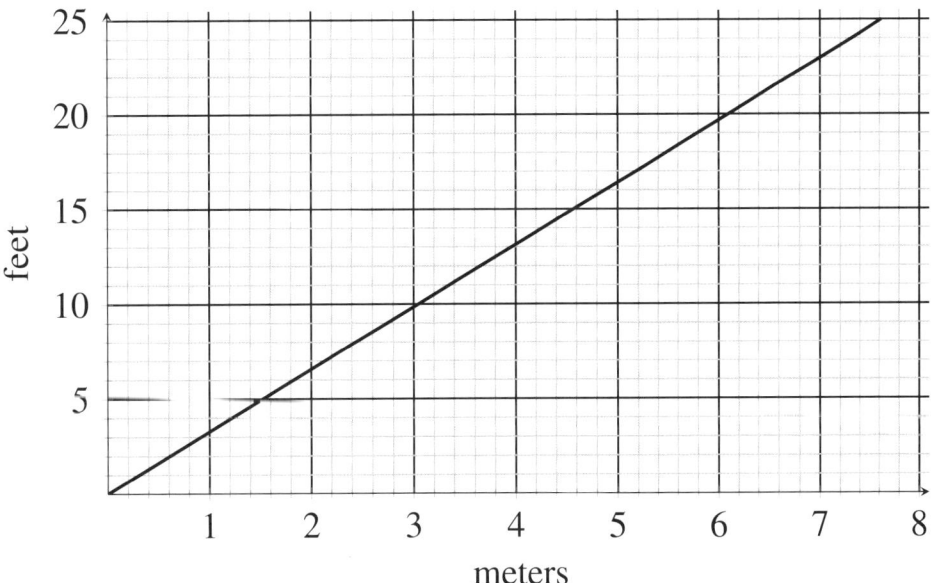

(a) Use the conversion graph to change 7 meters to feet.

(b) Use the conversion graph to change 20 feet to meters.

16.2 Distance vs. Time Graphs

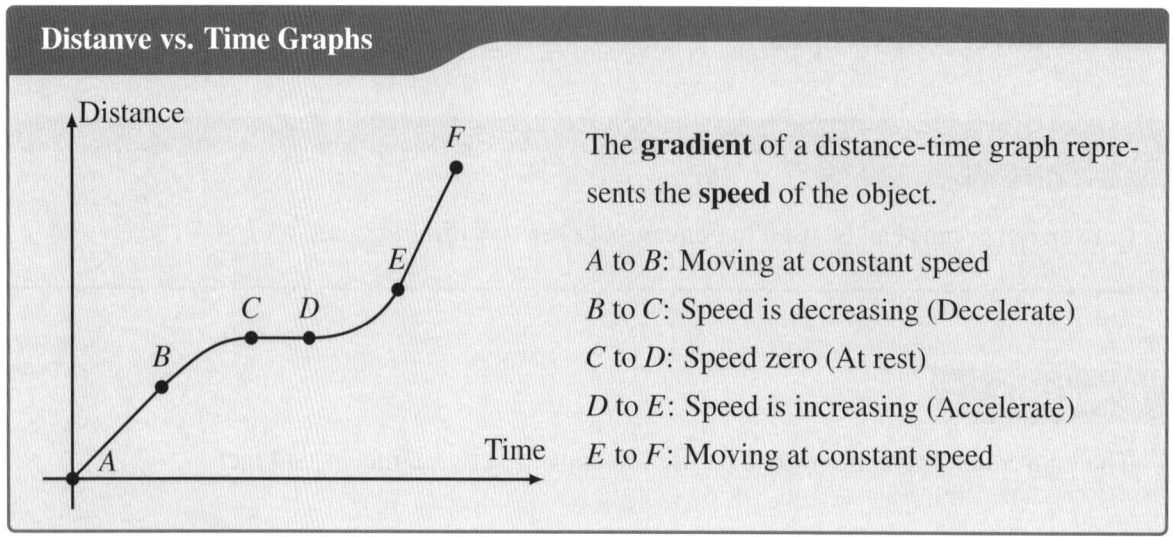

The **gradient** of a distance-time graph represents the **speed** of the object.

A to B: Moving at constant speed
B to C: Speed is decreasing (Decelerate)
C to D: Speed zero (At rest)
D to E: Speed is increasing (Accelerate)
E to F: Moving at constant speed

Example 16.2.1

Joy cycled from her home to the post office. After completing the postal work, she headed back home. Her journey is represented as a distance-time graph below.

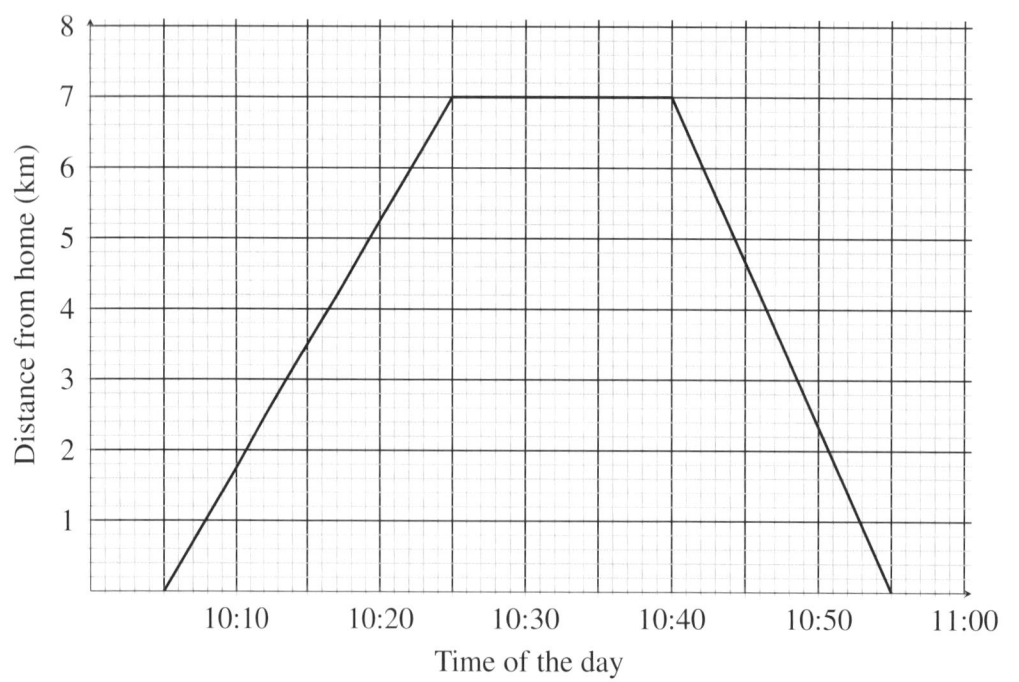

(a) What time did joy started cycling?

(b) How long did it take her to finish the postal work?

(c) Find the speed on her way to the post office and the speed on her way back home.(in km/h)

Example 16.2.2

Clara is on her way to work and her distance from home is graphed below. Estimate her speed at 9:30.

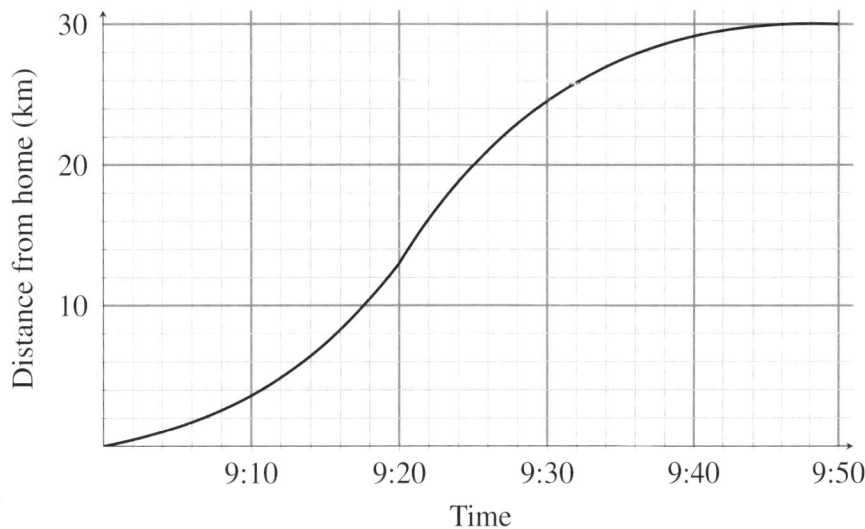

16.3 Speed vs. Time Graphs

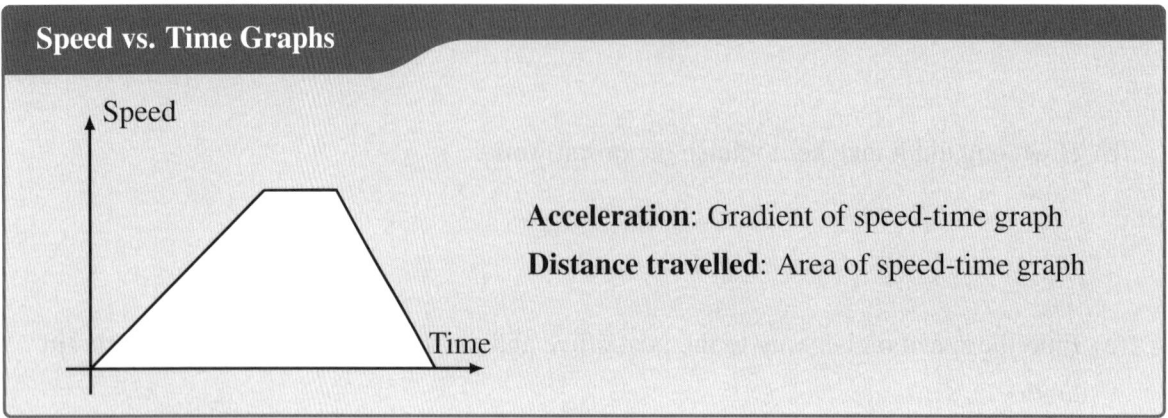

Acceleration: Gradient of speed-time graph

Distance travelled: Area of speed-time graph

Example 16.3.1

A speed-time graph is given blow, where speed is in meters per second and time is in seconds. Find:

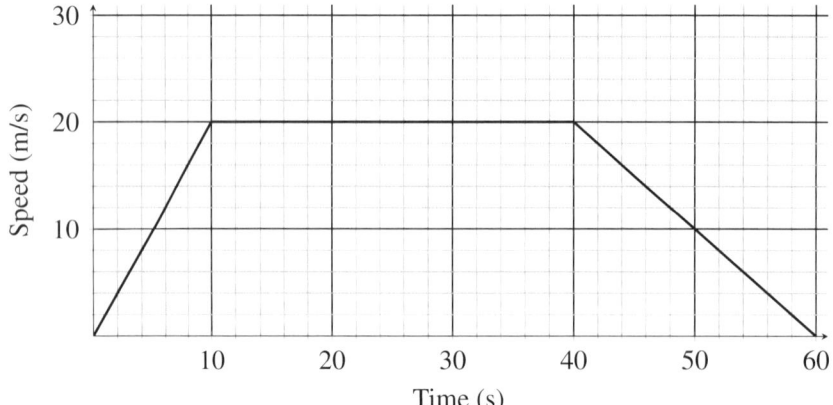

(a) the acceleration at $t = 43$.

(b) the total distance travelled.

(c) the average speed of the entire journey.

116   IGCSE & MYP Math

Unit 4

Mensuration

Ch.17 Measures
Ch.18 Geometrical Terms
Ch.19 Two Dimensional Figures
Ch.20 Three Dimensional Figures

17 Measures

17.1 Units of Length

Prefix	Symbol	Multiplication Factor	Scientific Notation
kilo	k	1000	1×10^3
–	–	1	1×10^0
centi	c	0.01	1×10^{-2}
milli	m	0.001	1×10^{-3}

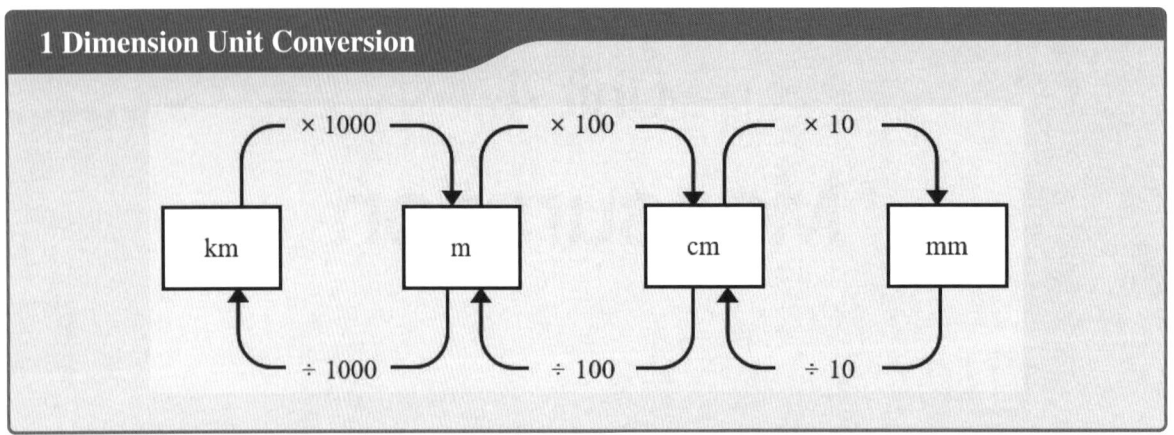

Example 17.1.1

Change

(a) 6.2 mm to m

(b) 9800 m to km

(c) 0.023 km to cm

118 IGCSE & MYP Math

17.2 Units of Area

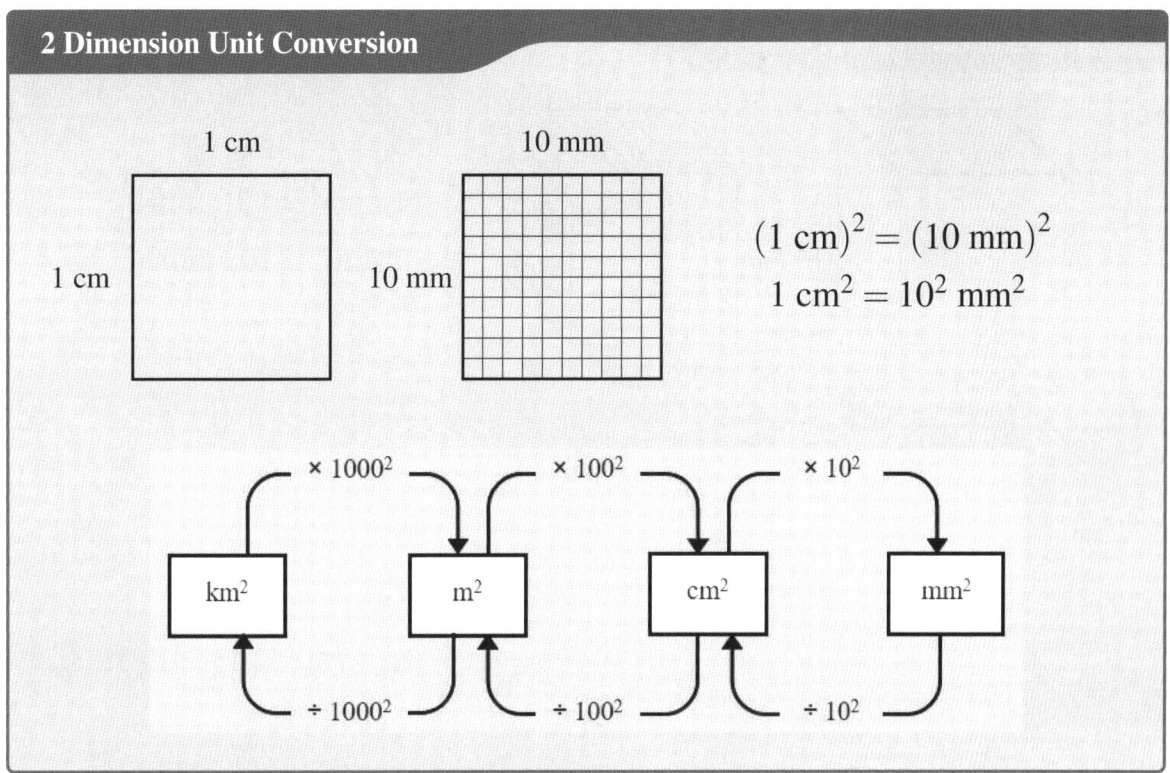

Example 17.2.1

Change

(a) 0.047 km^2 to m^2

(b) 18,000 mm^2 to cm^2

17.3 Units of Volume

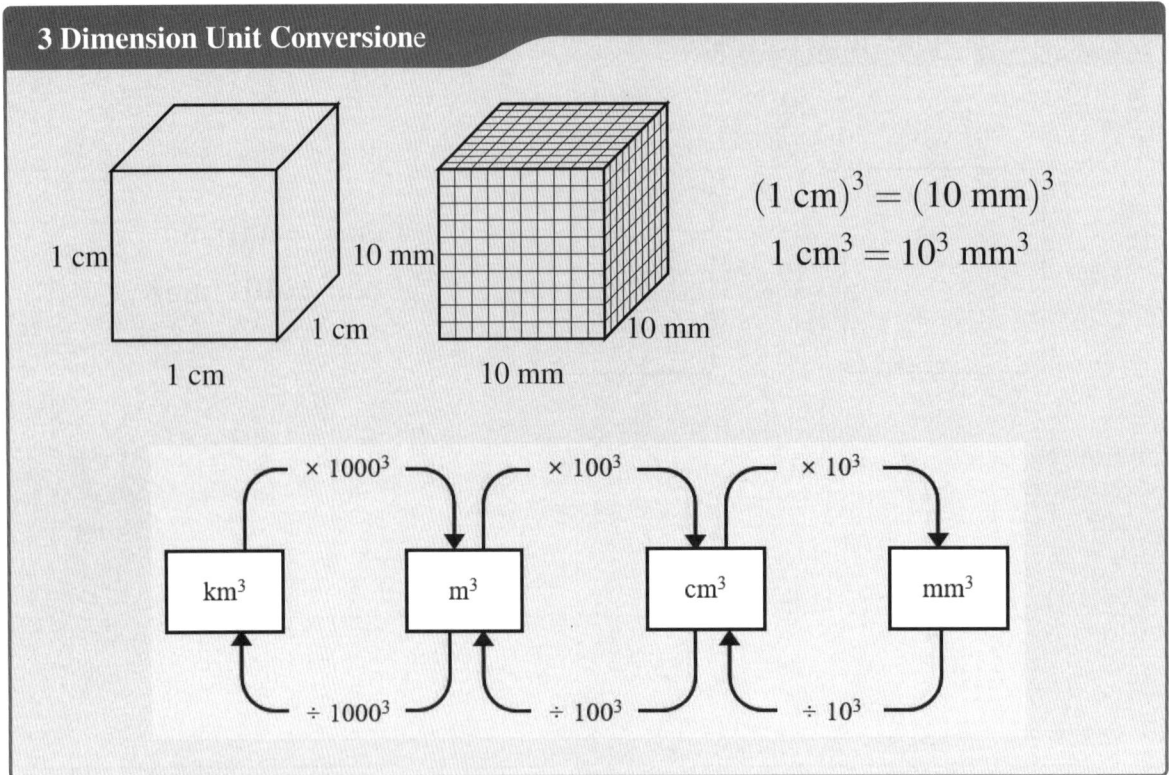

Example 17.3.1

Change

(a) 930,000 m^3 to km^3

(b) 0.034 m^3 to cm^3

17.4 Mass, Capacity, and Density

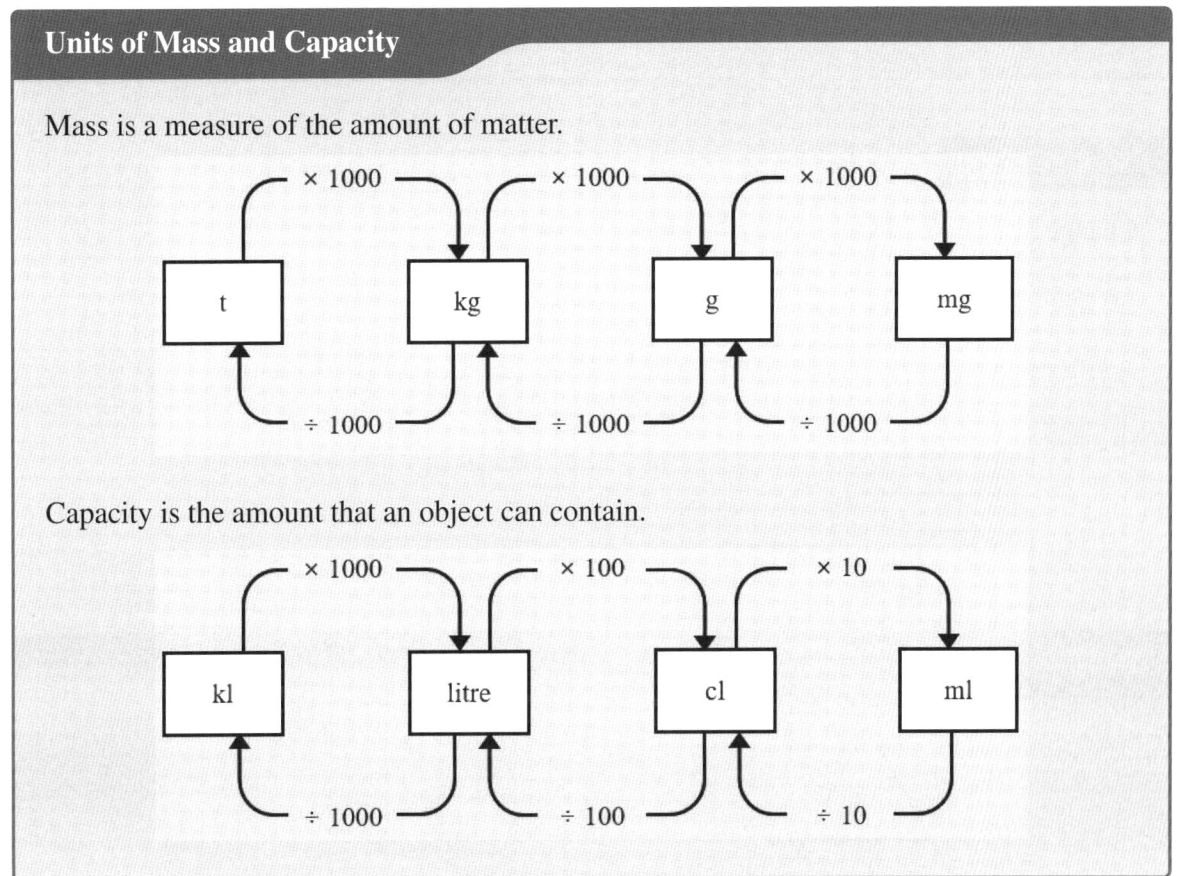

Example 17.4.1

Change

(a) 63,500 g to t

(b) 0.00593 litre to ml

Conversion Between Capacity and Volume

$1 \text{ ml} = 1 \text{ cm}^3$ $1 \text{ litre} = 1000 \text{ cm}^3$ $1000 \text{ litres} = 1 \text{ m}^3$

Example 17.4.2

Change

(a) 3.5 litres to cm^3

(b) 5.86 m^3 to litres

Density

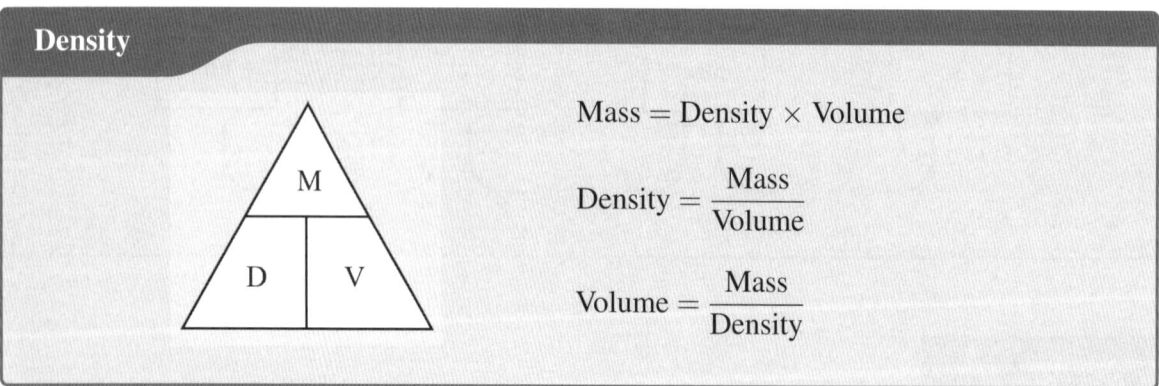

Mass = Density × Volume

$$\text{Density} = \frac{\text{Mass}}{\text{Volume}}$$

$$\text{Volume} = \frac{\text{Mass}}{\text{Density}}$$

Example 17.4.3

(a) Find the volume of wood that has a mass of 48g and density of 60 g/cm^3.

(b) Find the density of a piece of metal that has a mass of 0.4 kg and volume of 80 cm^3.

18 Geometrical Terms

18.1 Points and Lines

Points and Lines

Point (No Dimension): Points are used to represent positions.

Line (1-Dimension): A straight one-dimensional figure that extends infinitely in both directions.

(1) Parallel: Lines on a plane that never meet.

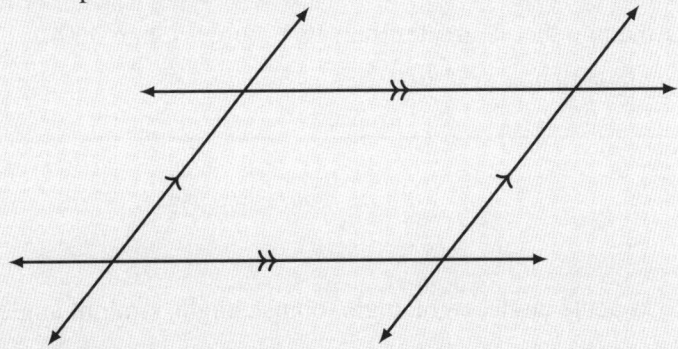

(2) Perpendicular: Lines that meet each other at 90°.

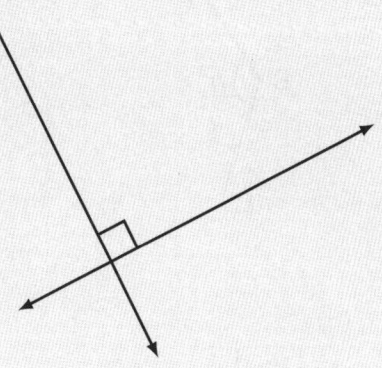

18.2 Angles

Angles

Angle: The amount of turn between two lines.

Types of Angles
(1) Acute angle: An angle that is greater than 0° but less than 90°.
(2) Right angle: An angle that is exactly 90°.
(3) Obtuse angle: An angle that is greater than 90° but less than 180°.
(4) Straight angle: An angle that is exactly 180°.
(5) Reflex angle: An angle that is greater than 180° but less than 360°.
(6) Revolution: An angle that is exactly 360°.

Example 18.2.1

Identify each angle as acute angle, right angle, obtuse angle, straight angle, reflex angle, or revolution.

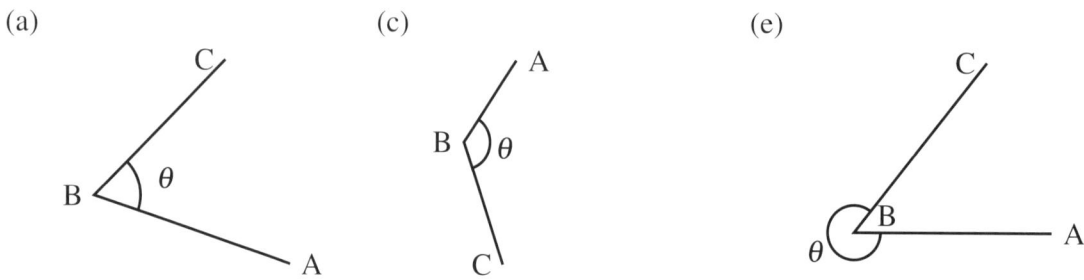

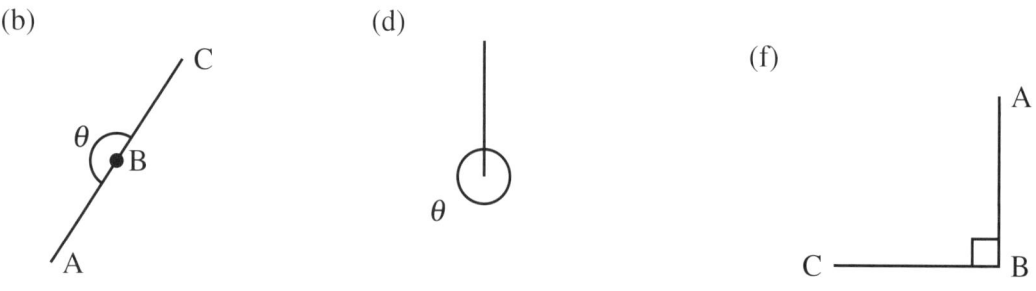

18.3 Polygons

Polygons

Polygon: Closed 2-dimensional shape formed with straight lines.

Regular Polygon: Polygons with congruent sides and congruent interior angles.

Regular Triangle   **Regular Quadrilateral**   **Regular Pentagon**   **Regular Hexagon**

  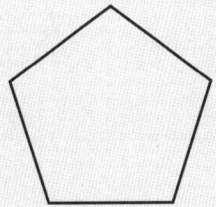 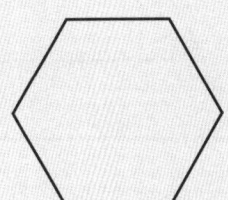

Triangles

Triangle: A three-sided polygon with three angles, vertices, and sides.

Triangles Classified by Angles
(1) Acute triangle: A triangle with three acute angles.
(2) Right triangle: A triangle with one right angle.
(3) Obtuse triangle: A triangle with one obtuse angle.

Acute Triangle   **Right Triangle**   **Obtuse Triangle**

 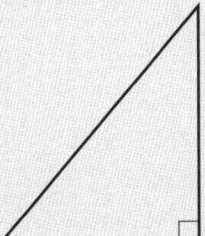 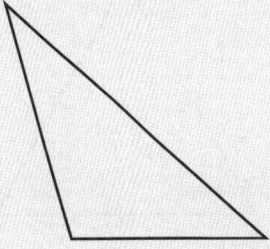

Triangles Classified by Sides

(1) Equilateral triangle: A triangle with three equal sides.

(2) Isosceles triangle: A triangle with two equal sides.

(3) Scalene triangle: A triangle with no equal sides.

Equilateral Triangle

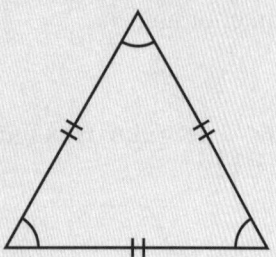

Isosceles Triangle

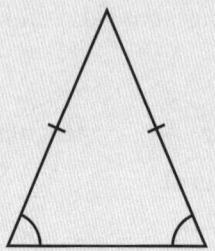

Scalene Triangle

Example 18.3.1

Classify each triangle by its angles and sides.

(a)

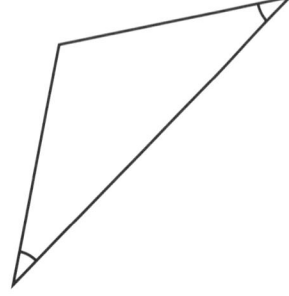

(c)

(b)

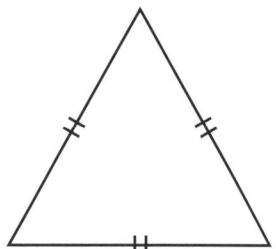

Quadrilaterals

Quadrilateral: A four-sided polygon with four angles, vertices, and sides.

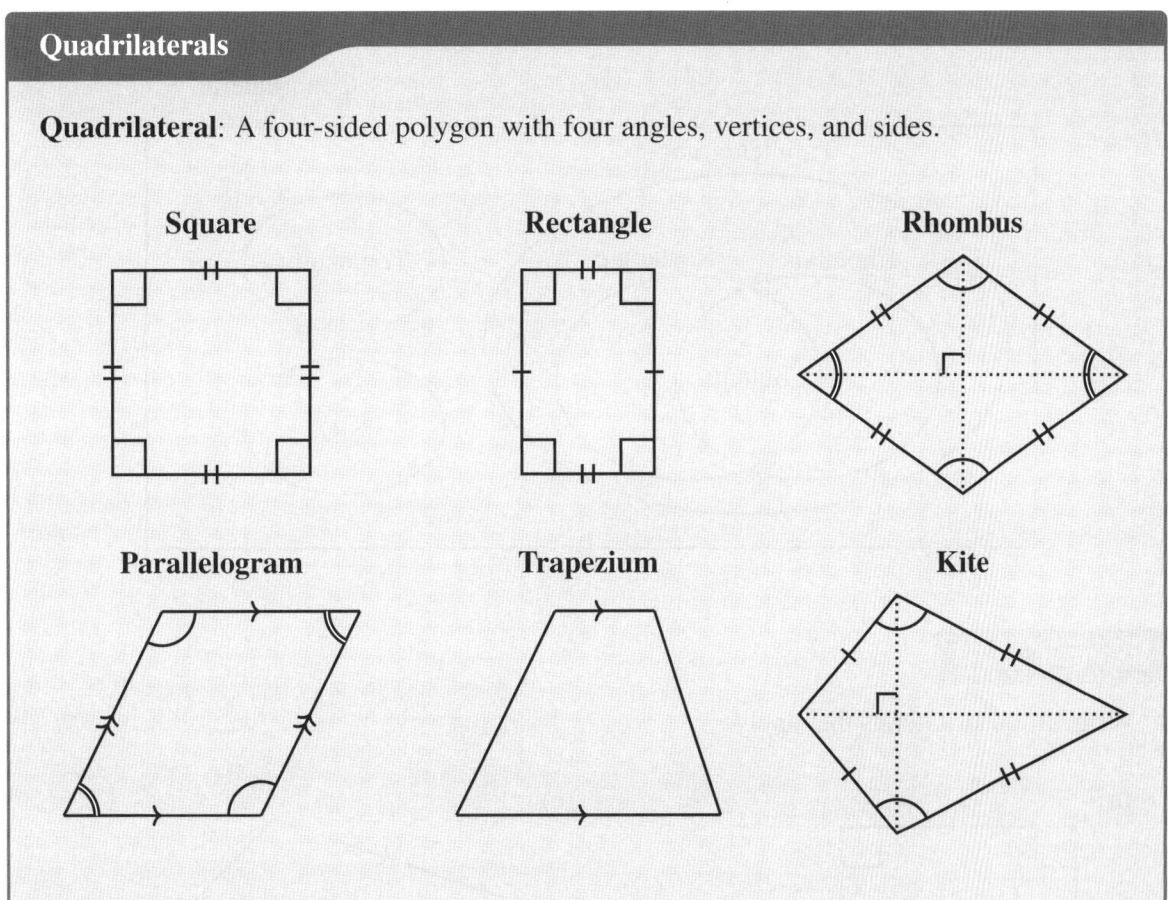

Properties of Quarilaterals

	Square	Rectangle	Rhombus	Parallelogram	Trapezium	Kite
All sides equal	✓		✓			
Opposite sides equal	✓	✓	✓	✓		
All angles right angles	✓	✓				
Parallel sides	2	2	2	2	1	
Opposite angles equal	2	2	2	2		1
Diagonals equal in length	✓	✓				
Diagonals perpendicular	✓		✓			✓
Diagonals bisect each other	✓	✓	✓	✓		
Diagonals bisect angle	✓		✓			✓

Relationships of Quadrilaterals

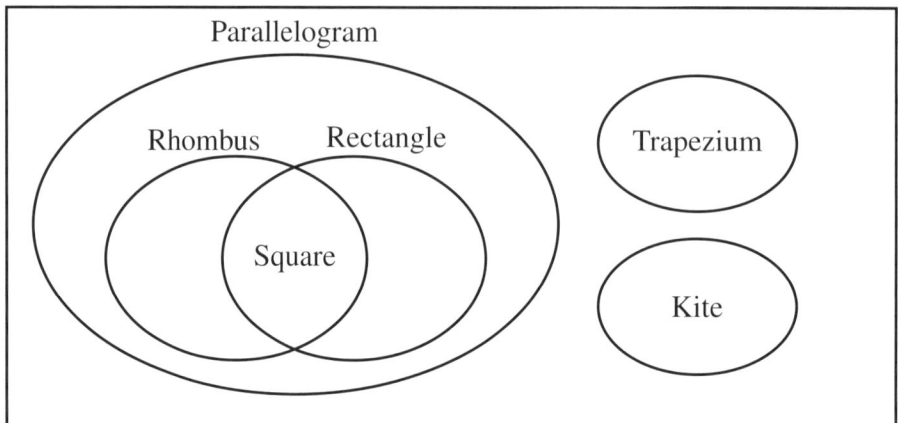

Example 18.3.2

Write all quadrilaterals that apply.

(a)

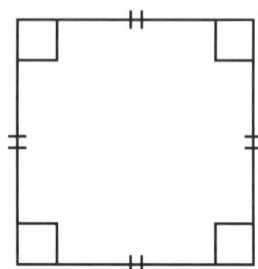

(c)

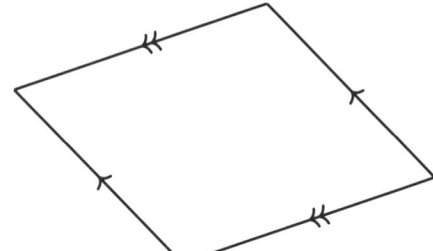

(b)

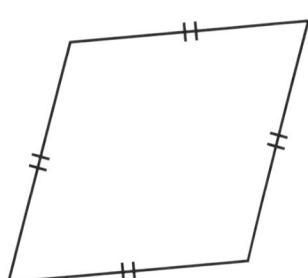

19 Two Dimensional Figures

19.1 Triangles

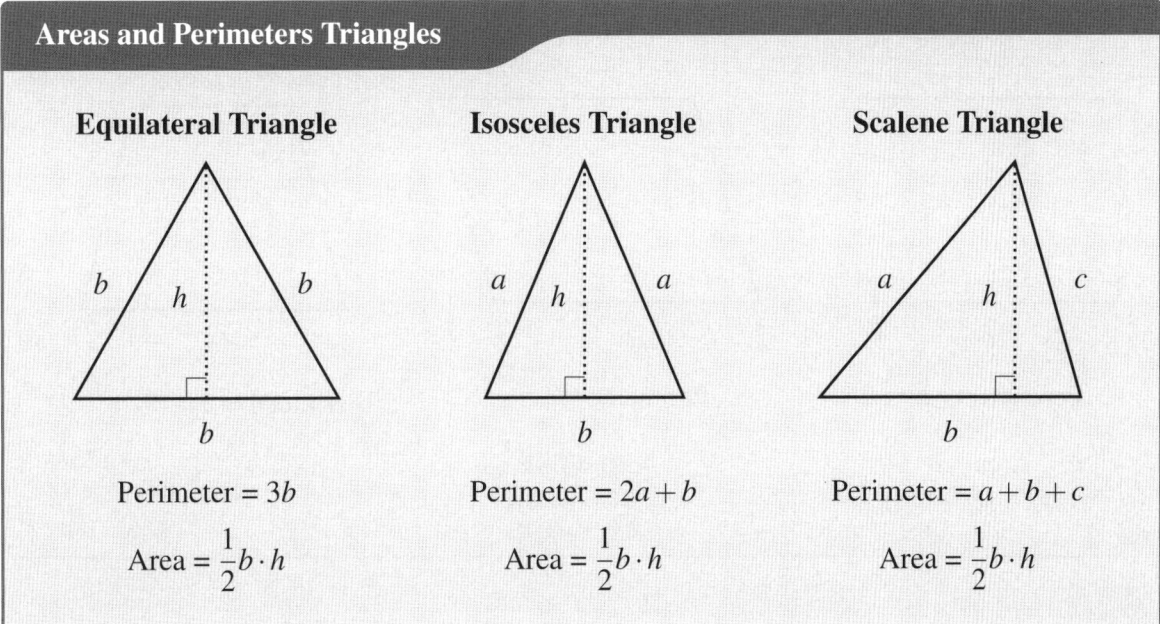

Example 19.1.1

Find the perimeter and the area of each triangle below.

(a)

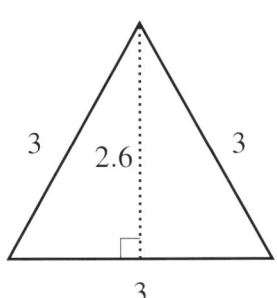

(b)

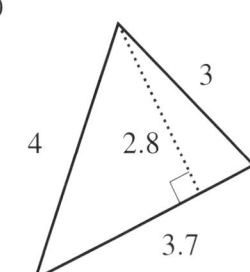

19.2 Quadrilaterals

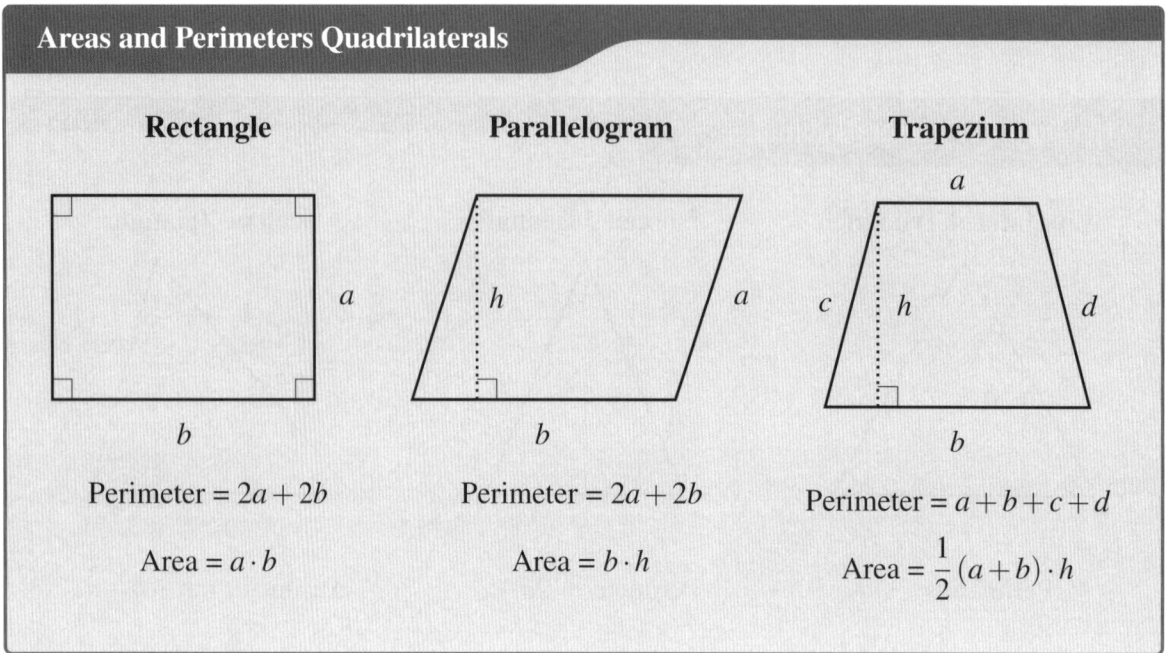

Example 19.2.1

Find the perimeter and the area of each triangle below.

(a)   (b)

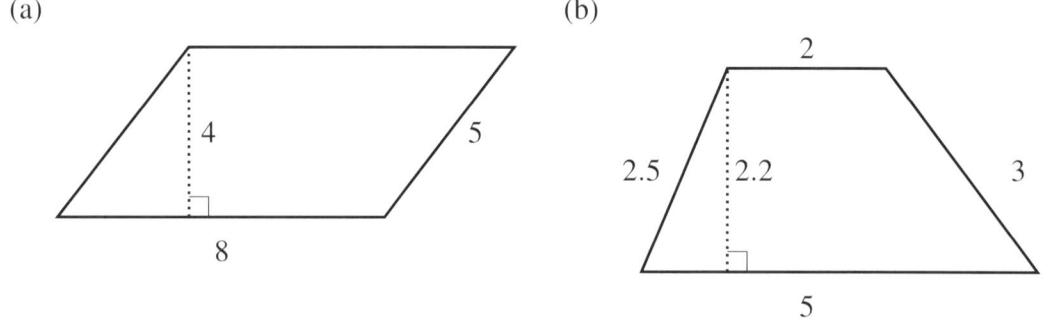

19.3 Circles

Circumference and Area of Circles

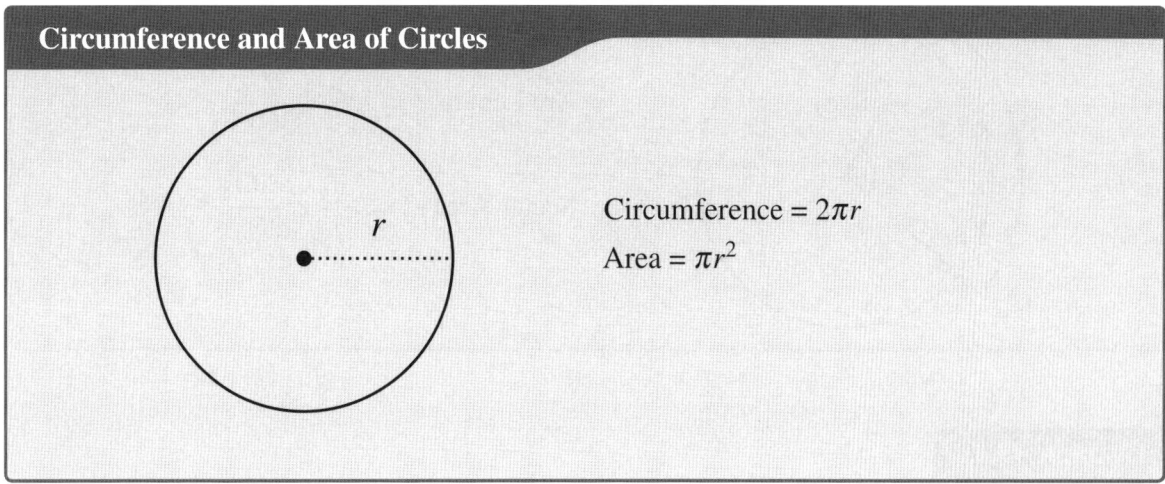

Circumference = $2\pi r$
Area = πr^2

Example 19.3.1

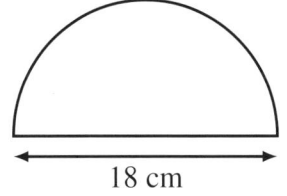

Find the perimeter and area of the semicircle on the left.
Give your answers in terms of π.

Arc Length and Sector Area

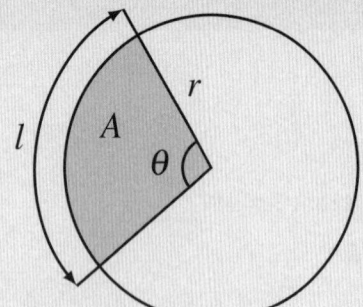

Arc Length $l = 2\pi r \times \dfrac{\theta}{360}$

Sector Area $A = \pi r^2 \times \dfrac{\theta}{360}$

Example 19.3.2

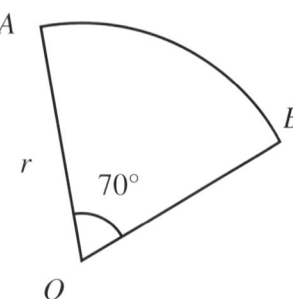

OAB is a sector with central angle $70°$.
The area of the sector AOB is 22cm^2.

(a) Find the radius of the circle to the nearest cm.

(b) Find the perimeter of the sector to the nearest cm.

20 Three Dimensional Figures

20.1 Prisms and Cylinders

Volumes of Prisms and Cylinders

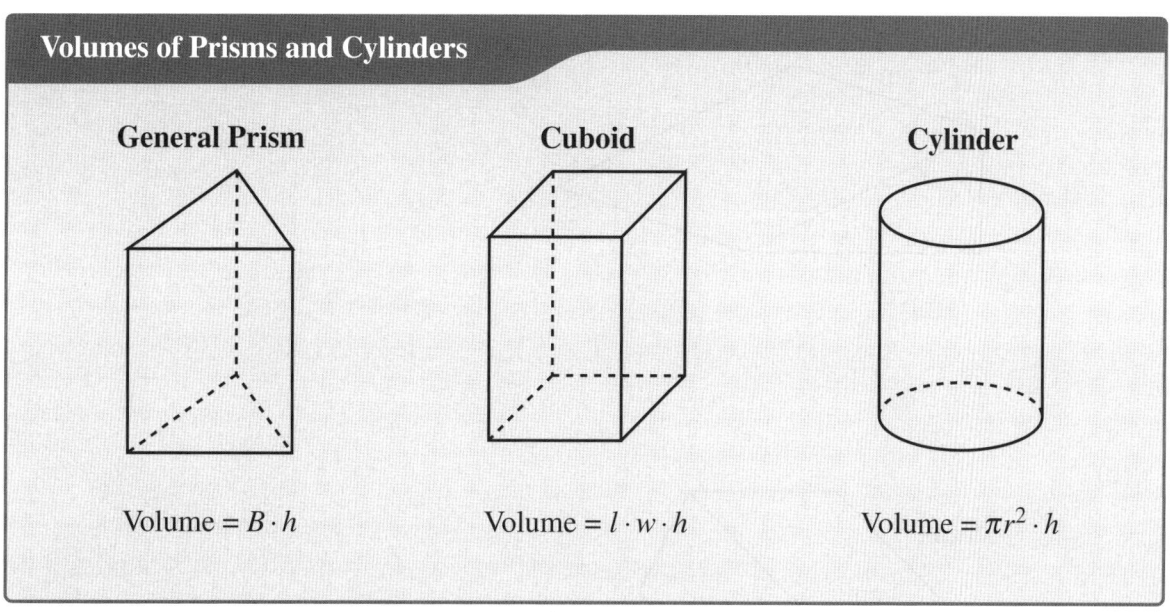

General Prism	Cuboid	Cylinder
Volume = $B \cdot h$	Volume = $l \cdot w \cdot h$	Volume = $\pi r^2 \cdot h$

Surface Area and Nets of Prisms and Cylinders

Nets: A two dimensional figure which can be produced by unfolding a three dimensional figure.

General Prism	Cuboid	Cylinder
Area = $2B + P \cdot h$	Area = $2lw + 2(l+w)h$	Area = $2\pi r^2 + 2\pi r \cdot h$

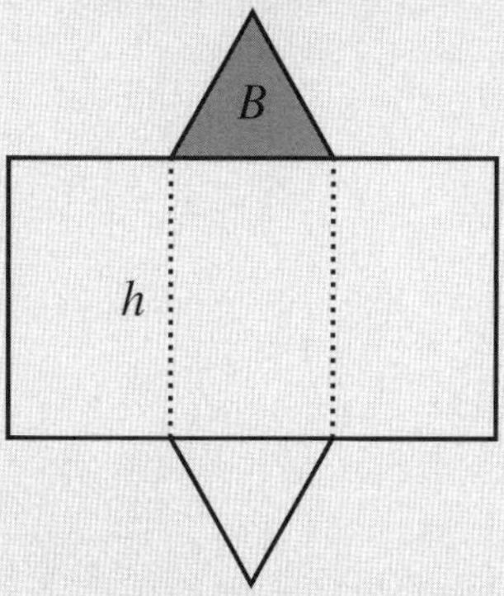

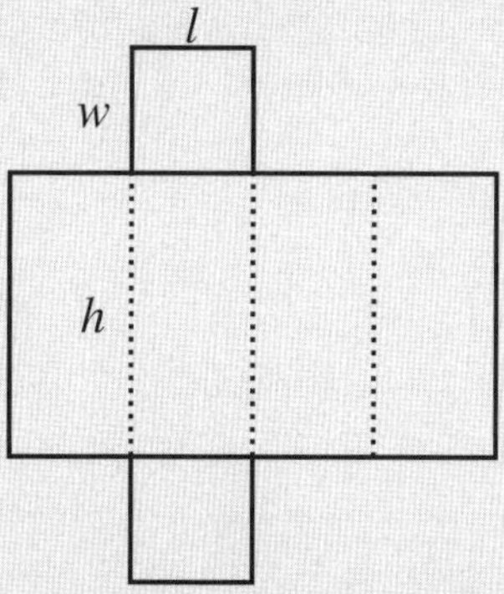

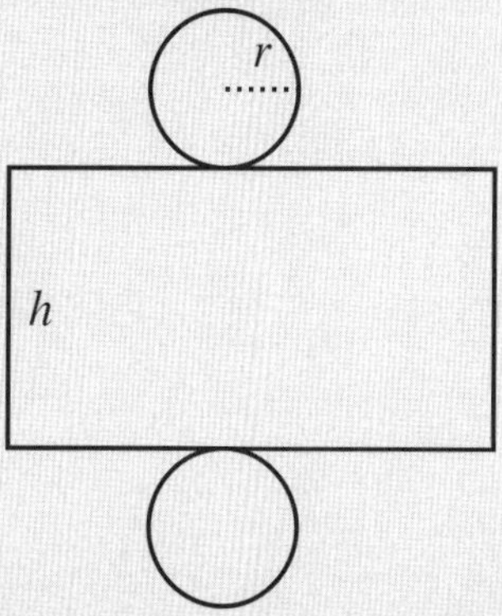

Unit 4. Mensuration

Example 20.1.1

Find the volume and surface area of each three dimensional figure.

(a)

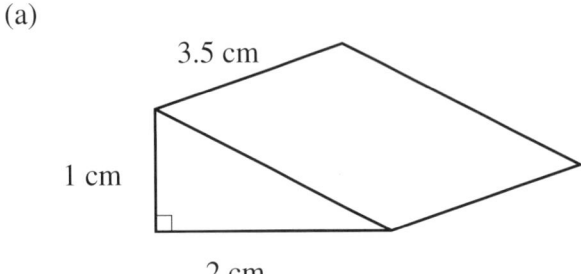

(b)

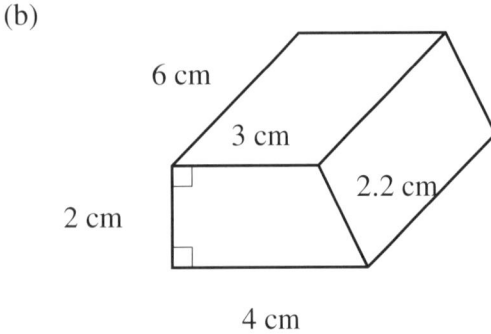

20.2 Pyramids and Cones

Volumes of Pyramids and Cones

Triangular Pyramid

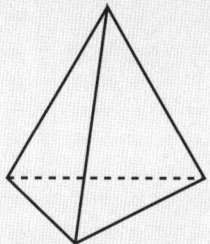

Volume = $\frac{1}{3} B \cdot h$

Rectangular Pyramid

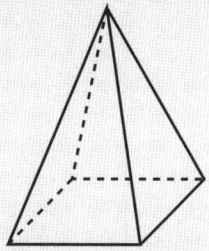

Volume = $\frac{1}{3} l \cdot w \cdot h$

Cone

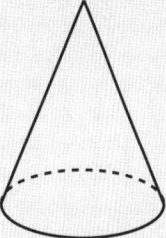

Volume = $\frac{1}{3} \pi r^2 h$

Surface Area and Nets of Prisms and Cylinders

Triangular Pyramid

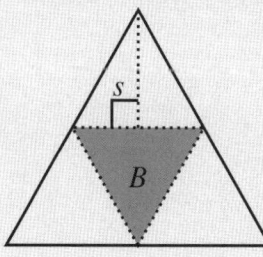

Area = $B + \frac{1}{2} P \cdot s$

Rectangular Pyramid

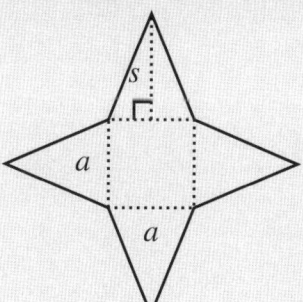

Area = $a^2 + 2as$

Cone

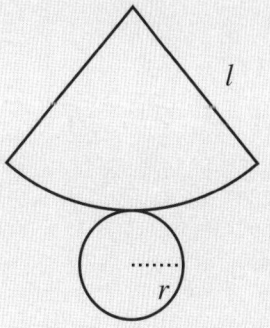

Area = $\pi r^2 + \pi r l$

Example 20.2.1

Find the volume and surface area of each three dimensional figure.

(a) A pyramid with a square base of side 3 m and vertical height 4 m.

(b) A cone with radius of 7cm and vertical height 5cm.

20.3 Spheres

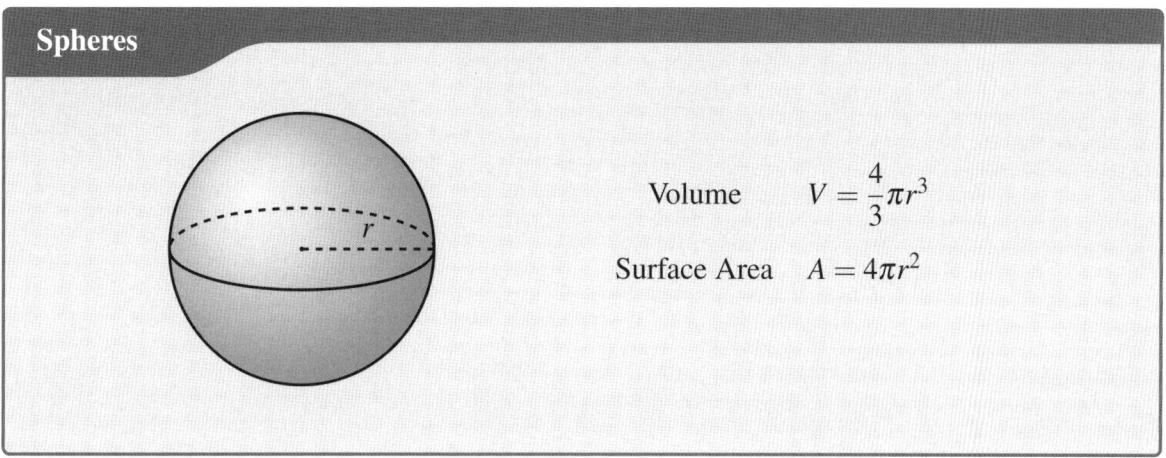

Spheres

Volume $V = \dfrac{4}{3}\pi r^3$

Surface Area $A = 4\pi r^2$

Example 20.3.1

A sphere has a volume of 600 cm³.

(a) Calculate the radius of the sphere.

(b) Calculate the surface area of the sphere.

Unit 5
Geometry

- Ch.21 Geometrical Constructions
- Ch.22 Similarity
- Ch.23 Congruent Triangles
- Ch.24 Symmetry
- Ch.25 Basic Angle Properties
- Ch.26 Angles in Polygons
- Ch.27 Angles in Circles

21 Geometrical Constructions

21.1 Measuring and Drawing Angles

Measuring Acute and Obtuse Angles

(1) Place the center of the protractor at the vertex.
(2) Align the base line.
(3) Move around the scale starting from zero and read the scale where the other line passes.

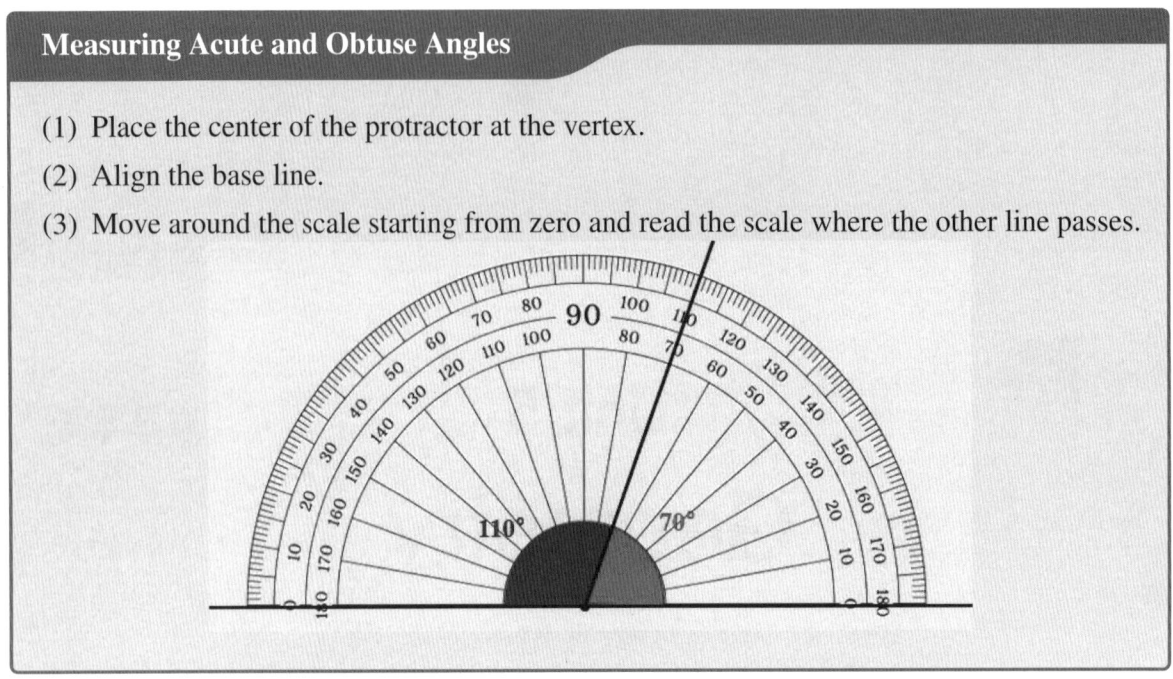

Measuring Reflex Angles

(1) Measure the inner angle.
(2) Subtract the angle from 360°.

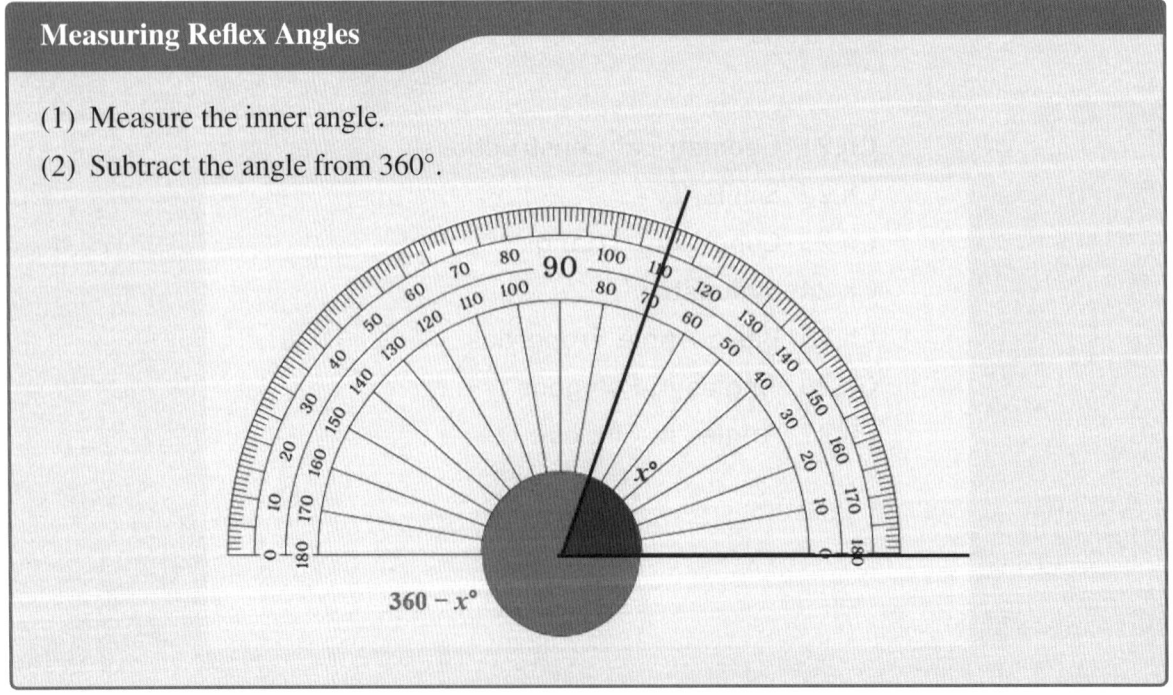

Example 21.1.1

Measure the following angles.

(a)
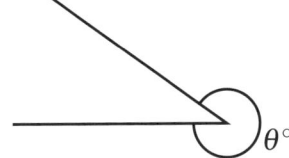

(c)
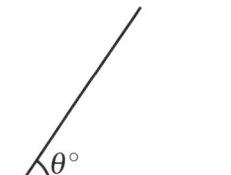

(b)
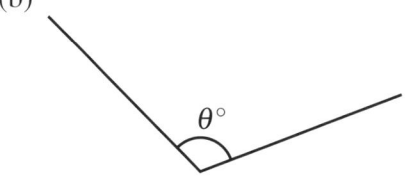

Drawing Angles

(1) Draw the base line and draw the vertex on the line.
(2) Place the center of the protractor at the vertex and align the base line.
(3) Draw a point on the scale.
(4) Draw a straight line which passes the vertex and the point from (3).

Example 21.1.2

Draw an angle of 50°.

21.2 Constructing Triangles

Constructing Triangle $\triangle ABC$ Given Three Sides

(1) Draw segment BC.
(2) Draw an arc centered at B with radius equal to the length of AB.
(3) Draw an arc centered at C with radius equal to the length of AC.
(4) Label the intersection point of the arcs as A.
(5) Join AB and AC.

Example 21.2.1

Construct a triangle that has side lengths 4cm, 5cm, and 6cm.

22 Similarity

22.1 Lengths of Similar Figures

Properties of Similar Figures

(1) Corresponding angles are congruent
(2) Corresponding sides are proportional

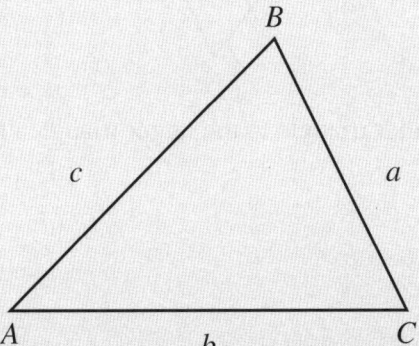 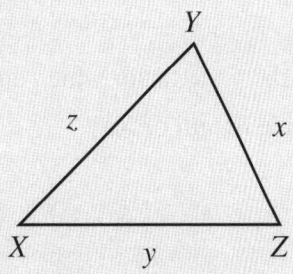

Scale Factor $\quad \dfrac{x}{a} = \dfrac{y}{b} = \dfrac{z}{c} = k$

Example 22.1.1

Triangles ABC and XYZ are shown in the diagram below

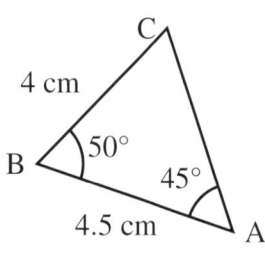
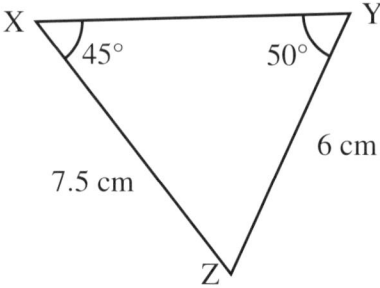

(a) Find the scale factor which enlarges the smaller triangle to the larger triangle. Then find the side length of XY.

(b) Find the scale factor which reduces the larger triangle to the smaller triangle. Then find the side length of AC.

22.2 Areas of Similar Figures (EXTENDED ONLY)

Areas of Similar Figures

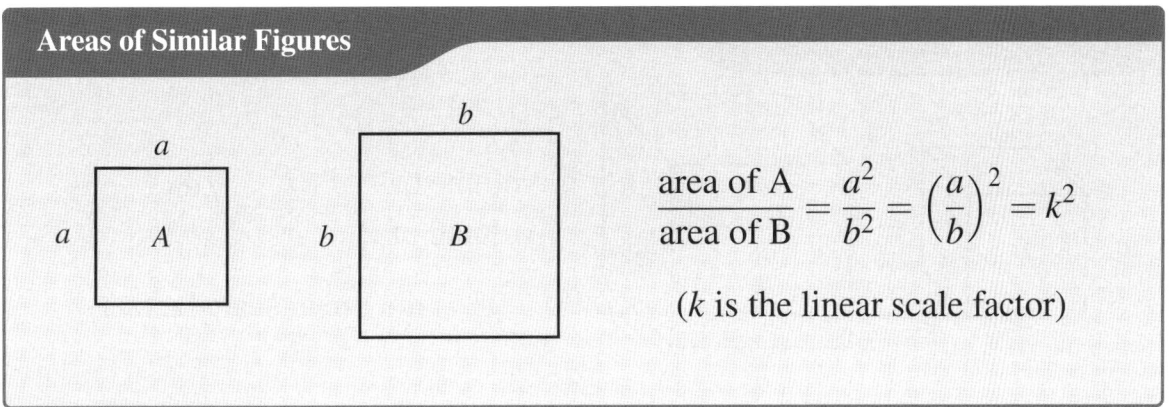

$$\frac{\text{area of A}}{\text{area of B}} = \frac{a^2}{b^2} = \left(\frac{a}{b}\right)^2 = k^2$$

(k is the linear scale factor)

Example 22.2.1 EXTENDED ONLY

The triangles in the diagram are similar triangles. If the area of the larger triangle is 72cm², find the area of the smaller triangle.

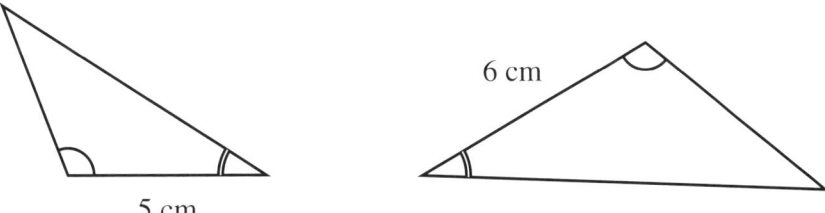

Example 22.2.2 EXTENDED ONLY

Two similar parallelograms have areas of 12cm² and 75cm². If the base of the smaller parallelogram is 8cm, find the base of the larger parallelogram.

22.3 Volumes of Similar Figures (EXTENDED ONLY)

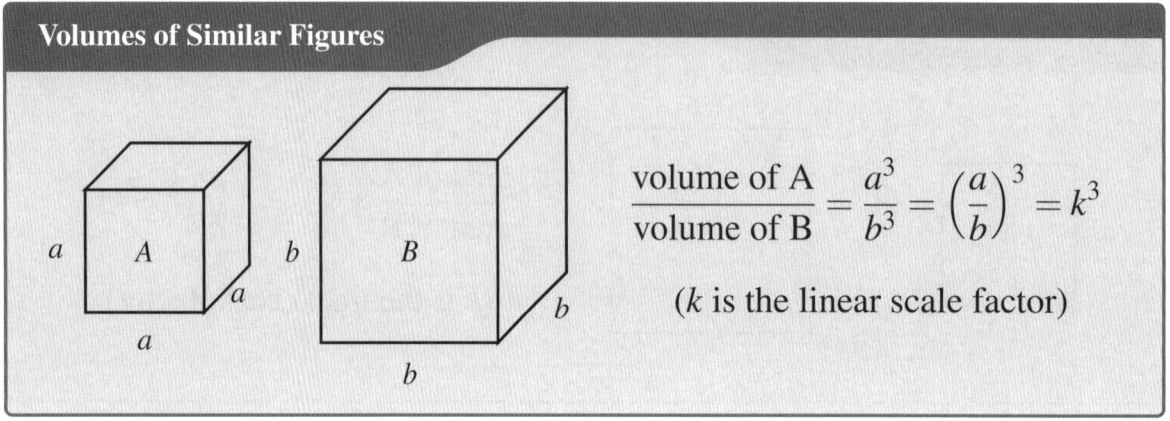

Volumes of Similar Figures

$$\frac{\text{volume of A}}{\text{volume of B}} = \frac{a^3}{b^3} = \left(\frac{a}{b}\right)^3 = k^3$$

(k is the linear scale factor)

Example 22.3.1 EXTENDED ONLY

Two similar cones have radius of 3cm and 4cm. If the volume of the smaller cone is 81cm³, find the volume of the larger cone.

Example 22.3.2 EXTENDED ONLY

Two similar cylinders have volumes of 48m³ and 162m³. If the height of the larger cylinder is 6m, find the height of the smaller cylinder.

22.4 Scale Drawings

Scale Drawing

Scale Drawing: A drawing which is reduced or enlarged from its original size according to a certain scale.

Example 22.4.1

1cm on a map represents an actual distance of 2km.

(a) If the distance between town A and town B on the map is 4cm, find the actual distance.

(b) If the actual distance between town A and town C is 9km, find the distance between the two towns on the map.

(c) (EXTENDED ONLY) The area of town C on the map is 6cm^2. Find the actual area of the town.

23 Congruent Triangles (EXTENDED ONLY)

23.1 SSS Congruency (EXTENDED ONLY)

SSS Congruency

If three sides of a triangle is equal to the three sides of another triangle, the two triangles are congruent by **SSS(Side-Side-Side) congruency**.

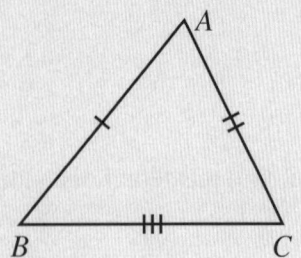 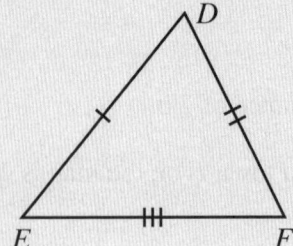

$$\overline{AB} = \overline{DE}$$
$$\overline{BC} = \overline{EF}$$
$$\overline{CA} = \overline{FD}$$
$$\implies \triangle ABC \cong \triangle DEF$$

Example 23.1.1 EXTENDED ONLY

State whether each of the following pairs of triangles is congruent.

(a)

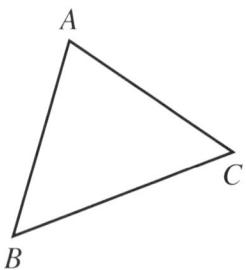 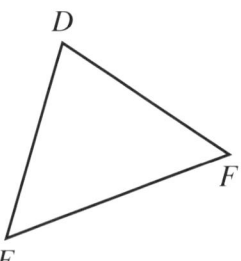

(b)

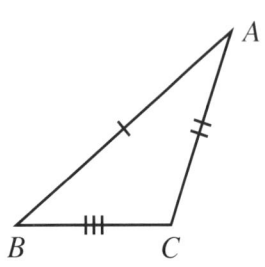 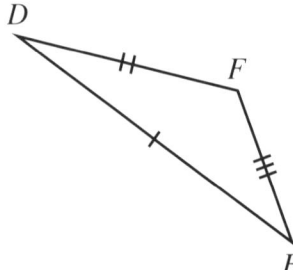

148 IGCSE & MYP Math

23.2 SAS Congruency (EXTENDED ONLY)

SAS Congruency

If two sides of a triangle is equal to the two sides of another triangle and the included angles are equal, the two triangles are congruent by **SAS(Side-Angle-Side) congruency**.

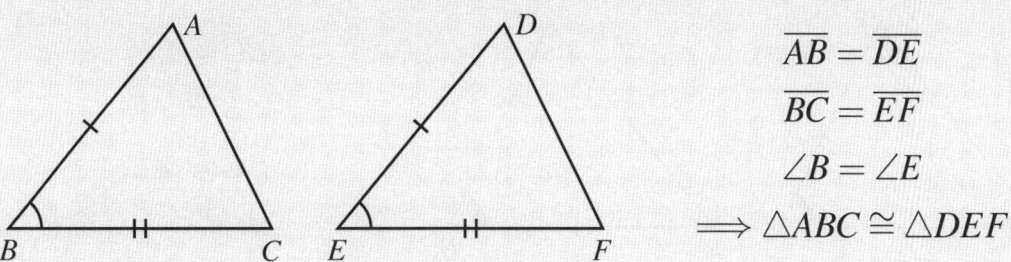

$$\overline{AB} = \overline{DE}$$
$$\overline{BC} = \overline{EF}$$
$$\angle B = \angle E$$
$$\implies \triangle ABC \cong \triangle DEF$$

Example 23.2.1 EXTENDED ONLY

State whether each of the following pairs of triangles is congruent.

(a)

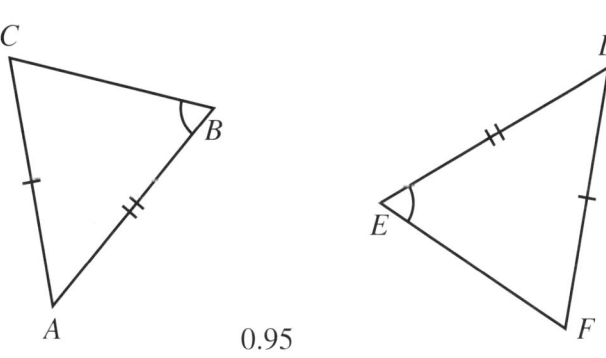

(b)

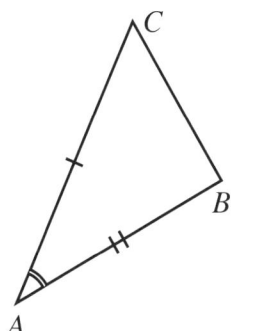
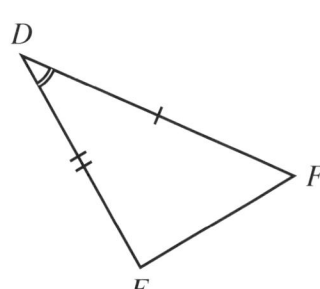

23.3 ASA Congruency (EXTENDED ONLY)

ASA Congruency

If two angles of a triangle is equal to the two angles of another triangle and the included sides are equal, the two triangles are congruent by **ASA(Angle-Side-Angle) congruency**.

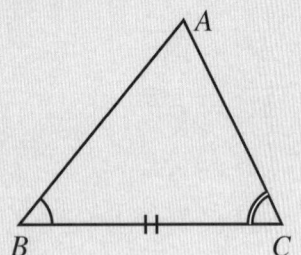
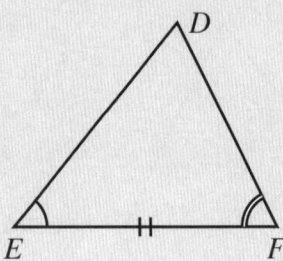

$\overline{BC} = \overline{EF}$
$\angle B = \angle E$
$\angle C = \angle F$
$\implies \triangle ABC \cong \triangle DEF$

Example 23.3.1 EXTENDED ONLY

State whether each of the following pairs of triangles is congruent.

(a)

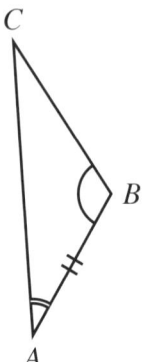
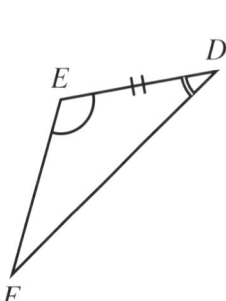

(b)

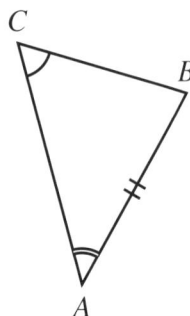
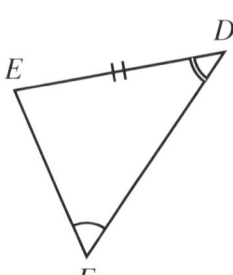

23.4 RHS Congruency (EXTENDED ONLY)

> **Title**
>
> If two right triangles have equal length of hypotenuse and one other side equal, the two triangles are congruent by **RHS(Right angle-Hypotenuse-Side) congruency**.
>
>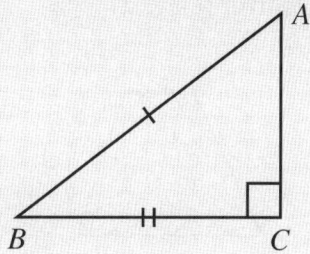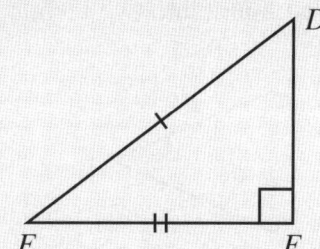
>
> $\angle C = \angle F = 90°$
> $\overline{AB} = \overline{DE}$
> $\overline{BC} = \overline{EF}$
> $\implies \triangle ABC \cong \triangle DEF$

Example 23.4.1 EXTENDED ONLY

State whether each of the following pairs of triangles is congruent.

(a)

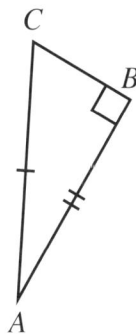 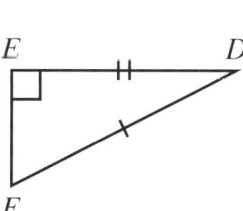

(b)

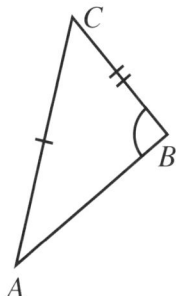 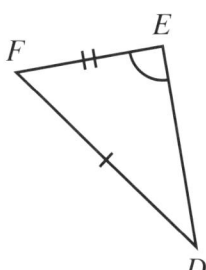

24 Symmetry

24.1 Symmetry in Two Dimension

> **Line Symmetry**
>
> **Line Symmetry**: Line which divides the figure into two identical mirror images.
>
>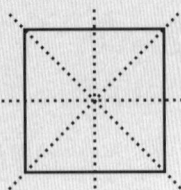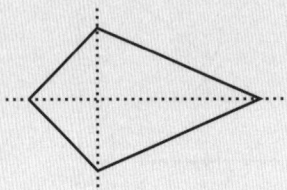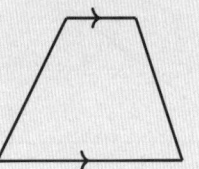

Example 24.1.1

Write down the number of lines of symmetry and draw the lines of symmetry on each diagram.

(a)

(b)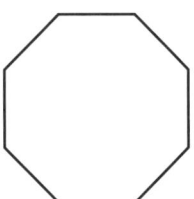

Example 24.1.2

Write down the number of lines of symmetry and draw the lines of symmetry on each diagram.

(a)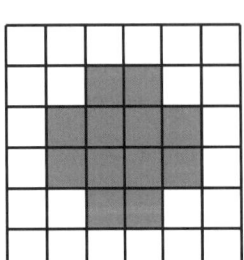

(b)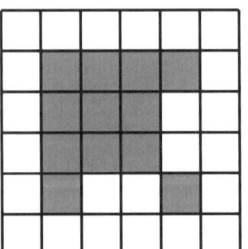

Rotational Symmetry

Rotational Symmetry: When the shape is rotated 360° with the center fixed and the shape fits into itself, the shape has a rotational symmetry.

Order of Rotational Symmetry: The number of times the figure fits into itself during the 360° rotation.

Original	(1) 90°	(2) 180°	(3) 270°	(4) 360°
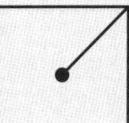		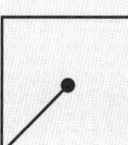	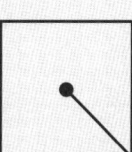	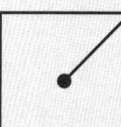

Example 24.1.3

State the order of rotational symmetry of each polynomial.

(a)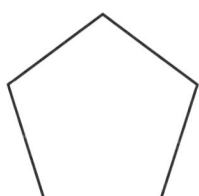

(b)

Example 24.1.4

State the order of rotational symmetry of each polynomial.

(a)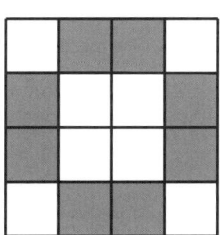

(b)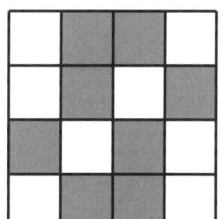

Unit 5. Geometry   153

24.2 Symmetry in Three Dimension (EXTENDED ONLY)

Plane Symmetry

Plane Symmetry: Plane which divides the three dimensional figure into two identical mirror shapes.

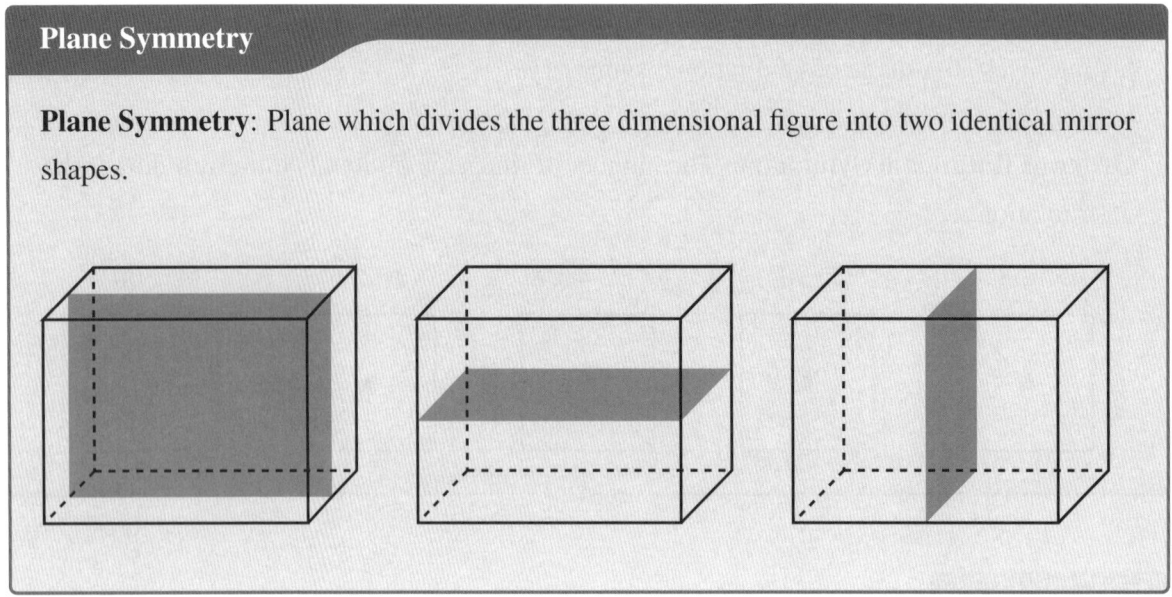

Example 24.2.1 EXTENDED ONLY

State the number of planes of symmetry of each shape.

(a)

(b)

Rotational Symmetry in Three Dimension

Rotational Symmetry: When the shape is rotated 360° about a certain axis and the shape fits into itself, the shape has a rotational symmetry.

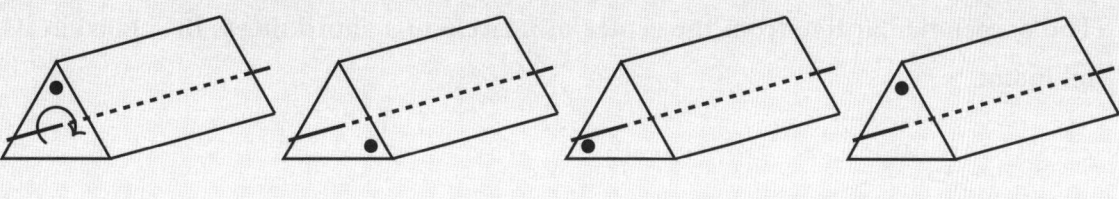

Example 24.2.2   EXTENDED ONLY

State the order of rotational symmetry of each three dimensional figure about the given axis.

(a)

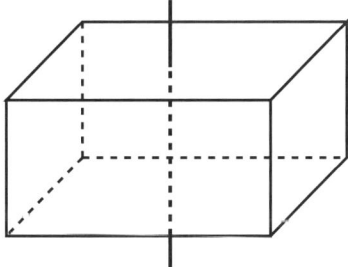

(b)

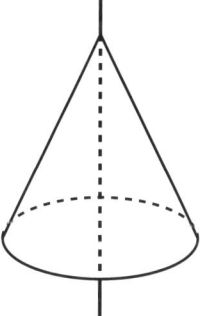

24.3 Symmetry in Circles (EXTENDED ONLY)

Circle Theorem (1)

(1) The perpendicular bisector of a chord passes through the centre.
The perpendicular line from the centre of a circle to a chord meets the chord at its midpoint.

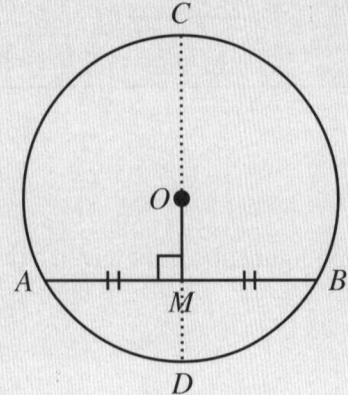

If $\overline{AB} \perp \overline{CD}$ and $AM = BM$,
then the centre O is on line CD.

If $\overline{AB} \perp \overline{OM}$, then $AM = BM$.

Example 24.3.1   EXTENDED ONLY

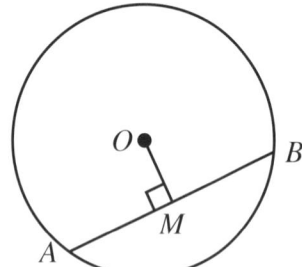

Chord AB is drawn in a circle with radius of 5 cm. If the $OM = 3$ cm, find the length of the chord AB.

Circle Theorem (2)

(2) Equal chords are equidistant from the centre.

Chords Equidistant from the centre are equal in length.

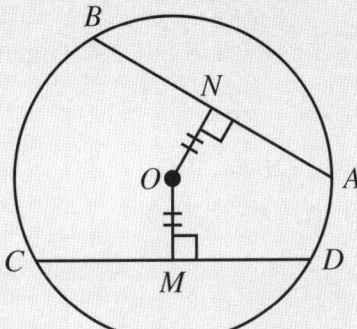

If $AB = CD$, then $ON = OM$

If $ON = OM$, then $AB = CD$.

Example 24.3.2   EXTENDED ONLY

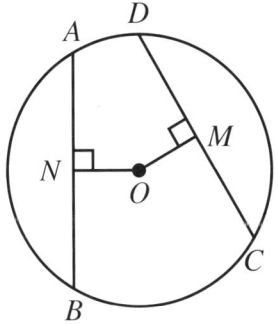

The radius of the circle is 13 cm. If $AB = CD = 24$cm, find the length of OM.

Circle Theorem (3)

(3) Tangents from an external point are equal in length.

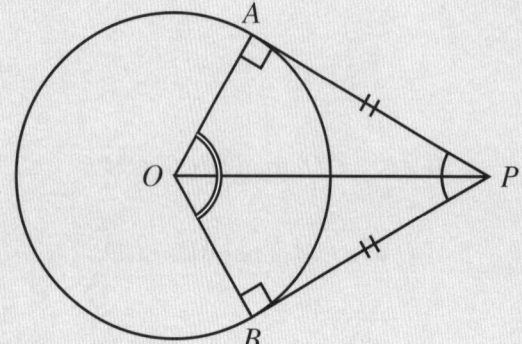

If $\overline{OA} \perp \overline{AP}$ and $\overline{OB} \perp \overline{BP}$, then

(1) $AP = BP$
(2) $\angle AOP = \angle BOP$
(3) $\angle APO = \angle BPO$

Example 24.3.3 EXTENDED ONLY

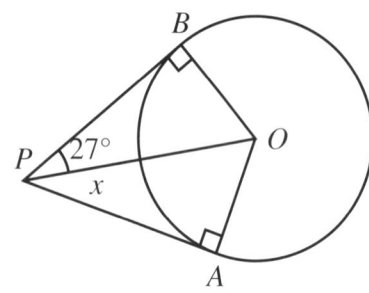

If $BP = 12$cm and $\angle OBP = \angle OAP = 90°$,

(a) find the length of AP.

(b) find the size of angle x.

25 Basic Angle Properties

25.1 Angle Relationships

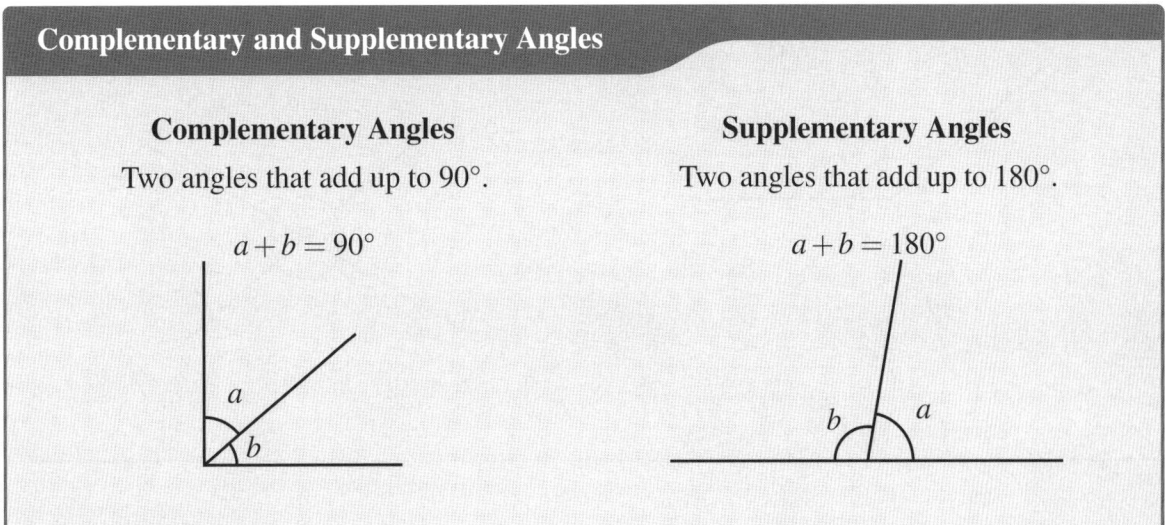

Example 25.1.1

Find the size of angles marked x.

(a)

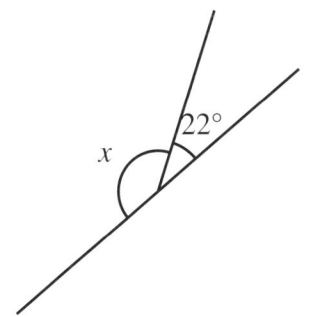

(b)

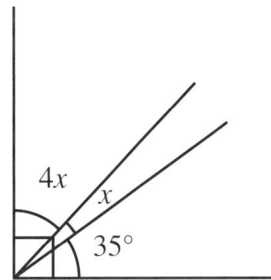

Angles Around a Point and Vertically Opposite Angles

Angles Around a Point

Angles at a point make a revolution.

$a + b + c = 360°$

Vertically Opposite Angles

Two pairs of vertical angles are formed between intersecting lines.

$a = c$ and $b = d$

Example 25.1.2

Find x, y and z.

(a)

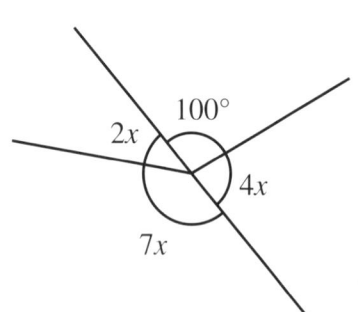

(b)

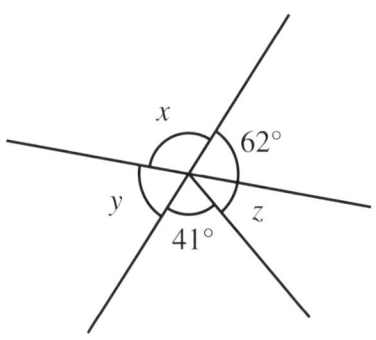

25.2 Angles Formed Within Parallel Lines

Corresponding Angles (F-shaped)

When a pair of parallel lines is cut by a transversal, it creates four pairs of corresponding angles. Corresponding angles are equal to each other.

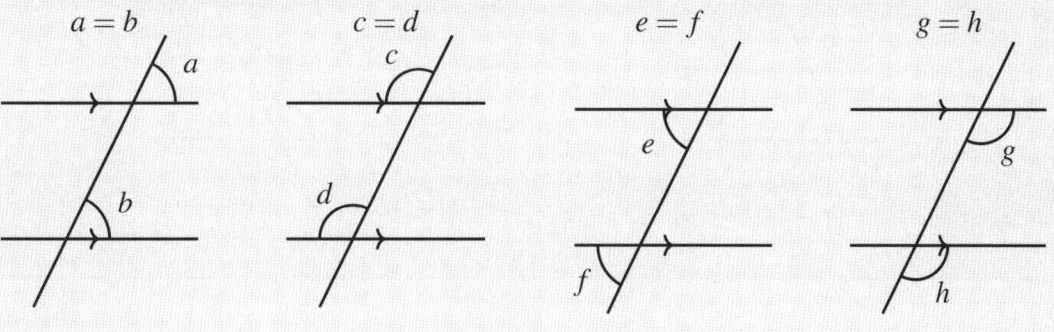

Example 25.2.1

Find the size of angles x and y.

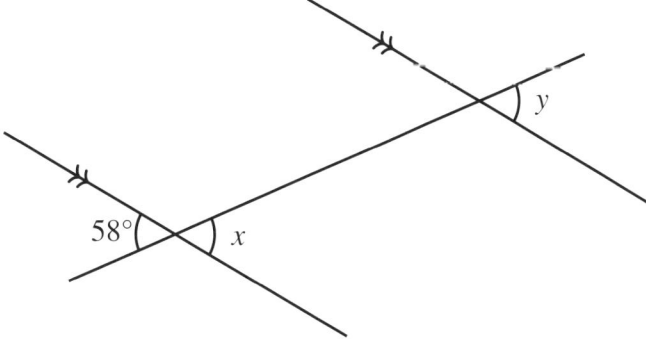

Alternate Angles (Z-shaped)

When a pair of parallel lines is cut by a transversal, it creates two pairs of alternate angles. Alternate angles are equal to each other.

Example 25.2.2

Find the size of angles x, y, and z.

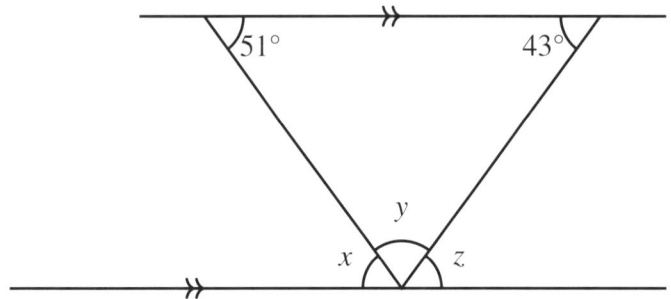

Co-interior Angles (C-shaped)

When a pair of parallel lines is cut by a transversal, it creates two pairs of co-interior angles. Co-interior angles add up to 180°.

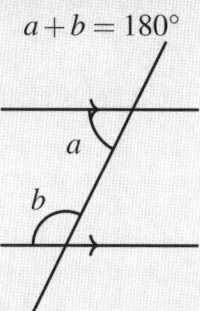

$a + b = 180°$

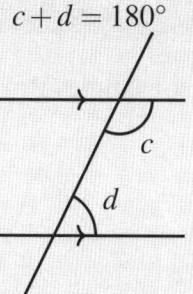

$c + d = 180°$

Example 25.2.3

Find the size of angles x, y, and z.

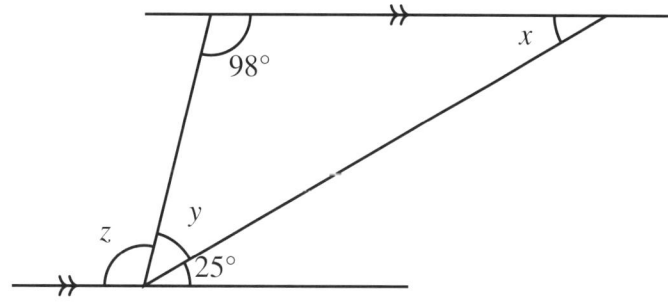

26 Angles in Polygons

26.1 Angles in Triangles

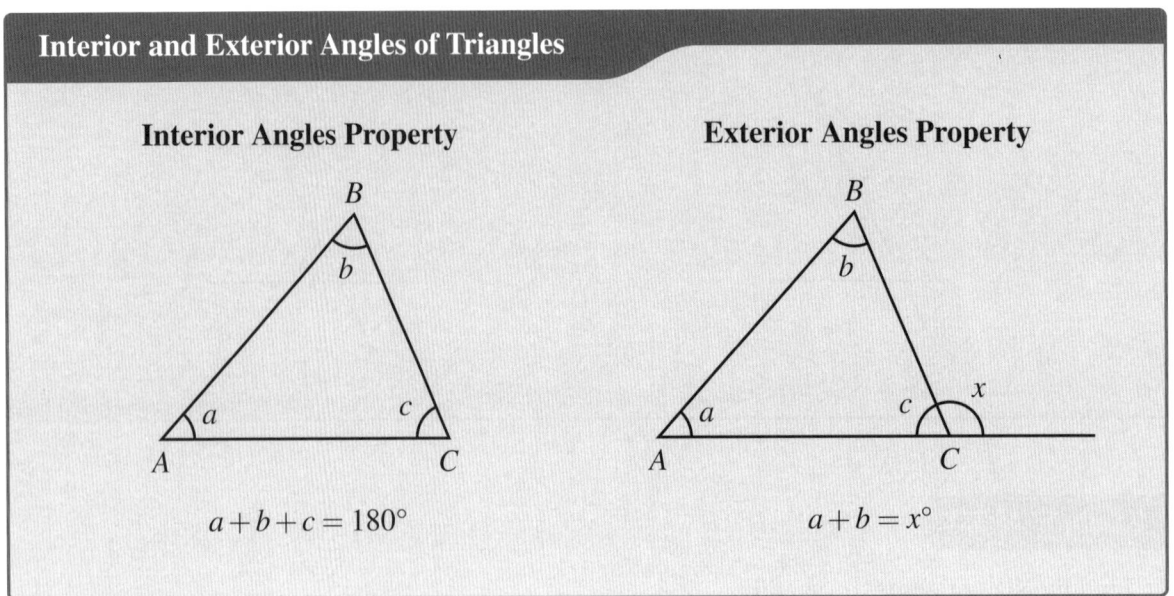

Interior and Exterior Angles of Triangles

Interior Angles Property

$a + b + c = 180°$

Exterior Angles Property

$a + b = x°$

Example 26.1.1

Find the values x and y.

(a) (b)

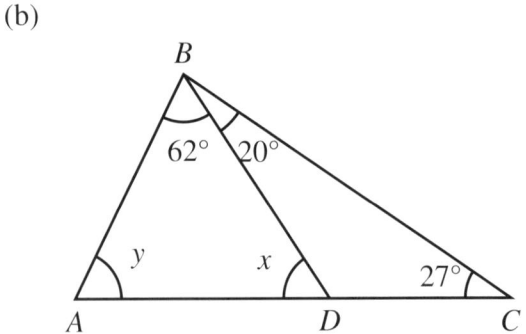

26.2 Angles in Quadrilaterals

Interior Angles of Quadrilaterals

Any quadrilateral can be divided into two triangles. So the sum of the interior angles of a quadrilateral is 360°.

$$a + b + c + d = 360°$$

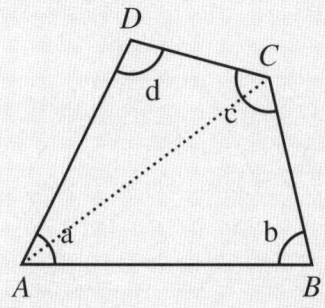
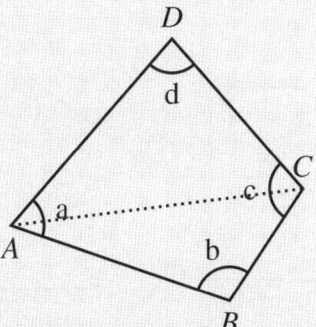
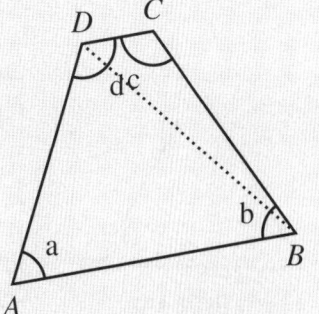

Example 26.2.1

Find the size of angles x and y.

(a)

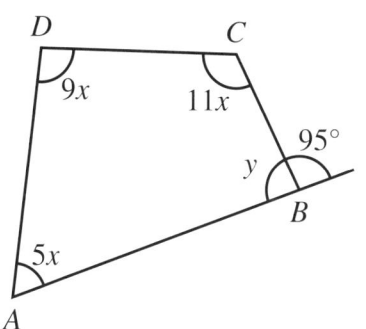

(b)

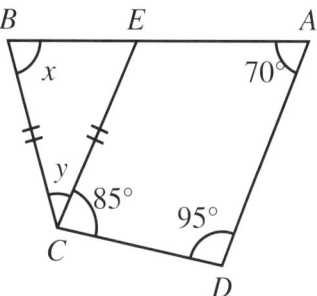

26.3 Angles in Polygons

Interior Angles of Polygons

Sum of the interior angles of polygons can be worked out by dividing the polygons into triangles.

Sum of interior angles of n-gon $= 180 \times (n-2)$

$n = 3$
180×1

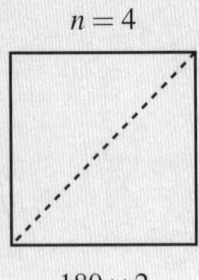
$n = 4$
180×2

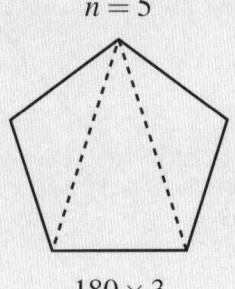
$n = 5$
180×3

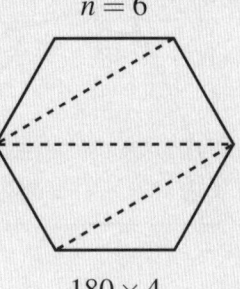
$n = 6$
180×4

Example 26.3.1

(a) Find the sum of the interior angle of a decagon (10-gon).

(b) Find the size of each interior angle of a regular decagon.

Example 26.3.2

A polygon has an interior angle sum of 2700°. How many sides does this polygon have?

166   IGCSE & MYP Math

27 Angles in Circles

27.1 Angles in Semicircles

Angles in Semicircles

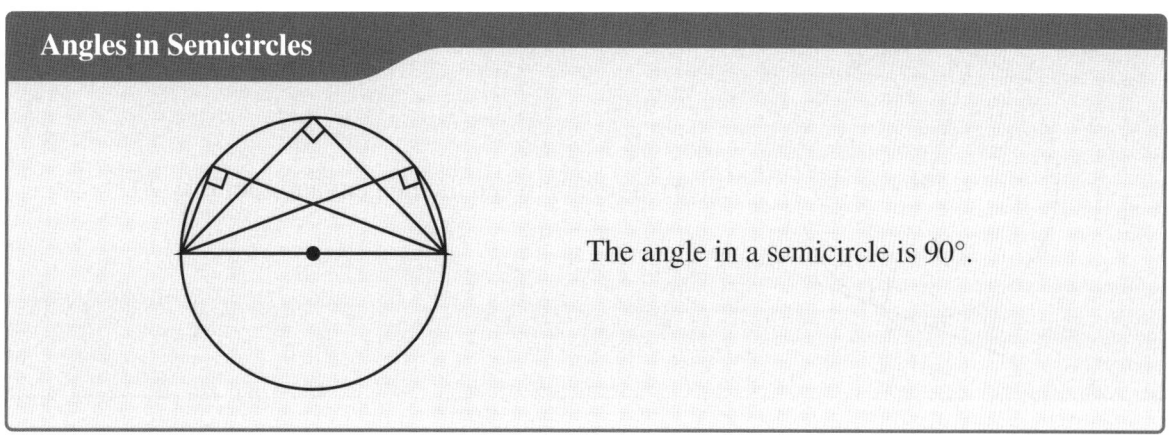

The angle in a semicircle is 90°.

Example 27.1.1

Find the angle x.

(a)

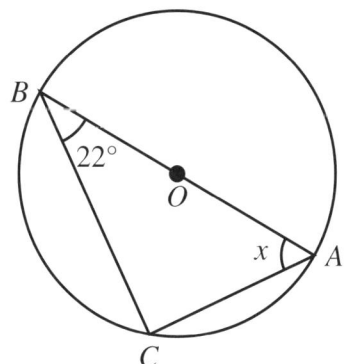

(b)

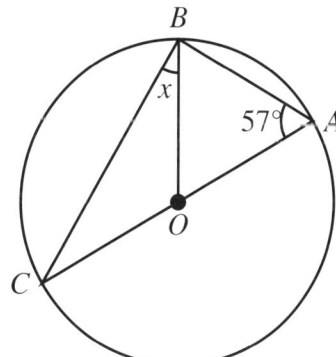

27.2 Angle Between Tangent and Radius

Angle Between Tangent and Radius

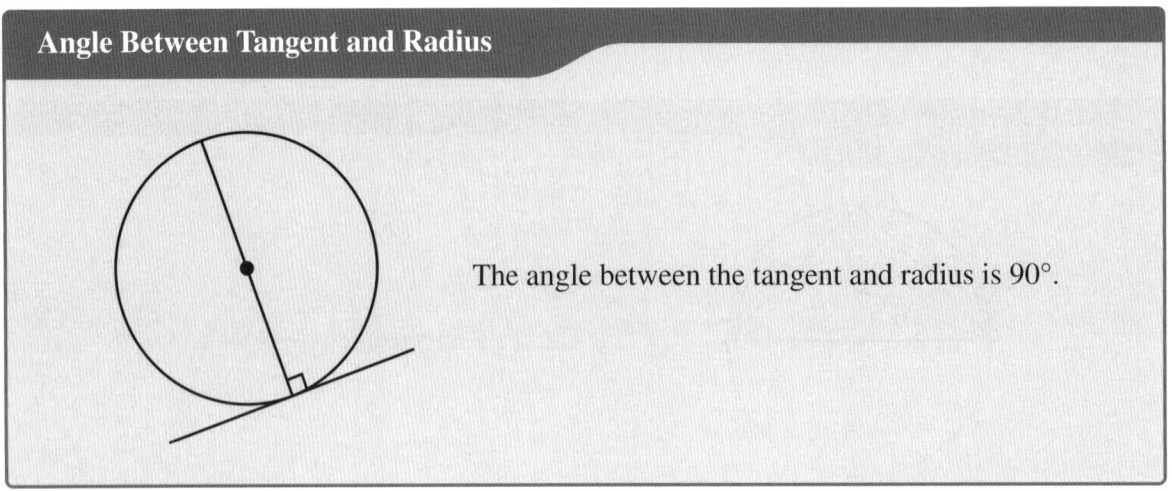

The angle between the tangent and radius is 90°.

Example 27.2.1

Find the angle x.

(a) (b)

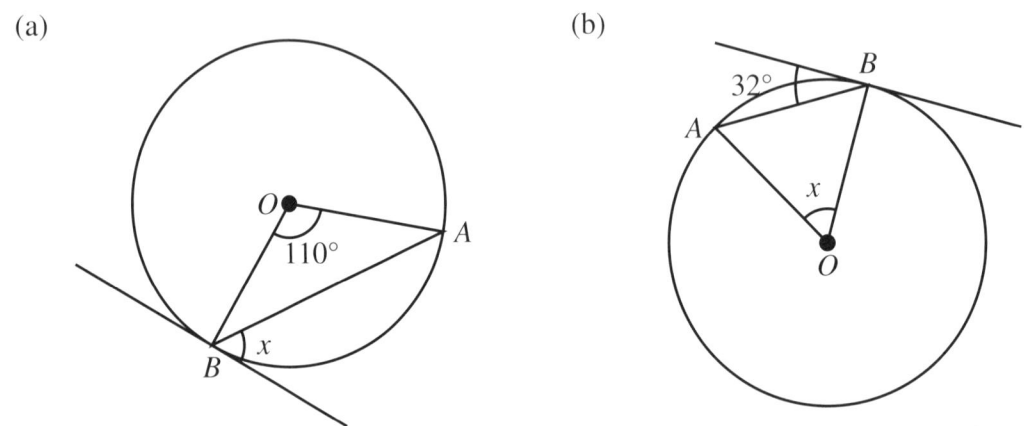

27.3 Angle at Center and Angle at Circumference (EXTENDED ONLY)

Angle at Center and Angle at Circumference

The angle at the center of a circle is twice the angle at the circumference.

$$\angle AOB = 2 \times \angle ACB$$

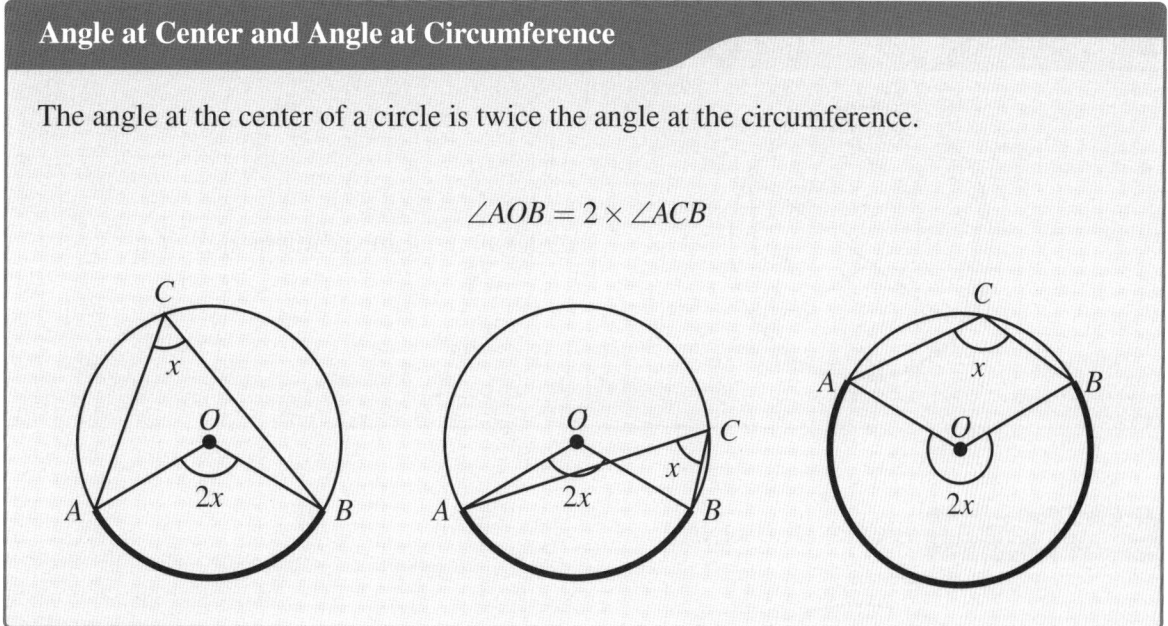

Example 27.3.1 EXTENDED ONLY

Find the angle x.

(a)

(b)

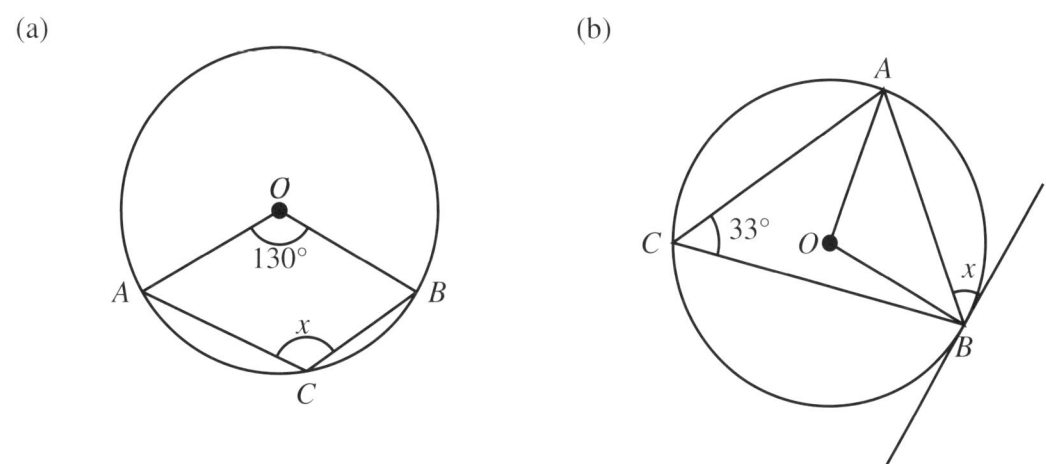

27.4 Angles in the Same Segment (EXTENDED ONLY)

Angles in the Same Segment

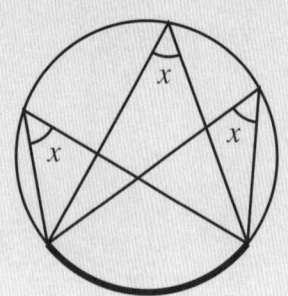

Angles in the same segment are equal.

Example 27.4.1 EXTENDED ONLY

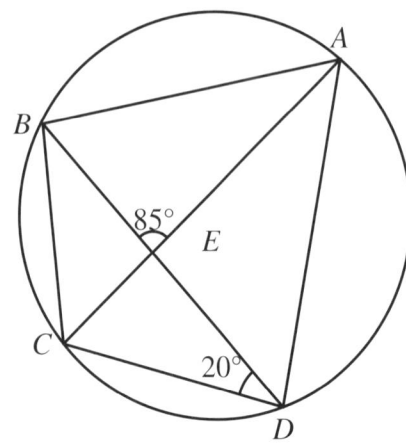

It is given that
$\angle AEB = 85°$ and
$\angle BDC = 20°$.

Complete the following statements.

(a) Angle $CED = $ _____ because _____

_____

(b) Angle $ABD = $ _____ because _____

_____

170   IGCSE & MYP Math

27.5 Angles in Opposite Segment (EXTENDED ONLY)

Angles in Opposite Segment

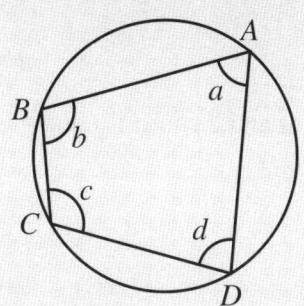

Cyclic Quadrilateral: A quadrilateral with all four vertices on the circumference of a circle.

Opposite angles of a cyclic quadrilateral are supplementary. Angles in opposite segments are supplementary.

$$a + c = 180° \quad \text{and} \quad b + d = 180°$$

Example 27.5.1 EXTENDED ONLY

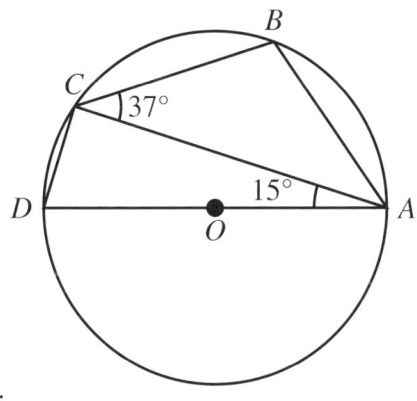

It is given that
$\angle ACB = 37°$ and
$\angle CAD = 15°$.

Find:

(a) angle ADC

(b) angle ABC

(c) angle BAC

27.6 Alternate Angle Theorem (EXTENDED ONLY)

> **Alternate Angle Theorem**
>
>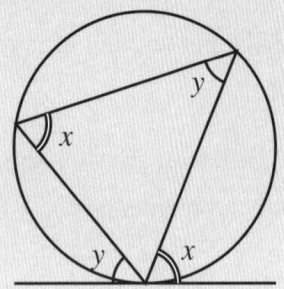
>
> The angle between a tangent and a chord is equal to the angle in the alternate segment.

Example 27.6.1   EXTENDED ONLY

Find the value of x in each diagram.

(a)

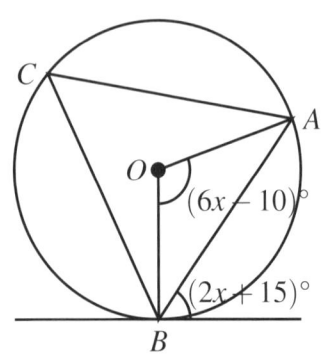

(b)

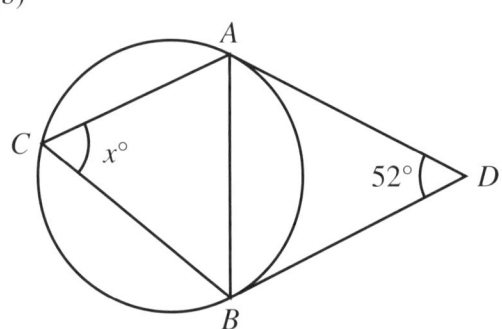

Unit 6
Trigonometry

Ch.28 Right Triangles
Ch.29 Trigonometric Functions
Ch.30 Non-right Triangles

28 Right Triangles

28.1 Finding Side Lengths

Pythagorean Theorem

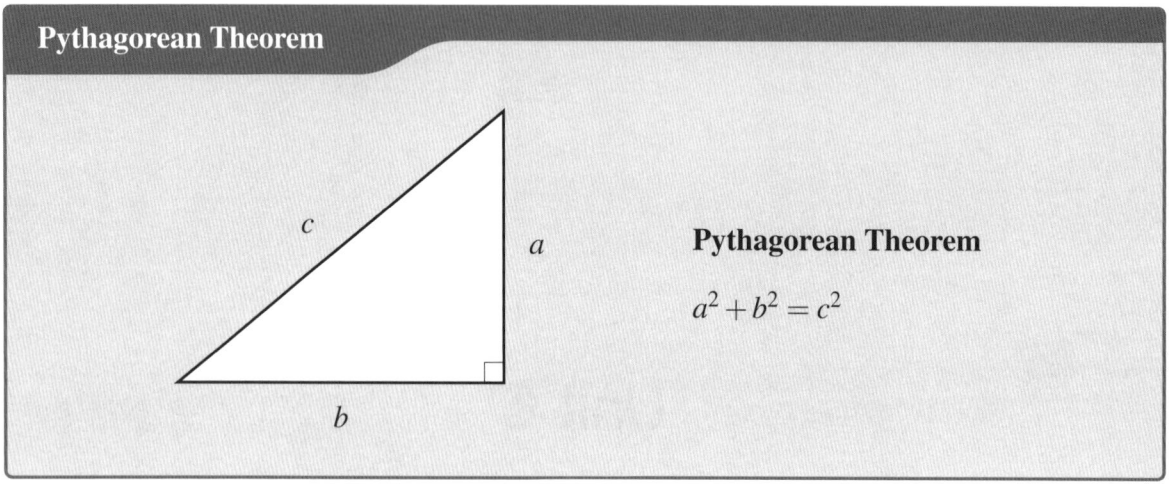

Pythagorean Theorem

$a^2 + b^2 = c^2$

Example 28.1.1

Find the side lengths marked x in each diagram.

(a)

(b)

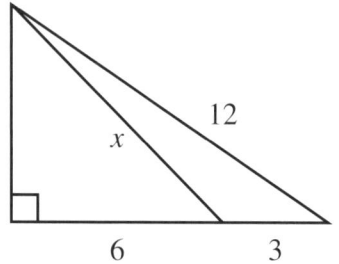

Sine, Cosine, and Tangent

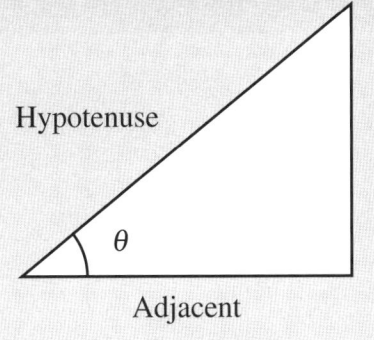

SOH CAH TOA

$$\sin \theta = \frac{\text{Opp}}{\text{Hyp}}$$

$$\cos \theta = \frac{\text{Adj}}{\text{Hyp}}$$

$$\tan \theta = \frac{\text{Opp}}{\text{Adj}}$$

Example 28.1.2

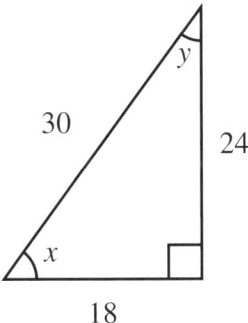

Calculate each of the following.

(a) $\sin x$

(b) $\cos y$

(c) $\tan y$

Example 28.1.3

Find the value of x in each diagram. Give your answer to the nearest whole number.

(a)

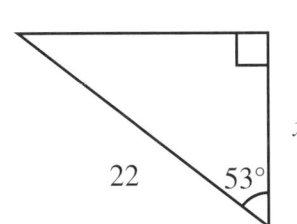

(b)

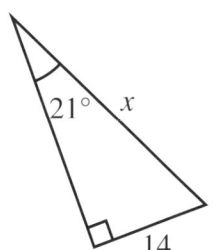

(c)

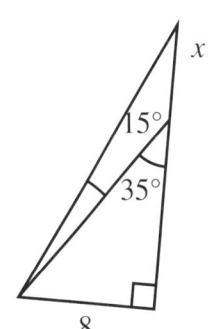

Unit 6. Trigonometry 175

28.2 Finding Angles

Inverse Trigonometry

If $\sin x = y$, then $x = \sin^{-1}(y)$.

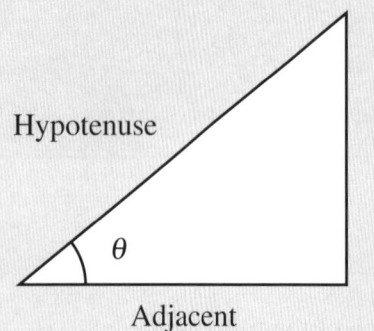

Inverse Trigonometry

$\theta = \sin^{-1}\left(\dfrac{\text{Opp}}{\text{Hyp}}\right)$

$\theta = \cos^{-1}\left(\dfrac{\text{Adj}}{\text{Hyp}}\right)$

$\theta = \tan^{-1}\left(\dfrac{\text{Opp}}{\text{Adj}}\right)$

※ Angles should be written in degrees and decimals to one decimal place.

Example 28.2.1

Calculate the angle x correct to 1 decimal place.

(a)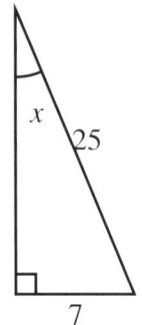

(b)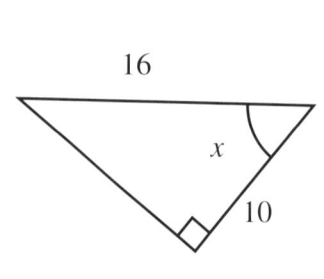

(c)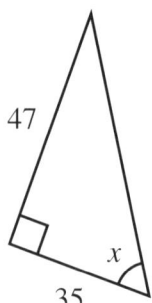

28.3 Angles of Elevation and Depression (EXTENDED ONLY)

Angles of Elevation and Depression

Line of Sight: Line drawn from the observer's eyes to the object being observed.

Angle of Elevation or Depression: The angle measured from the horizontal to the line of sight.

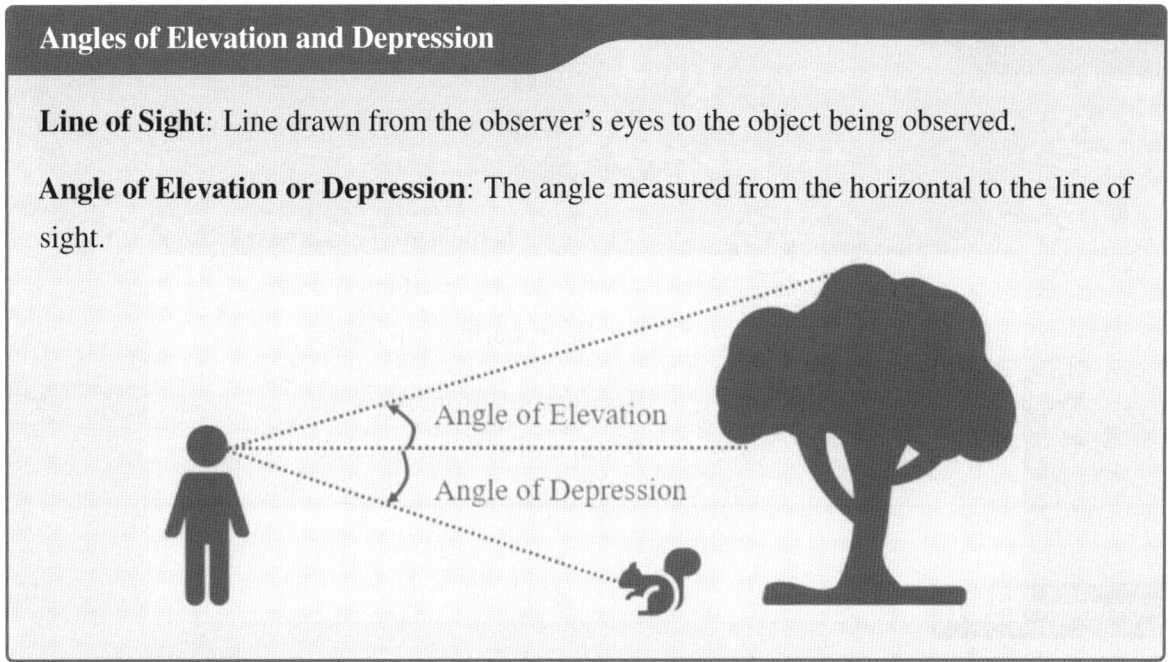

Example 28.3.1 EXTENDED ONLY

Two trees can be seen from the top of a tower of height 100 m. If the angles of depression of the trees are 12° and 20° each, calculate the distance between the two trees.

28.4 Bearings

Bearings

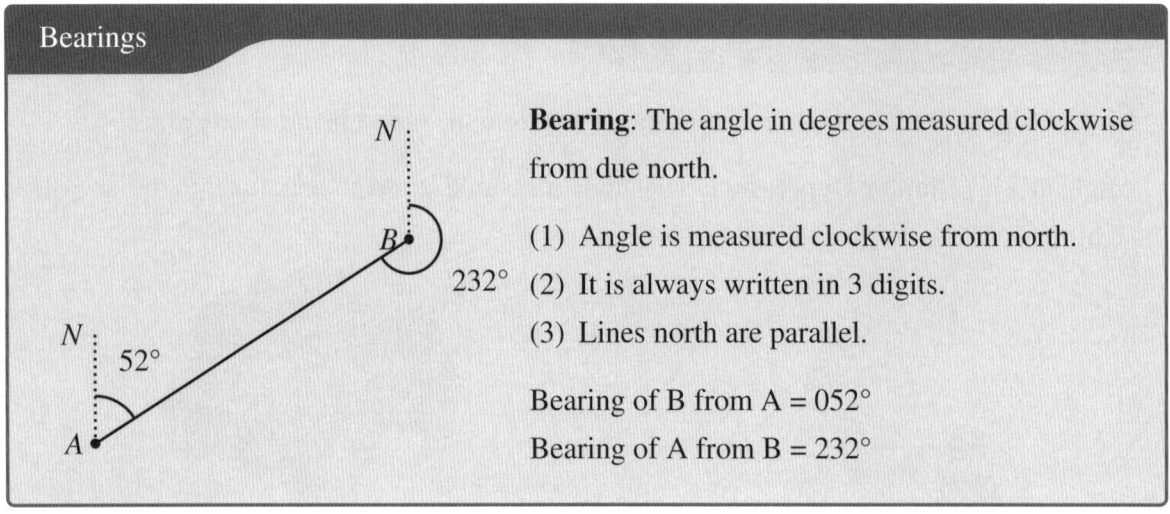

Bearing: The angle in degrees measured clockwise from due north.

(1) Angle is measured clockwise from north.
(2) It is always written in 3 digits.
(3) Lines north are parallel.

Bearing of B from A = 052°
Bearing of A from B = 232°

Example 28.4.1

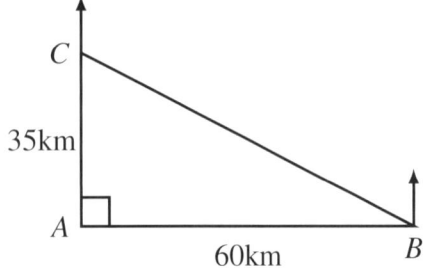

The diagram shows the positions of town A, B, and C. Town B is due east of town C, and town A is due south of town C.

(a) Write the bearing of town B from town C.

(b) Work out the bearing of town C from town B.

(c) (EXTENDED ONLY) Find the shortest distance from town A to $\overline{BC}$.

178 IGCSE & MYP Math

28.5 Three-Dimensional Problems Involving Trigonometry (EXTENDED ONLY)

Example 28.5.1 EXTENDED ONLY

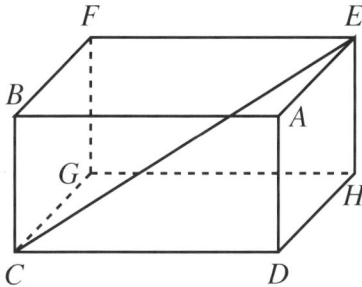

$AB = 8$cm $BF = 6$cm $AD = 2$cm

(a) Calculate the length of CE.

(b) Calculate the angle between CE and the plane $CDHG$.

29 Trigonometric Functions (EXTENDED ONLY)

29.1 Sine Functions (EXTENDED ONLY)

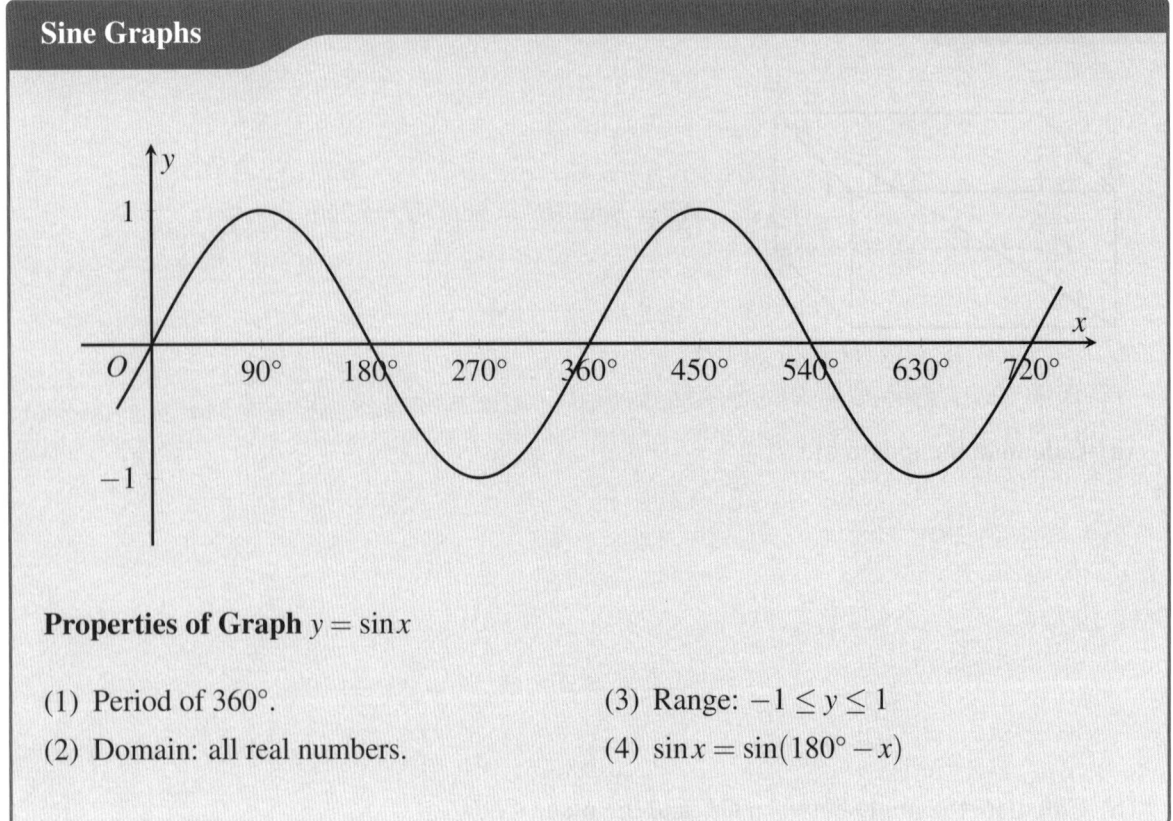

Sine Graphs

Properties of Graph $y = \sin x$

(1) Period of 360°.
(2) Domain: all real numbers.
(3) Range: $-1 \leq y \leq 1$
(4) $\sin x = \sin(180° - x)$

Example 29.1.1 — EXTENDED ONLY

Find the angle, between 0° and 360°, which has the same sine value as

(a) 45°

(b) 150°

(c) 220°

Solving Sine Equations

(1) Use the calculator to find one solution.

(2) Use the symmetry of the sine graph and find the other solutions.

Example 29.1.2 EXTENDED ONLY

Solve each equation for $0° \leq x \leq 360°$

(a) $\sin x = \dfrac{\sqrt{3}}{2}$

(b) $4\left(\sin x + \dfrac{1}{2}\right) = 1$

(c) $(\sin x)^2 = \dfrac{1}{4}$

29.2 Cosine Functions (EXTENDED ONLY)

Cosine Graphs

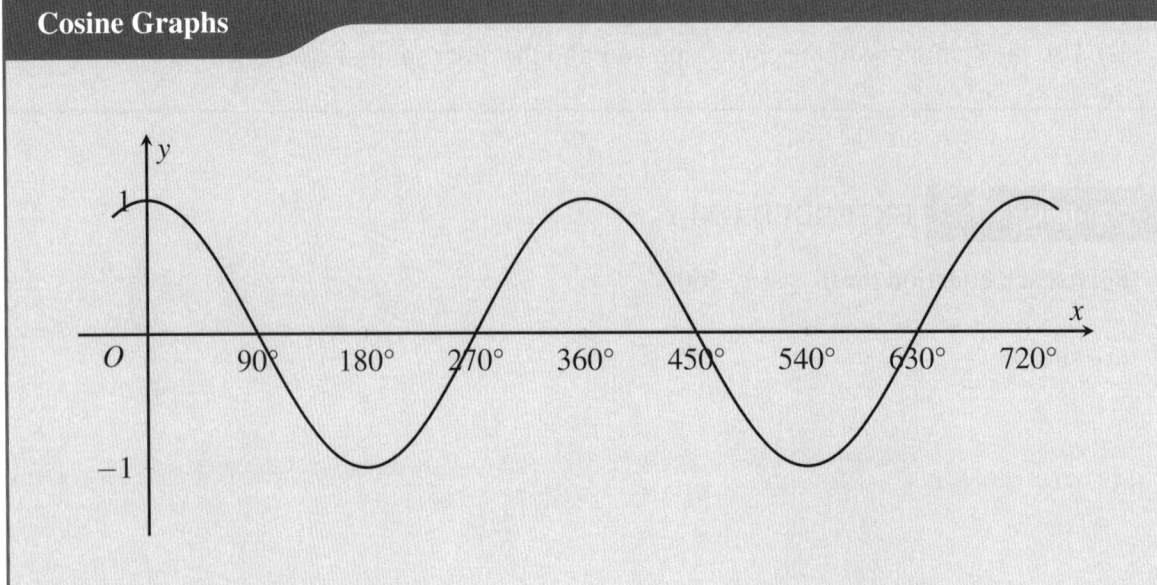

Properties of Graph $y = \cos x$

(1) Period of 360°.
(2) Domain: all real numbers.
(3) Range: $-1 \leq y \leq 1$
(4) $\cos x = \cos(360° - x)$
(5) $\cos x = -\cos(180° - x)$

Example 29.2.1 EXTENDED ONLY

Find the angle, between 0° and 360°, which has the same cosine value as

(a) 60°

(b) 190°

(c) 320°

Solving Cosine Equations

(1) Use the calculator to find one solution.

(2) Use the symmetry of the cosine graph and find the other solutions.

Example 29.2.2 EXTENDED ONLY

Solve each equation for $0° \leq x \leq 360°$

(a) $5\sqrt{2} - 2\cos x = 6\sqrt{2}$

(b) $\cos(x) = \cos(215°)$

29.3 Tangent Functions (EXTENDED ONLY)

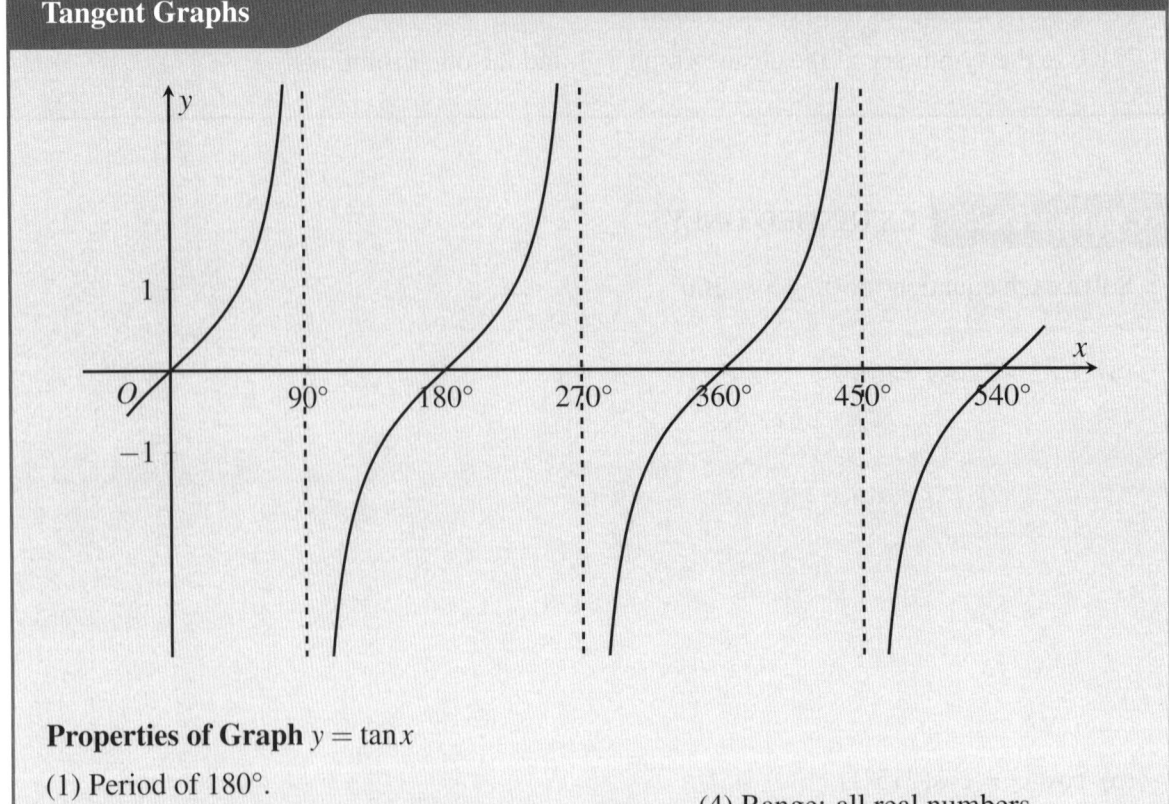

Properties of Graph $y = \tan x$

(1) Period of 180°.
(2) Vertical asymptotes at $x = 90° + 180°n$
(3) Domain: $x \neq 90° + 180°n$, where n is an integer.
(4) Range: all real numbers
(5) $\tan x = \tan(180° + x)$

Example 29.3.1   EXTENDED ONLY

Find the angle, between 0° and 360°, which has the same tangent value as

(a) 25°

(b) 100°

(c) 300°

Solving Tangent Equations

(1) Use the calculator to find one solution.

(2) Use the symmetry of the tangent graph and find the other solutions.

Example 29.3.2 EXTENDED ONLY

Solve each equation for $0° \leq x \leq 360°$

(a) $\tan x = 3.5$

(b) $\tan x = \tan 315°$

30 Non-Right Triangles (EXTENDED ONLY)

30.1 Sine Rule (EXTENDED ONLY)

Sine Rule

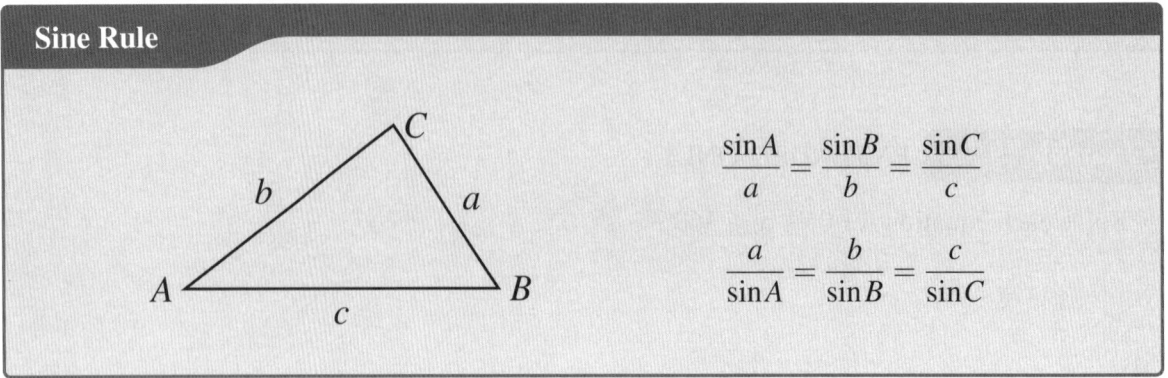

$$\frac{\sin A}{a} = \frac{\sin B}{b} = \frac{\sin C}{c}$$

$$\frac{a}{\sin A} = \frac{b}{\sin B} = \frac{c}{\sin C}$$

Example 30.1.1   EXTENDED ONLY

Calculate the length of x. Give your answer correct to 3 significant figures.

(a)

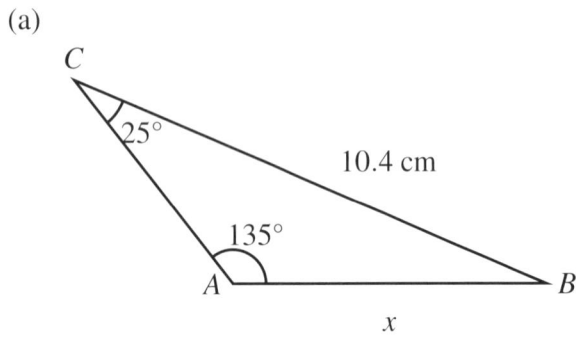

(b)

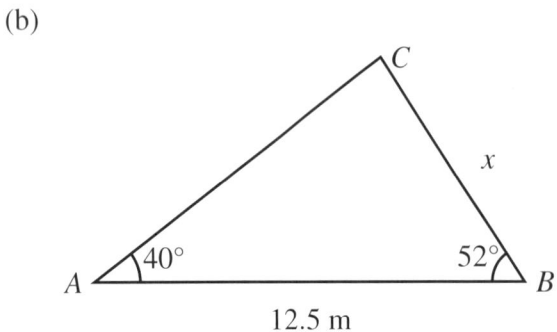

186   IGCSE & MYP Math

Example 30.1.2 EXTENDED ONLY

Calculate the value of x.

(a)

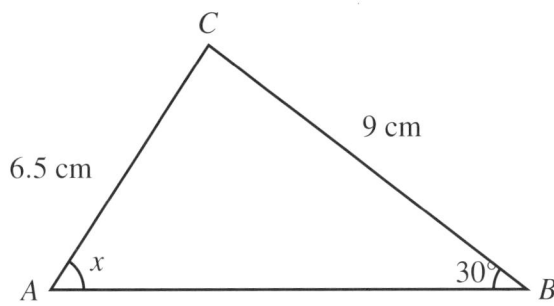

(b)

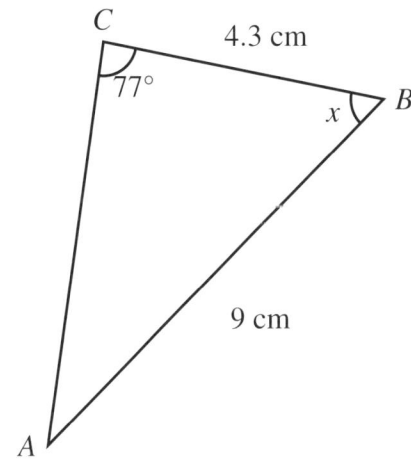

30.2 Cosine Rule (EXTENDED ONLY)

Cosine Rule

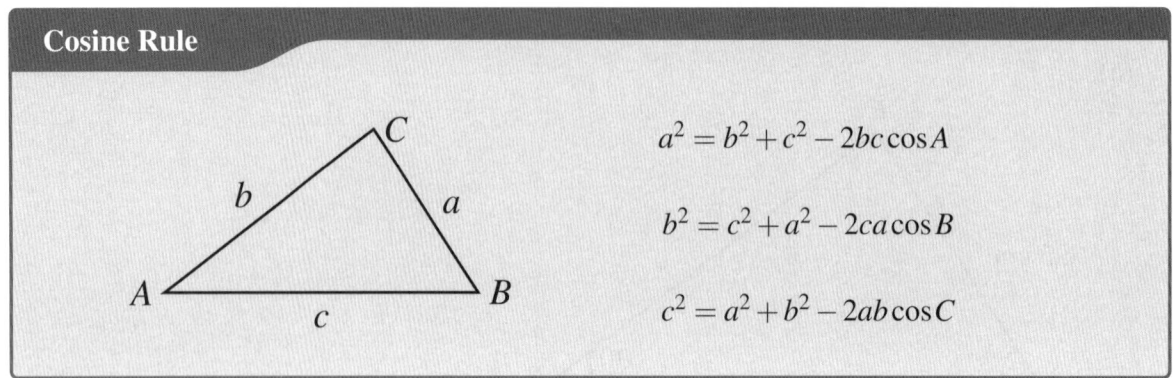

$$a^2 = b^2 + c^2 - 2bc\cos A$$

$$b^2 = c^2 + a^2 - 2ca\cos B$$

$$c^2 = a^2 + b^2 - 2ab\cos C$$

Example 30.2.1   EXTENDED ONLY

Calculate the length of x. Give your answer correct to 3 significant figures.

(a)

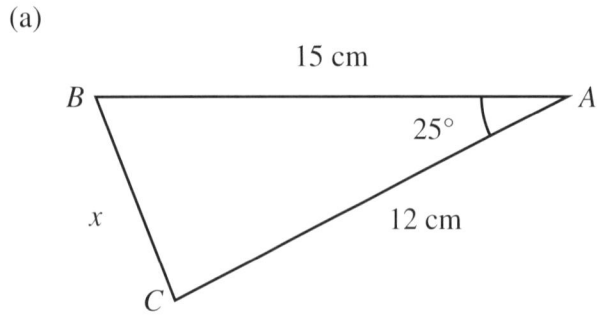

(b)

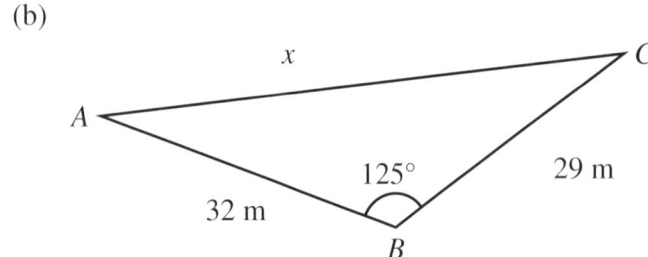

Example 30.2.2 EXTENDED ONLY

Calculate the value of x.

(a)

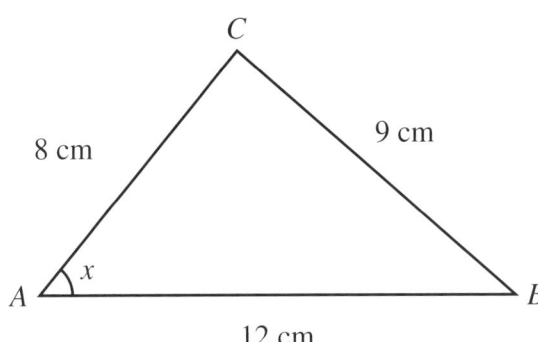

(b)

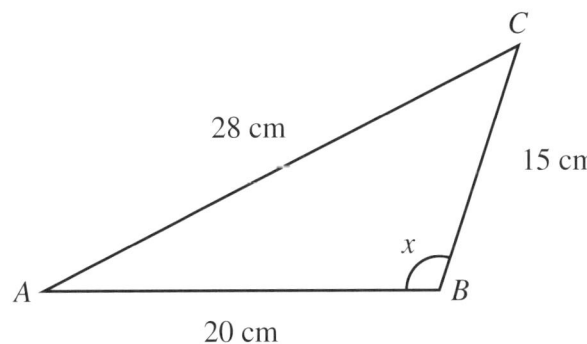

30.3 Area of a Triangle (EXTENDED ONLY)

Area of a Triangle

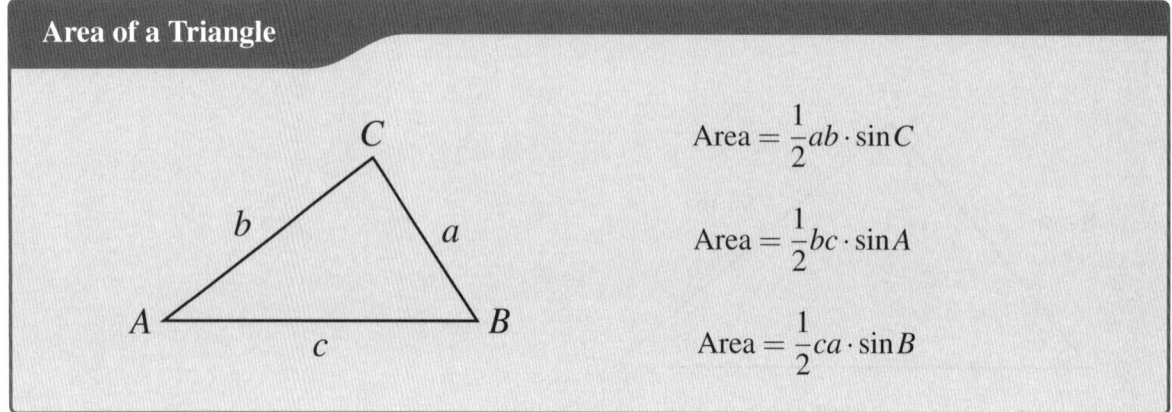

$$\text{Area} = \frac{1}{2}ab \cdot \sin C$$

$$\text{Area} = \frac{1}{2}bc \cdot \sin A$$

$$\text{Area} = \frac{1}{2}ca \cdot \sin B$$

Example 30.3.1 EXTENDED ONLY

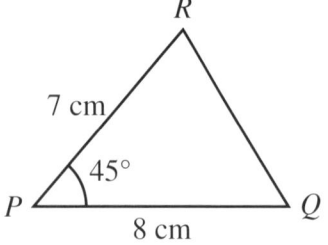

Find the area of the triangle in the diagram.

Example 30.3.2 EXTENDED ONLY

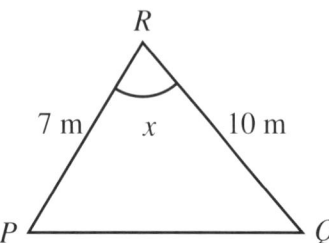

If the area of the triangle is 33.5 m², find the angle x.

Example 30.3.3 EXTENDED ONLY

Find the area of each polygon.

(a)

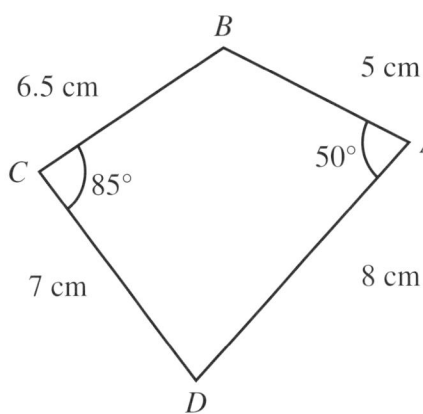

(b)

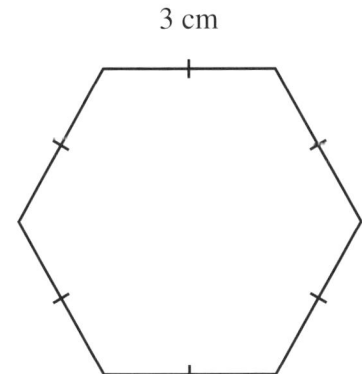

Unit 7
Vectors and Transformations

Ch.31 Vectors
Ch.32 Transformations

31 Vectors

31.1 Column Vectors

Column Vectors and Translation

We can use **column vectors** to represent translations.

Translation from P to Q

$$\overrightarrow{PQ} = \begin{pmatrix} a \\ b \end{pmatrix}$$

a: Translation in the x direction.
b: Translation in the y direction.

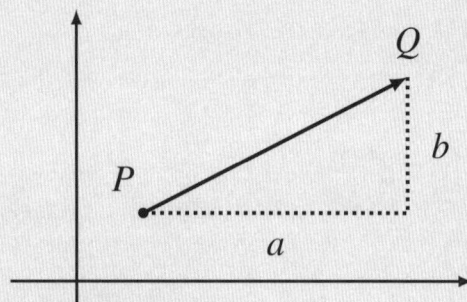

Position and Displacement Vectors

Position Vector:
The vector from the origin O to point A is called a position vector, and it is written as $\overrightarrow{OA}$ or **a**.

Displacement Vector:
$\overrightarrow{AB}$ represents a vector which originates at point A and terminates at point B.

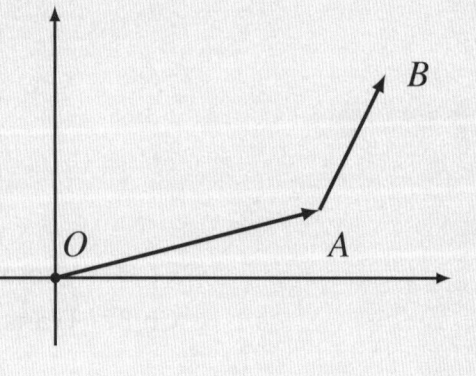

Equality of Vectors

Two vectors are equal if they have the same magnitude and direction.

$$\vec{AB} = \vec{CD} = \vec{EF}$$

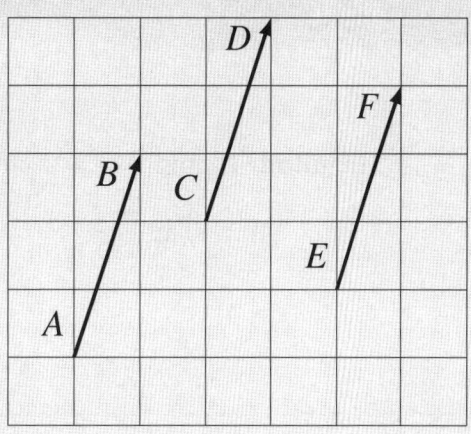

Example 31.1.1

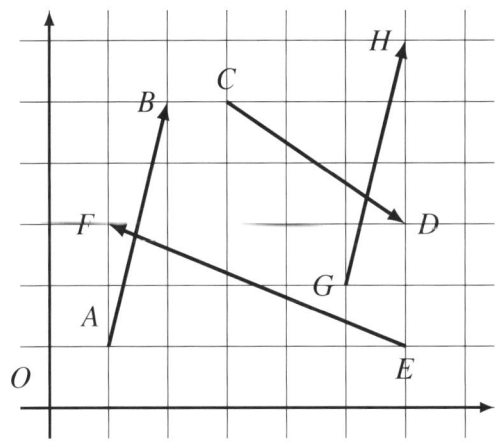

(a) Represent the following vectors in column vector form.

  (i) $\vec{AB}$

  (ii) $\vec{EF}$

  (iii) Displacement vector from G to H

  (iv) Position vector of point D

(b) Find another vector that is equal to $\vec{AB}$

31.2 Magnitude of Vectors (EXTENDED ONLY)

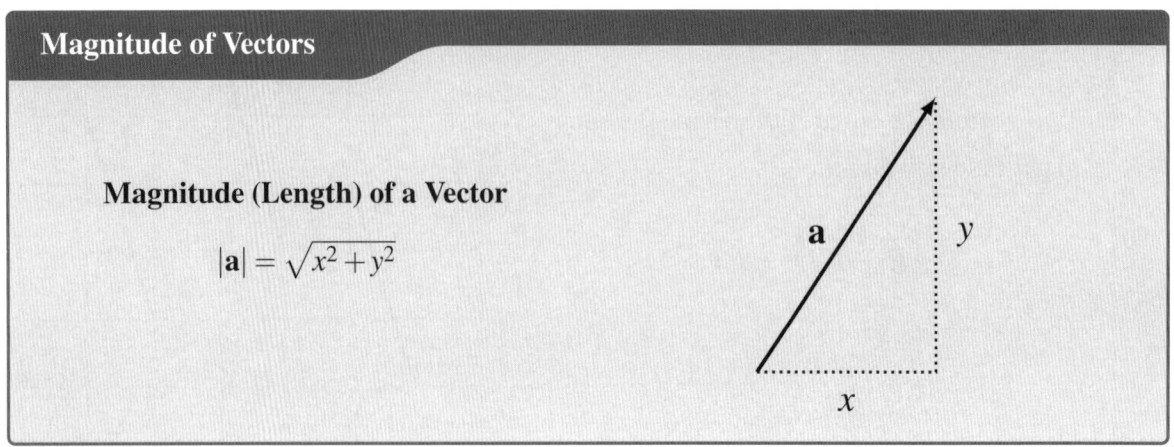

Magnitude of Vectors

Magnitude (Length) of a Vector

$$|\mathbf{a}| = \sqrt{x^2 + y^2}$$

Example 31.2.1 EXTENDED ONLY

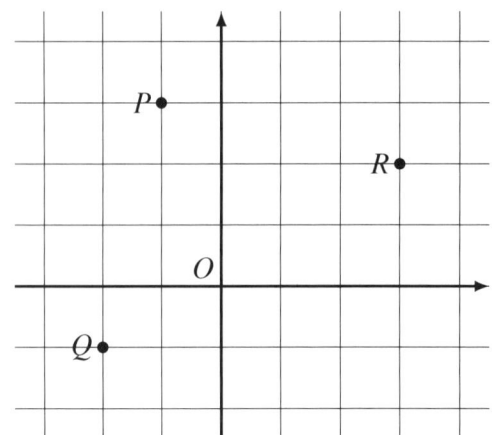

Find the magnitude of the following vectors

(a) Position vector of point Q

(b) Displacement vector from P to R

31.3 Vector Addition and Subtraction

Vector Addition

Adding Vectors Geometrically

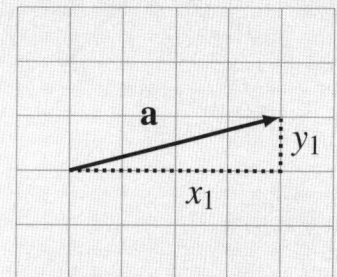 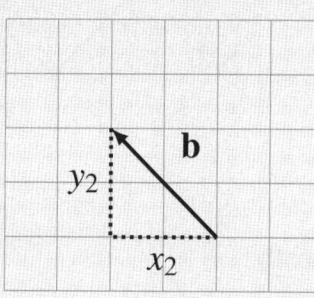 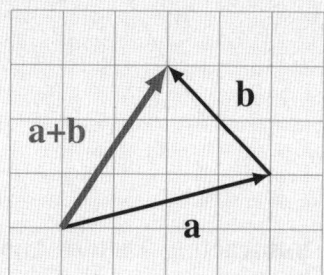

Adding Vectors Algebraically

$$\mathbf{a} + \mathbf{b} = \begin{pmatrix} x_1 \\ y_1 \end{pmatrix} + \begin{pmatrix} x_2 \\ y_2 \end{pmatrix} = \begin{pmatrix} x_1 + x_2 \\ y_1 + y_2 \end{pmatrix}$$

Example 31.3.1

Given $\mathbf{p} = \begin{pmatrix} 5 \\ 1 \end{pmatrix}$ and $\mathbf{q} = \begin{pmatrix} -3 \\ 2 \end{pmatrix}$, find $\mathbf{p} + \mathbf{q}$

(a) graphically

(b) algebraically

Vector Subtraction

Subtracting Vectors Geometrically

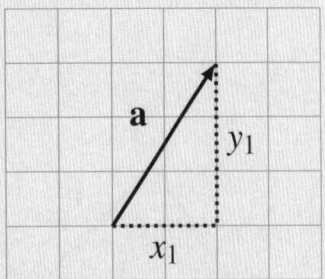
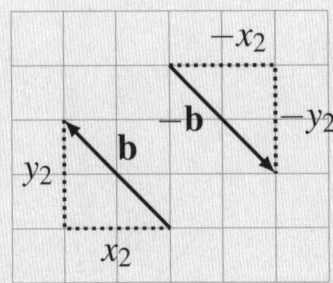
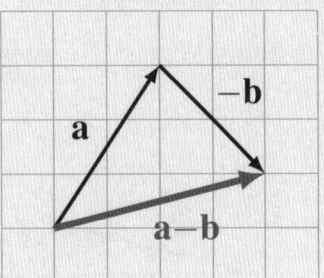

Subtracting Vectors Algebraically

$$\mathbf{a} - \mathbf{b} = \mathbf{a} + (-\mathbf{b}) = \begin{pmatrix} x_1 \\ y_1 \end{pmatrix} - \begin{pmatrix} x_2 \\ y_2 \end{pmatrix} = \begin{pmatrix} x_1 - x_2 \\ y_1 - y_2 \end{pmatrix}$$

Example 31.3.2

Given $\mathbf{p} = \begin{pmatrix} -3 \\ -1 \end{pmatrix}$ and $\mathbf{q} = \begin{pmatrix} 2 \\ 2 \end{pmatrix}$, find $\mathbf{p} - \mathbf{q}$

(a) graphically

(b) algebraically

31.4 Scalar Multiplication

Scalar Multiplication

Multiplying a Vector with a Scalar Geometrically

If a vector **a** is multiplied by a scalar k, the resultant vector $k \cdot \mathbf{a}$ is **parallel** to the original vector **a**.

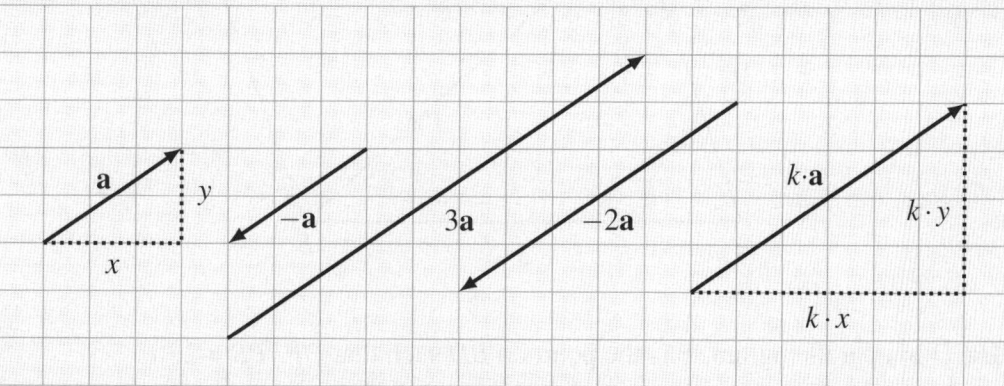

Multiplying a Vector with a Scalar Algebraically

$$k \cdot \mathbf{a} = k \begin{pmatrix} x \\ y \end{pmatrix} = \begin{pmatrix} k \cdot x \\ k \cdot y \end{pmatrix}$$

Example 31.4.1

Given $\mathbf{p} = \begin{pmatrix} 4 \\ -2 \end{pmatrix}$,

(a) represent $2\mathbf{p}$ and $-\dfrac{1}{2}\mathbf{p}$ on the grid.

(b) find the column vector of $2\mathbf{p}$ and $-\dfrac{1}{2}\mathbf{p}$

31.5 Vector Geometry (EXTENDED ONLY)

Example 31.5.1 EXTENDED ONLY

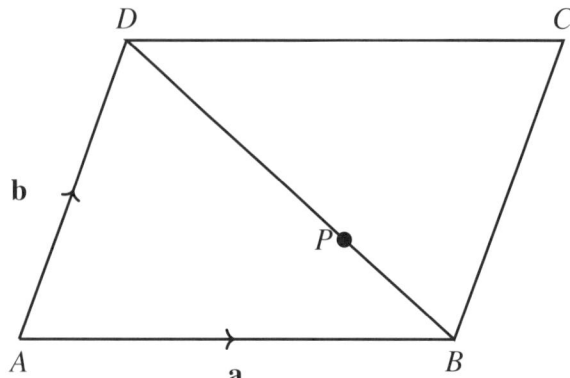

ABCD is a parallelogram. *P* is the point on *BD* such that *DP*: *PB* = 2 : 1. If $\overrightarrow{AB} = \mathbf{a}$ and $\overrightarrow{AD} = \mathbf{b}$,

(a) write down an expression for $\overrightarrow{DB}$ in terms of **a** and **b**.

(b) express $\overrightarrow{PC}$ in terms of **a** and **b**.

32 Transformations

Transformation: Change in position or size of a shape. Transformation produces an **image**.

Types of Transformation

(1) Reflection (Flip): Produces a congruent image.
(2) Rotation (Turn): Produces a congruent image.
(3) Translation (Slide): Produces a congruent image.
(4) Enlargement (Change size): Produces a similar image.

32.1 Reflection

Reflection

Reflection: Mirror image of a shape.

Properties of Reflection

(1) A point and its image are the same distance from the mirror line.
(2) The mirror line and the line joining a point and its image meet perpendicularly.
(3) A point on the mirror line is invariant.
(4) Reflection produces a congruent image.

Reflection Over x-axis

Reflection Over y-axis

Example 32.1.1

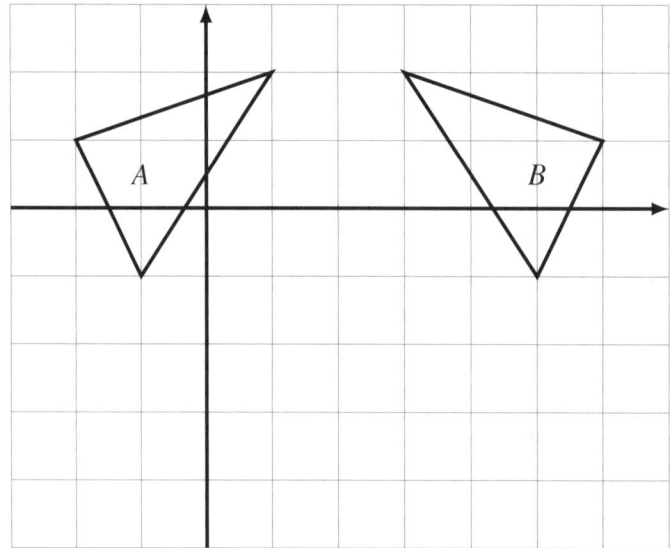

Two triangles A and B are shown in the grid.

(a) Describe a single transformation that maps triangle A onto B.

(b) Reflect triangle B in the line $y = -1$ and label the image C.

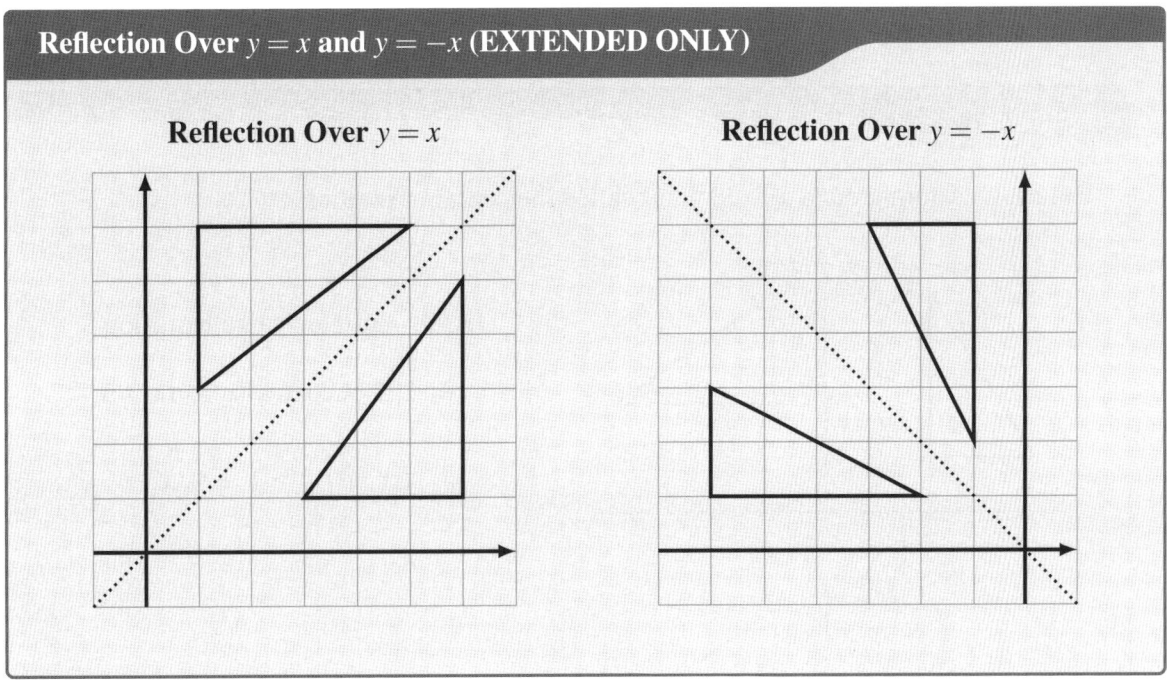

Example 32.1.2   EXTENDED ONLY

Reflect the triangle in the line $y = x$ and label the image Q.

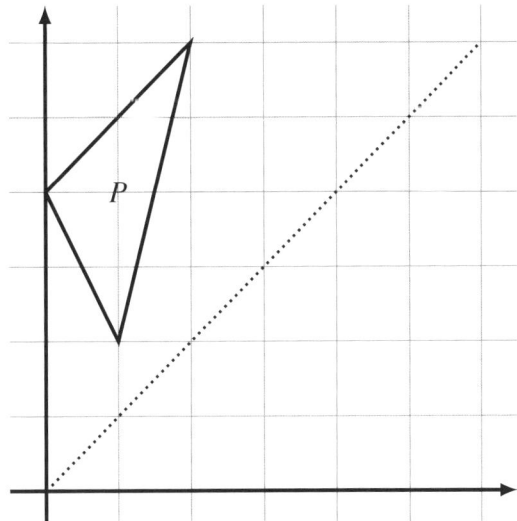

32.2 Rotation

Rotation

Rotation: A turn around a fixed point called the center of rotation.

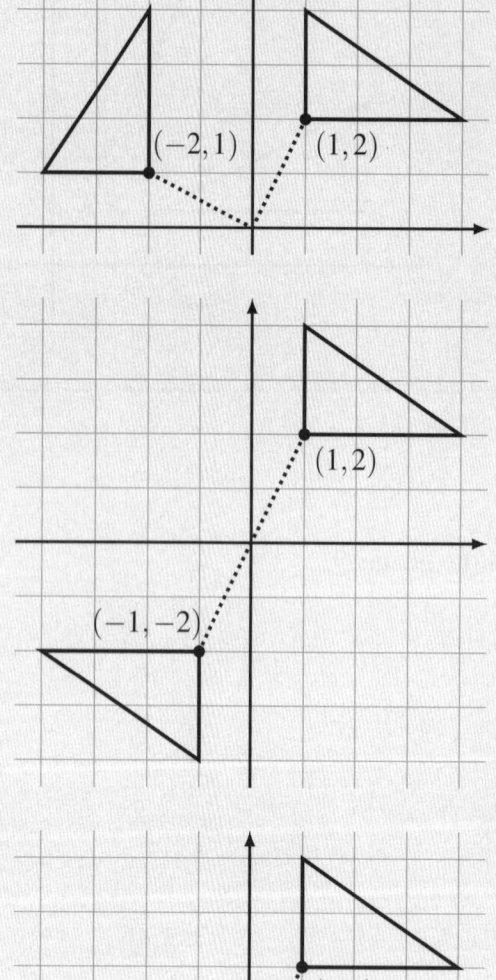

**90° Anticlockwise Rotation
or 270° Clockwise Rotation**

$$(x,y) \Rightarrow (-y,x)$$

**180° Anticlockwise Rotation
or 180° Clockwise Rotation**

$$(x,y) \Rightarrow (-x,-y)$$

**270° Anticlockwise Rotation
or 90° Clockwise Rotation**

$$(x,y) \Rightarrow (y,-x)$$

Properties of Rotation

(1) Direction can be either clockwise or anticlockwise.
(2) A point and its image are equidistant from the center of rotation.
(3) The center of rotation is invariant.
(4) Rotation produces a congruent image.
(5) The perpendicular bisector of a line joining a point and its image passes through the center of rotation.

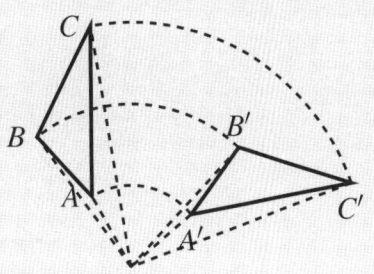

How to Draw Perpendicular Bisectors

(1) Draw a line joining point A and its image A'.
(2) Draw equal arcs from point A and A'. The radii of the arcs have to be greater than half of length AA'.
(3) Connect the two intersection points with a straight line.

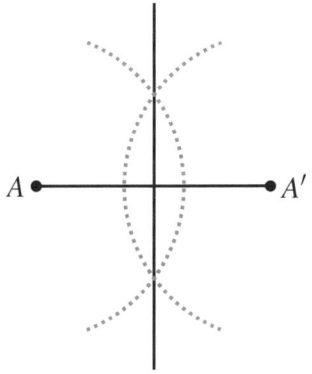

How to Find Center of Rotation

(1) Connect the corresponding points.
(2) Draw perpendicular bisectors of the lines drawn in (1).
(3) The intersection point of the perpendicular bisectors is the center of rotation.

Example 32.2.1

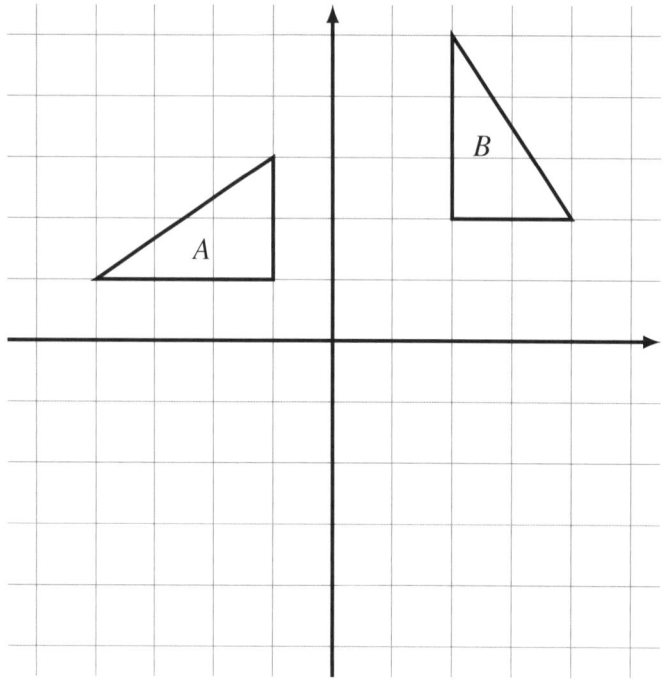

Two triangles A and B are shown in the grid.

(a) Describe a single transformation that maps triangle A onto B.

(b) Rotate A through 90° anticlockwise about $(0, -1)$. Label the image C.

32.3 Translation

Translation

Translation: Movement of an object without changing its orientation.

Properties of Translation
(1) Every point moves the same distance in the same direction.
(2) No part of the shape is invariant.
(3) Translation produces a congruent image.

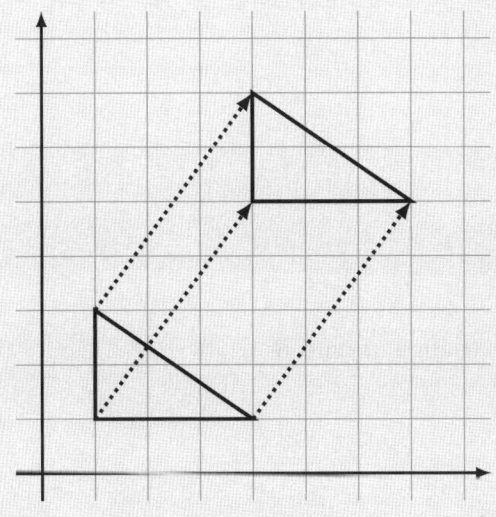

Meaning of Translation Vector $\begin{pmatrix} a \\ b \end{pmatrix}$

a: Horizontal shift
    positive a: move to the right
    negative a: move to the left
b: Vertical Shift
    positive b: move up
    negative b: move down

Example 32.3.1

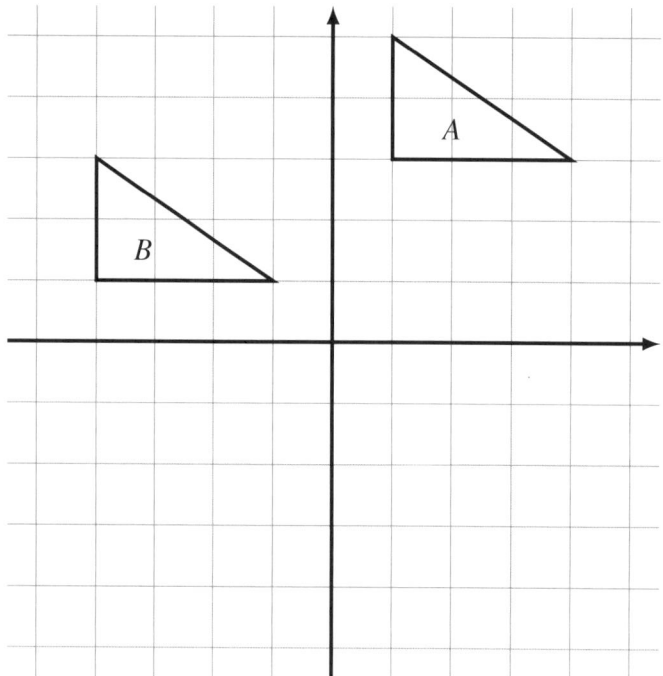

Two triangles A and B are shown in the grid.

(a) Describe a single transformation that maps triangle A onto B.

(b) Translate triangle B by the vector $\begin{pmatrix} 1 \\ -3 \end{pmatrix}$. Label the image C.

32.4 Enlargement

Enlargement

Enlargement: Resizing a shape by a scale factor from a point called center of enlargement.

Properties of Enlargement
(1) If the scale factor is greater than 1, the image is larger than the original shape. If the scale factor is smaller than 1, the image is smaller than the original shape.
(2) If the scale factor is negative, the image will be on the opposite side of the center of enlargement.
(3) Angles and orientation of the shape are invariant.
(4) Enlargement produces a similar image.

Enlargement by a Positive Scale Factor

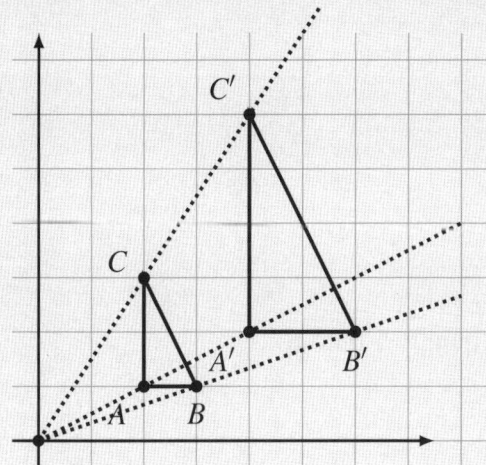

Positive Scale Factor

Scale factor $k = \dfrac{OA'}{OA} = \dfrac{OB'}{OB} = \dfrac{OC'}{OC}$

$OA' = k \cdot OA$
$OB' = k \cdot OB$
$OC' = k \cdot OC$

How to Enlarge a Shape by a Positive Scale Factor
(1) Draw lines connecting the center of enlargement O to each vertex A, B, and C.
(2) Plot a point A' so that the distance from A' to the center of enlargement O is k times the distance from A to O, where k is the scale factor. Make sure the points A and A' are on the same side of the center of enlargement.
(3) Do the same process with points B and C.

How to Find Center of Enlargement

(1) Draw lines connecting the corresponding points.

(2) The intersection point of the lines is the center of enlargement.

Example 32.4.1

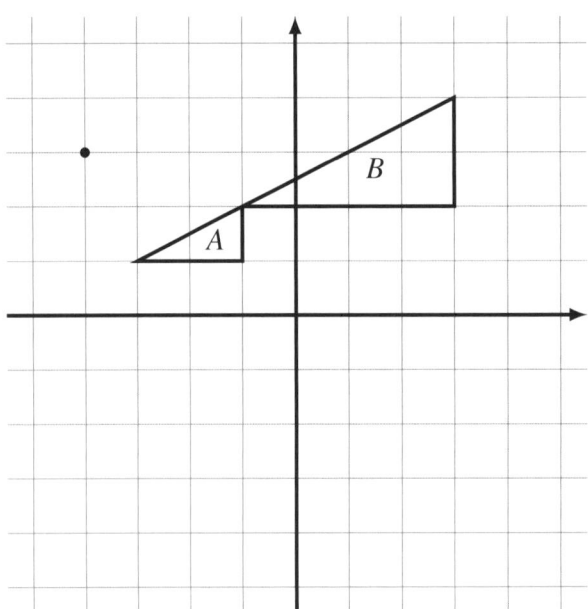

Two triangles A and B are shown in the grid.

(a) Describe a single transformation that maps triangle A onto B.

(b) Enlarge triangle A by scale factor of 3 with center of enlargement $(-4,3)$. Label the image C.

Enlargement by a Negative Scale Factor (EXTENDED ONLY)

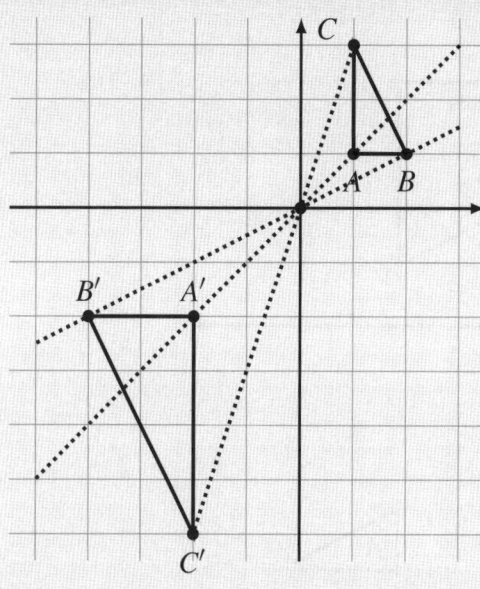

Negative Scale Factor

Scale factor $|k| = \dfrac{OA'}{OA} = \dfrac{OB'}{OB} = \dfrac{OC'}{OC}$

$OA' = |k| \cdot OA$
$OB' = |k| \cdot OB$
$OC' = |k| \cdot OC$

How to Enlarge a Shape by a Negative Scale Factor

(1) Draw lines connecting the center of enlargement O to each vertex A, B, and C.

(2) Plot a point A' so that the distance from A' to the center of enlargement O is $|k|$ times the distance from A to O, where k is the scale factor. Make sure the points A and A' are on the opposite side of the center of enlargement.

(3) Do the same process with points B and C.

Example 32.4.2 EXTENDED ONLY

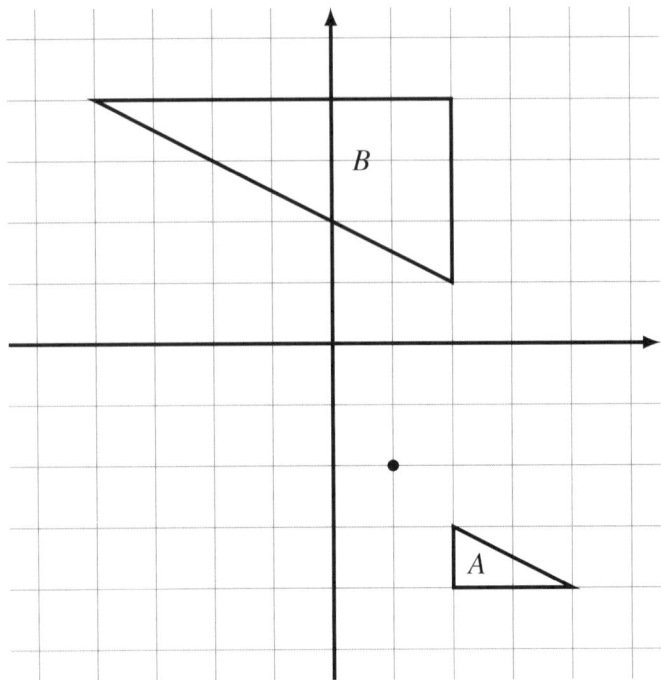

Two triangles A and B are shown in the grid.

(a) Describe a single transformation that maps triangle A onto B.

(b) Enlarge triangle A by scale factor of −2 with center of enlargement (1,−2). Label the image C.

Enlargement by Fractional Scale Factor

$|k| > 1$ means the image is larger than the original shape

$|k| < 1$ means the image is smaller than the original shape

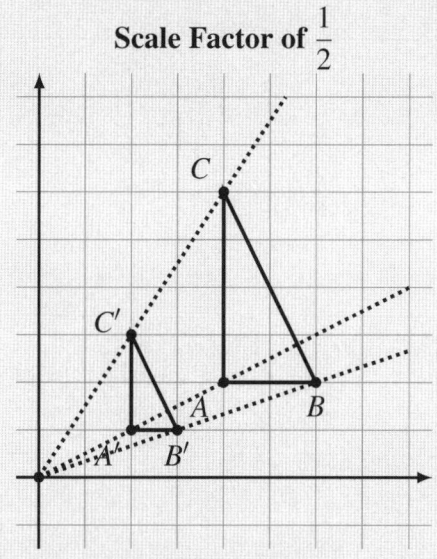

Scale Factor of $\dfrac{1}{2}$

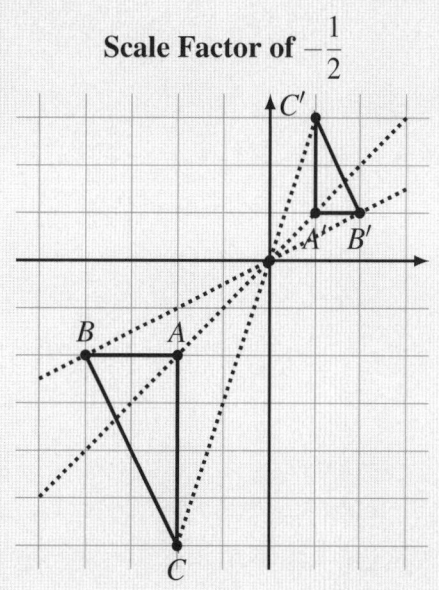

Scale Factor of $-\dfrac{1}{2}$

Example 32.4.3

Enlarge each shape with the given center of enlargement.

(a) Scale factor: $\dfrac{1}{3}$

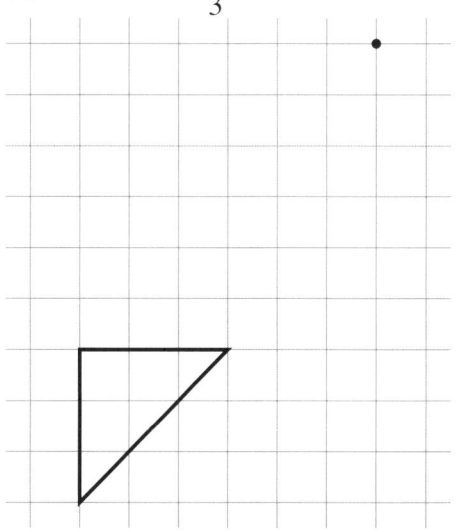

(b) (EXTENDED ONLY) Scale factor: $-\dfrac{1}{2}$

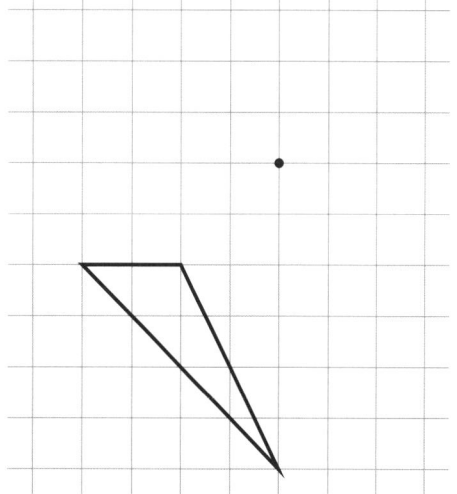

Unit 8
Probability

Ch.33 Simple Probability
Ch.34 Further Probability

33 Simple Probability

33.1 Probability

Probability

Probability: The chance that some event will happen.

Probability of an event A happening can be represented as

$$P(A) = \frac{\text{Number of outcomes in event } A}{\text{Total number of outcomes}}$$

```
         Decreasing Likelihood         Increasing Likelihood
        ◄─────────────────────        ─────────────────────►
        0                            0.5                           1
        ├─────────────┬───────────────┬──────────────┬─────────────┤
     Impossible    Unlikely      Even Chance       Likely       Certain
```

Properties of Probability

(1) All events occur with a probability of $0 \leq P(\text{event}) \leq 1$
(2) An even that is certain to happen has a probability of 1.
(3) An even that is impossible to happen has a probability of 0.

Example 33.1.1

An unbiased die is rolled. Find the probability of rolling

(a) a prime number

(b) a two

(c) a seven

(d) an integer

Ways to Express Probability

(1) Fraction   (2) Decimal   (3) Percentage

Example 33.1.2

A bag contains three blue balls, two yellow ball, and five red balls. If a ball is chosen at random from the bag, find the probability of selecting

(a) a yellow ball in decimals.

(b) a red ball in fraction.

(c) a blue ball in percentage.

Total Probability

The probabilities of all events should add up to 1.

Example 33.1.3

A spinner has letters P, Q, R, and S written on it. The probabilities of spinning a P or a Q is given in the table.

Letter	P	Q	R	S
Probability	0.1	0.3		

If spinning a R is three times as likely as spinning a S, complete the table.

33.2 Complementary Event

> **Complementary Event**
>
> **Complementary Event**: Complement of event A is the event A NOT occurring and is expressed as A'.
>
> $$P(A') = 1 - P(A)$$

Example 33.2.1

A card is drawn from a standard deck of 52 cards.

(a) What is the probability of drawing a king?

(b) What is the probability of drawing anything but a king?

33.3 Relative Frequency and Expected Frequency

Relative Frequency

Relative Frequency (Experimental Probability): Relative frequency is the number of times the event occurred during an experiment, divided by the total number of trials. It is used to estimate the probability of the event.

$$\text{Relative Frequency} = \frac{\text{Number of trials the event occurred}}{\text{Total number of trials}}$$

Example 33.3.1

One day, Chloe carries out a survey on the number of siblings of her classmates. The results are shown in the table.

Number of Siblings	0	1	2	3	4+
Frequency	40	84	56	17	3

Complete the table of relative frequencies.

Number of Siblings	0	1	2	3	4+
Relative Frequency					

Expected Frequency

Expected Frequency: Expected frequency is a theoretical predicted frequency of the event that we expect to occur in an experiment.

$$\text{Expected Frequency} = \text{Number of trials} \times \text{Probability of the event}$$

$$n(A) = n(\mathcal{E}) \times P(A)$$

Example 33.3.2

A bag contains purple, green, and blue marbles. The table shows the probability that a marble chosen at random from the bag will be purple or will be green. Claire chooses a marble at random from the bag.

Color	Purple	Green	Blue
Probability	0.35	0.2	

(a) Work out the probability that Claire chooses a blue marble.

Claire puts the marble back into the bag. Emily takes a marble at random from the bag. After recording the color, she puts the marble back into the bag. She does this 500 times.

(b) Work out an estimate for the number of times she chooses a blue marble.

34 Further Probability

34.1 Combined Events

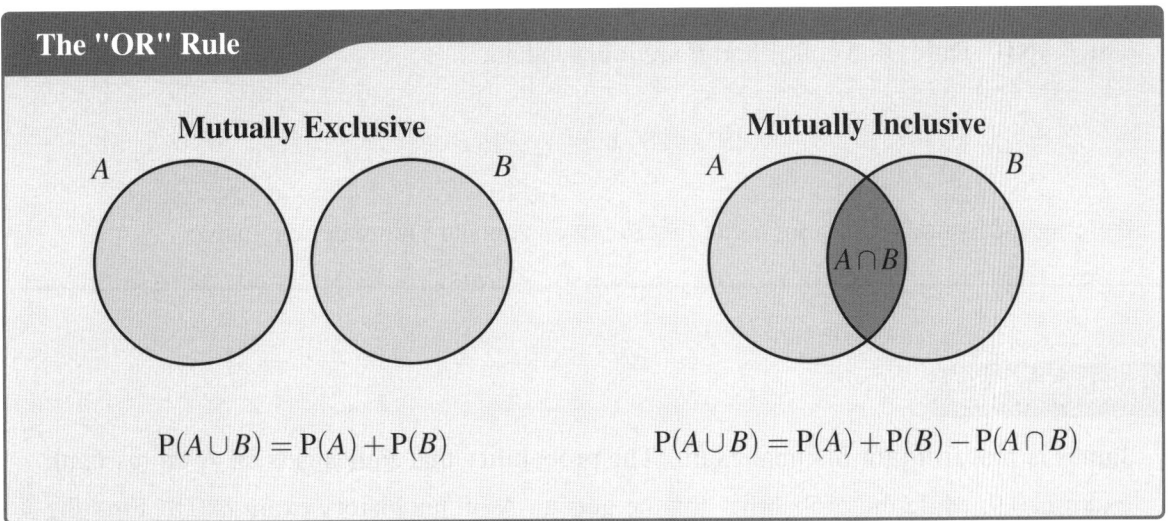

Example 34.1.1

A card is drawn from a standard deck of 52 cards. Find the probability of drawing

(a) a king or a queen.

(b) an diamond or a seven.

The "AND" Rule

Independent Events: Two events are independent if one event does not affect the other event, and vice versa.

The "AND" Rule: If events A and B are independent,

$$P(A \cap B) = P(A) \times P(B)$$

※ Being independent does not mean that the two events are mutually exclusive.

Example 34.1.2

James is preparing for his final exam. The probability that James gets an A on his math exam is 0.9, while the probability that he gets an A on his history exam is 0.8. Find the probability that:

(a) he receives A's on both classes.

(b) he doesn't receive an A in either class.

(c) he receives only one A.

(d) he receives at least one A.

34.2 Possibility Diagrams

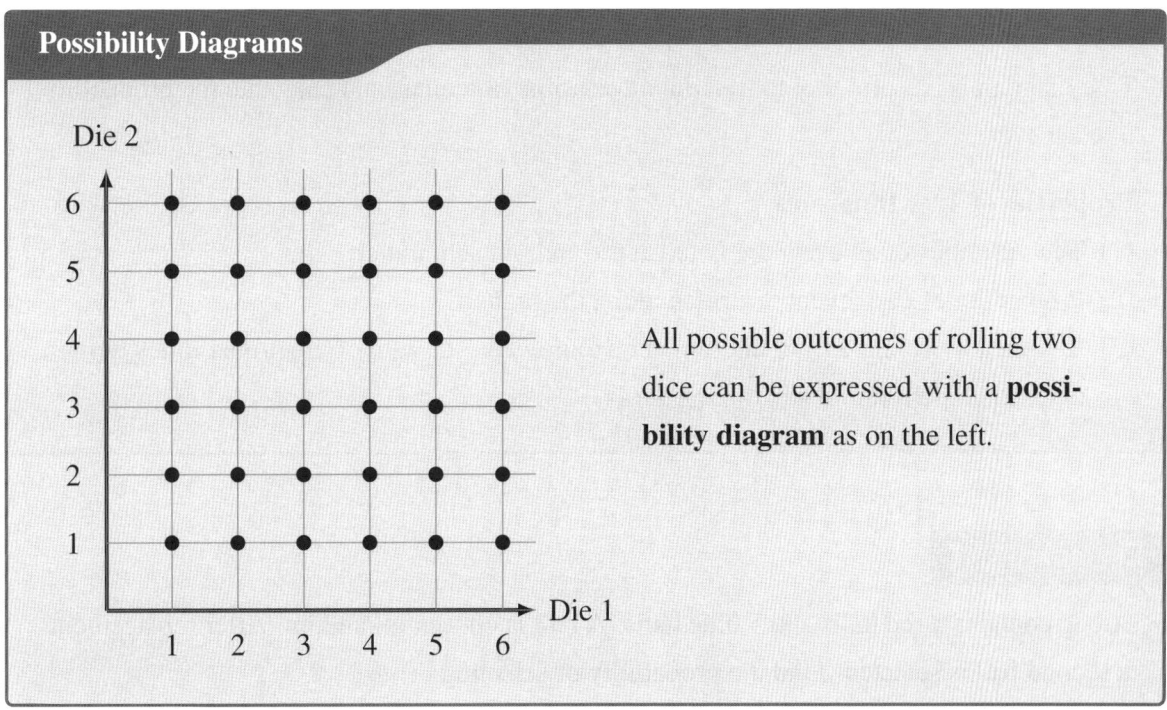

Possibility Diagrams

All possible outcomes of rolling two dice can be expressed with a **possibility diagram** as on the left.

Example 34.2.1

Two dice are thrown. Using a possibility diagram, find the probability that the sum is

(a) 8

(b) less than 9

(c) is greater than or equal to 10

34.3 Probability with Tree Diagrams

Tree Diagrams

Tree diagram is a useful tool to find out all possible outcomes and calculate the probability of each event.

Properties of Tree Diagrams
(1) The outcomes of an event are listed at the end of each branch.
(2) Probability of each event is written along the branch.
(3) If branches originate from the same previous event, the sum of the probabilities written on each branch should add up to a 1.

Example 34.3.1

A bag contains 3 red balls and 5 blue balls. A ball is chosen at random. After replacement, a second ball is selected. Find the probability of selecting:

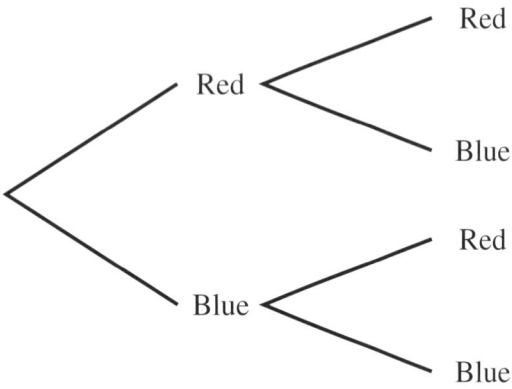

(a) two red balls

(b) one red ball and one green ball

224 IGCSE & MYP Math

34.4 Probability with Venn Diagrams

Example 34.4.1

There are 30 students in a class. 10 of the students own a cat, 15 of the students own a dog, and 8 of the students own neither. What is the probability that a randomly selected student will:

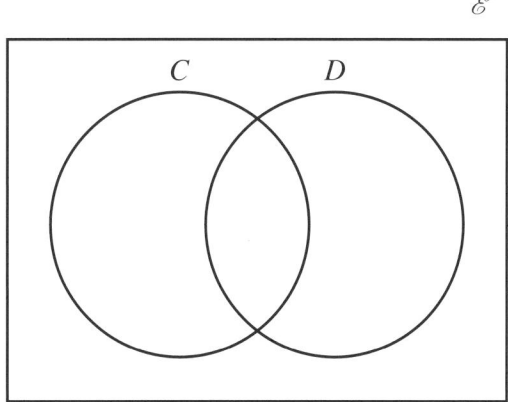

(a) own either a cat or a dog?

(b) only own a cat?

(c) not own a dog?

Unit 8. Probability

34.5 Conditional Probability (EXTENDED ONLY)

Conditional Probability

Conditional Probability: Probability of an event occurring, given that another event has already occurred.

$$\text{Probability of } A \text{ given } B = P(A|B) = \frac{P(A \cap B)}{P(B)} = \frac{n(A \cap B)}{n(B)}$$

Example 34.5.1 EXTENDED ONLY

A school provides two types of foreign language lessons: Spanish and Chinese. There are 39 students in Spanish class, 26 students in Chinese class, and 7 of them take both courses. If there are a total of 80 students in the school, what is the probability that a randomly selected student will:

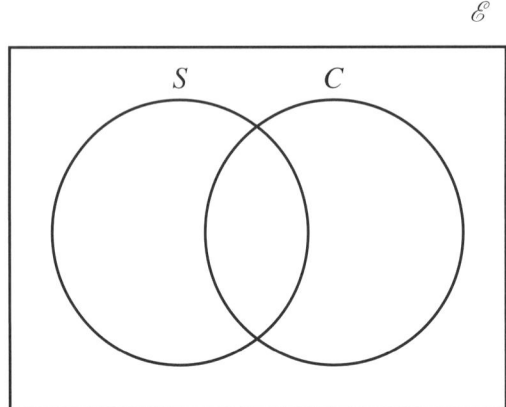

(a) be in both classes, given that the student is in Chinese class?

(b) be in Spanish class, given that the students is not in Chinese class?

Example 34.5.2 EXTENDED ONLY

A coin is biased so that it has 60% chance of landing heads. If it is thrown twice, what is the probability that:

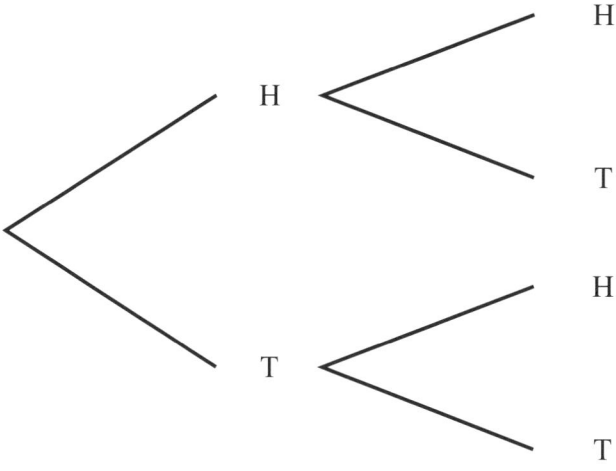

(a) one head is shown?

(b) it landed head on the second throw, given that it landed tail on the first throw?

Example 34.5.3 EXTENDED ONLY

A survey was conducted by a school district to determine the age distributions of teachers. The results are summarized in the table below.

Age	Male	Female	Total
Under 29	12	21	33
30-39	36	42	78
40-49	42	59	101
50 and above	21	67	88
Total	111	189	300

Find the probability that a randomly selected teacher from this school district is:

(a) a female between the ages of 30 and 39.

(b) a female given that the teacher is in their 30s.

Unit 9
Statistics

Ch.35 Classifying and Organizing Data
Ch.36 Displaying Data with Charts
Ch.37 Central Tendency and Spread
Ch.38 Continuous Data Representation
Ch.39 Scatter Diagram

35 Classifying and Organizing Data

35.1 Classifying Data

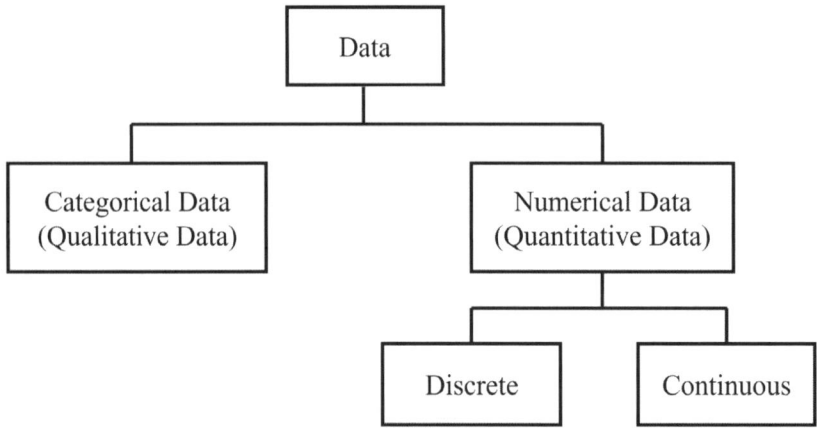

Types of Data

Categorical Data (Qualitative Data): Data that can be arranged into different groups of category. (Example: Favorite sports)

Numerical Data (Quantitative Data): Data that can be represented in numbers.
(1) **Discrete Data**: Numerical data that can consist of only certain numbers. (Example: Number of siblings)
(2) **Continuous Data**: Numerical data that can be consisted of any real number. (Example: Height, weight)

Example 35.1.1

Classify each data as categorical or numerical. If the data is numerical, state whether it is continuous or discrete.

(a) Number of pets per household.

(b) Volume of water in a cup of glass

(c) Hair color of classmates

35.2 Organizing Data

Frequency Table

Frequency table is constructed by writing each category or discrete numerical data with its frequencies.

Example 35.2.1

Construct a frequency table for the set of data values given.

(a) 1   5   2   4   1   1   3   4   2   5   1   2   5   1   1

Number	Tally	Frequency
1		
2		
3		
4		
5		

(b) red   blue   blue   black   red   blue   black   red   black   blue

Color	Tally	Frequency
Red		
Blue		
Black		

Grouped Frequency Table

Grouped Frequency Table: A table that shows **classes** or **intervals** of data with frequencies of each class. Usually continuous data are represented with grouped frequency tables.

Example 35.2.2

The final exam scores of students in Reina's class is given as below.

| 51 | 68 | 72 | 100 | 75 | 79 | 85 | 93 | 98 | 66 |
| 83 | 59 | 88 | 91 | 74 | 89 | 97 | 56 | 82 | 87 |

(a) Complete the grouped frequency table.

Score	Frequency
50-59	
60-69	
70-79	
80-89	
90-100	

(b) How many students scored above or equal to 70?

(c) How many students scored below 80?

Stem and Leaf Diagrame

Stem	Leaf
1	1 1 2 3 3 4 4 5 8
2	0 2 2 7 8
3	5 7 8 8
4	0 0 0 1 2 4 5 6 8 9

Stem and Leaf Diagrams: A plot where each data is separated into a leaf and stem. Usually leaf is the last digit, while stem is the other digits.

1 | 0 means 10.

Example 35.2.3

The heights of trees at a certain park is listed below in centimeters.

| 221 | 245 | 259 | 228 | 237 | 233 | 227 | 240 | 248 | 252 |
| 236 | 244 | 237 | 222 | 239 | 243 | 248 | 237 | 225 | 258 |

(a) Complete an ordered stem and leaf diagram to show this information.

Stem	Leaf
22	1 2 5 7 8
23	3 6 7 7 7 9
24	0 3 4 5 8 8
25	2 8 9

(b) How many trees are over or equal to 240 cm?

(c) If a tree at the park is chosen at random, find the probability of choosing a tree that is smaller than 240 cm.

36 Displaying Data with Charts

36.1 Pictograms

Pictogram

A chart that uses picture to represent quantities.

Example 36.1.1

The pictogram shows the amount of time four students spent studying during a week.

(a) Who spent the most time studying?

(b) How much time did Ben spend studying during the week?

(c) Draw symbols to represent $2\frac{1}{2}$ hours.

36.2 Bar Charts

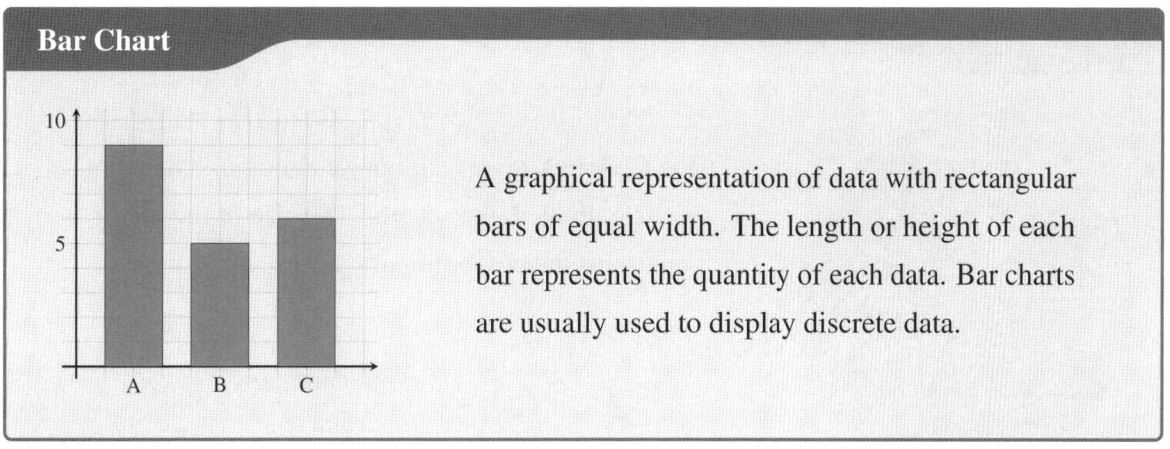

Bar Chart

A graphical representation of data with rectangular bars of equal width. The length or height of each bar represents the quantity of each data. Bar charts are usually used to display discrete data.

Example 36.2.1

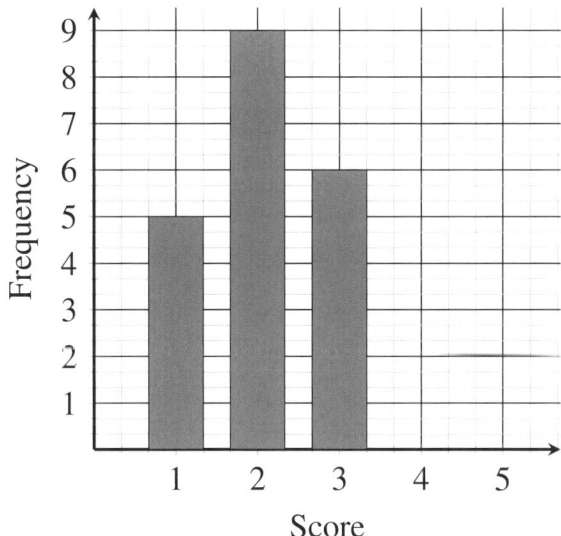

A bar chart on the left shows the scores of a football team in a season.

(a) If the team scored a 4 on four games, and scored a 5 on seven games, complete the bar chart to show this information.

(b) Work out the total score of the team during this season.

Unit 9. Statistics

36.3 Pie Charts

Pie Charts

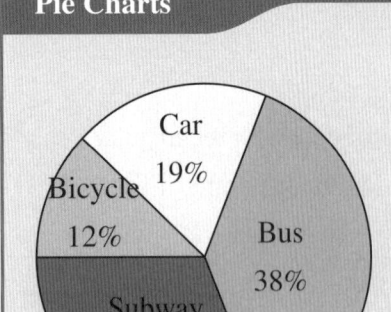

Pie Chart: A graphical representation of data with a circle divided into sectors. The size of the sector represents the proportion of the corresponding data.

$$\text{Central angle} = \frac{\text{Component part}}{\text{Total}} \times 360°$$

Example 36.3.1

The pie chart shows how Jasmine spent her allowance during a month.

(a) What did she spend the most money on?

(b) What fraction of the allowance did she spend on food?

Jasmine spent $180 on food.

(c) How much is her total allowance?

(d) If she spent $97.5 on games, work out the sector angle for games.

(e) How money did she save?

36.4 Histograms

Histogram

Histogram: A graphical representation of the distribution of numerical data.

Characteristics of Histograms
(1) Area represents the frequency of a data.
(2) The height of the rectangle represents the frequency density.

$$\text{Frequency density} = \frac{\text{Frequency}}{\text{Class width}}$$

Example 36.4.1

The grouped frequency table shows the weight, in kg, of 120 students in Troy High School. Draw a histogram of the distribution of the weights of the students.

Weight, x (kg)	Frequency	Class width	Frequency density
$45 \leq x < 50$	11		
$50 \leq x < 55$	34		
$55 \leq x < 65$	18		
$65 \leq x < 80$	48		
$80 \leq x < 90$	9		

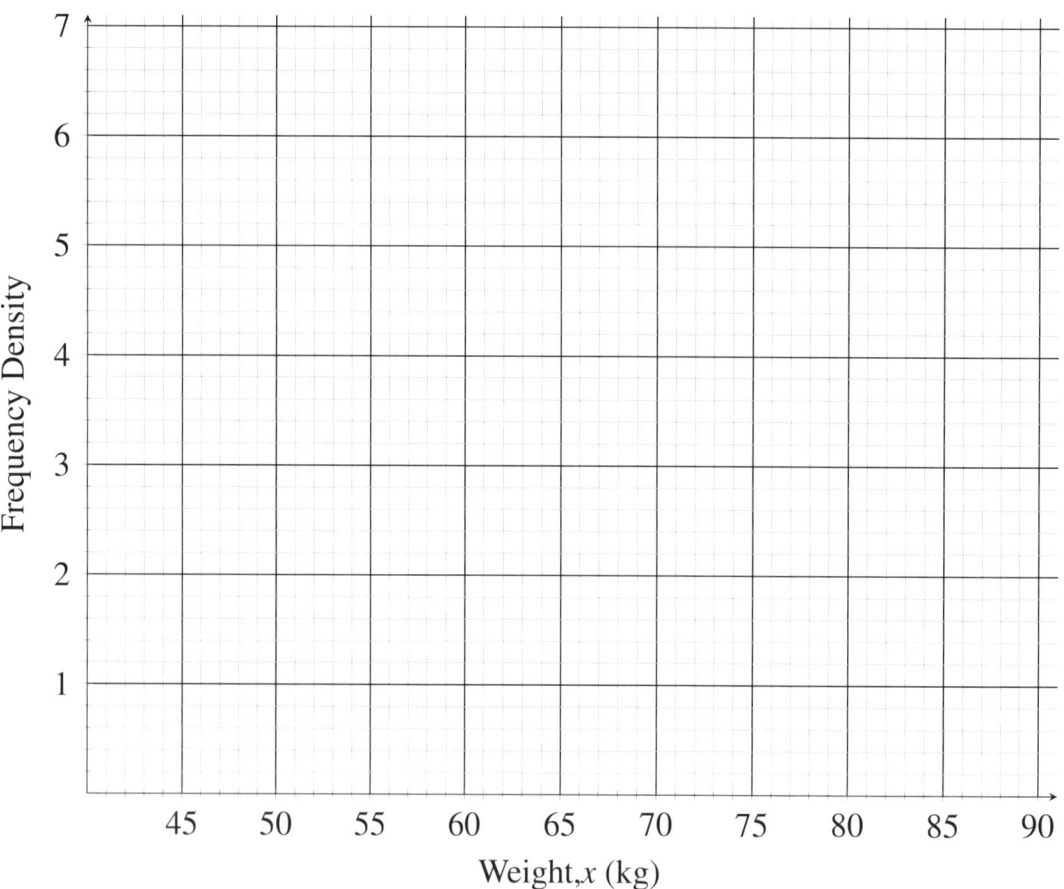

37 Central Tendency and Spread

37.1 Individual Data

Mean

Mean: The average value.

$$\text{Mean} = \frac{\text{Sum of all data values}}{\text{Number of data values}} = \frac{x_1 + x_2 + \ldots + x_n}{n}$$

Example 37.1.1

Find the mean of the data set below.

$$2 \quad 4 \quad 9 \quad 12 \quad 8 \quad 7 \quad 6 \quad 3$$

Median

Median: The middle value.

(1) List the numbers from least to greatest.

(2) Find the $\left(\dfrac{n+1}{2}\right)$ th number, which is the median.

Example 37.1.2

Find the median of each of the data set.

(a) 5 9 2 5 7 1 8

(b) 5 9 2 5 7 1 8 11

Mode

Mode: The most frequent value.//
(1) No Mode: All numbers occur the same amount of times.//
(2) Multiple Modes: More than one type of number is the most frequent.

Example 37.1.3

Find the mode of each of the data set.

(a) 5   2   3   5   3   1   3

(b) 2   6   2   5   5   9   1

(c) 2   3   7   5   9   1   0

Range

Range: The difference between the smallest and largest value.
$$\text{Range} = \text{Largest value} - \text{Smallest value}$$

Example 37.1.4

Find the range of each of the data set.

(a) 5   2   3   7   3   1   3

(b) −2   6   2   5   5   9   0

37.2 Frequency Table

Mean and Median of Frequency Tables

Mean: The average value.

$$\text{Mean} = \frac{\text{Sum of all data values}}{\text{Number of data values}} = \frac{\sum x \cdot f}{\sum f} = \frac{x_1 \cdot f_1 + x_2 \cdot f_2 + \ldots + x_n \cdot f_n}{f_1 + f_2 + \ldots + f_n}$$

Median: The middle value.
(1) Construct a cumulative frequency table.
(2) Find the $\left(\frac{n+1}{2}\right)$th number, which is the median.

Mode: The data value with the greatest frequency.

Example 37.2.1

Clara asked her 35 classmates how many siblings they had. Survey results are summarized in the table below.

Number of siblings	0	1	2	3	4
Frequency	4	13	9	7	2
Cumulative Frequency					

Determine the

(a) mean

(b) median

(c) mode

(d) range

37.3 Grouped Frequency Table (EXTENDED ONLY)

Grouped Frequency Table

When data is gathered in groups or classes, the mid-interval value represents all data values within each interval. We cannot find the exact mean, median, and mode of grouped data values.

Mean: The approximated average value.

$$\text{Mean} = \frac{\sum m \cdot f}{\sum f} = \frac{m_1 \cdot f_1 + m_2 \cdot f_2 + \ldots + m_n \cdot f_n}{f_1 + f_2 + \ldots + f_n}$$

(m_i represents the mid-interval value of each interval.)

Median Class: The class which includes the middle value.

Modal Class: The most frequent class.

Example 37.3.1 EXTENDED ONLY

The table below shows the ages of 50 members in a sport club.

Age	16-20	21-25	26-30	31-35	36-40
Frequency	6	12	15	8	9

Calculate the

(a) mean

(b) median

(c) mode

37.4 Stem and Leaf Diagram

Example 37.4.1

Stem	Leaf
4	1 2 4 4 5 7
5	0 2 2 7 8
6	5 7 8 8
7	0 0 0 5 6 8 9

Find each of the following.

(a) Mean

(b) Median

(c) Mode

(d) Range

38 Continuous Data Representation (EXTENDED ONLY)

38.1 Box-and-Whisker Plots (EXTENDED ONLY)

Box-and-Whisker Plots (Box Plot)

Box-and-Whisker Plots (Box Plot): A graphical way to display the distribution of data with five numbers: minimum, lower quartile, median, upper quartile, and maximum.

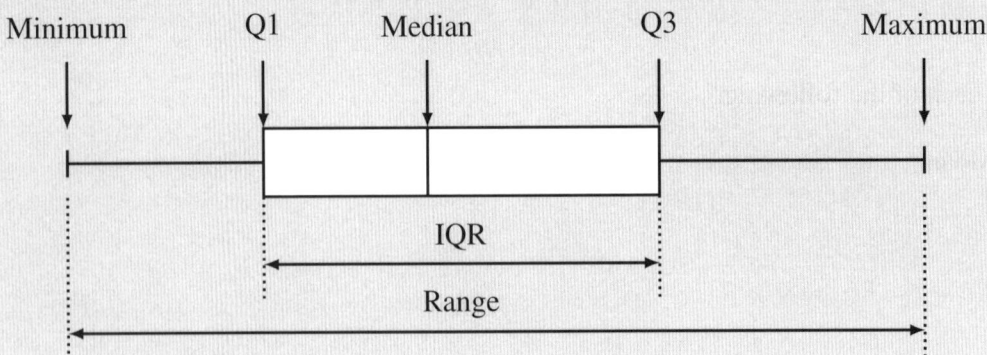

Five Number Summary
(1) Minimum: Smallest data
(2) Q1 (Lower Quartile): 25%
(3) Median: 50%
(4) Q3 (Upper Quartile): 75%
(5) Maximum: Largest data

Spread Tendency
(1) Range = Maximum − Minimum
(2) Interquartile Range (IQR) = Q3 − Q1

Example 38.1.1 EXTENDED ONLY

Find the minimum, lower quartile, median, upper quartile, and maximum of the data set and graph the box-and-whisker plot.

            49   51   59   63   67   69   73   75   82   88   93

Example 38.1.2 EXTENDED ONLY

The box plot shows the distribution of the height of apple trees in a garden.

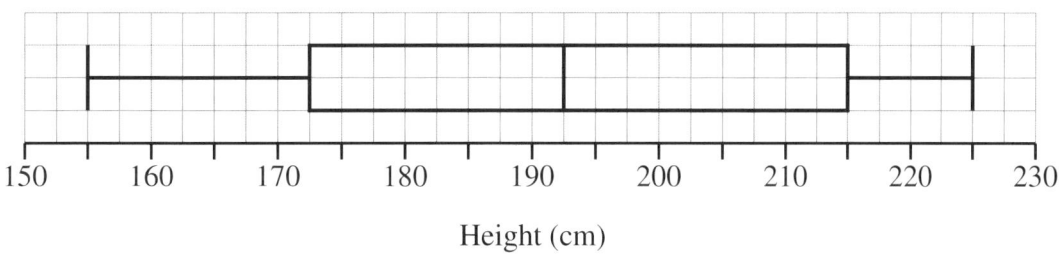

Height (cm)

(a) Write down the maximum height.

(b) Write down the median height.

(c) Work out the interquartile range of heights.

There are 120 trees in the garden.
(d) Work out the number of trees with a height of 215cm or less.

38.2 Cumulative Frequency (EXTENDED ONLY)

Example 38.2.1 EXTENDED ONLY

The frequency table below shows the weight distribution by cargo.

Weight, x (kg)	0-10	10-20	20-30	30-40	40-50	50-60
Frequency	3	11	22	46	24	14

(a) Plot a cumulative frequency curve.

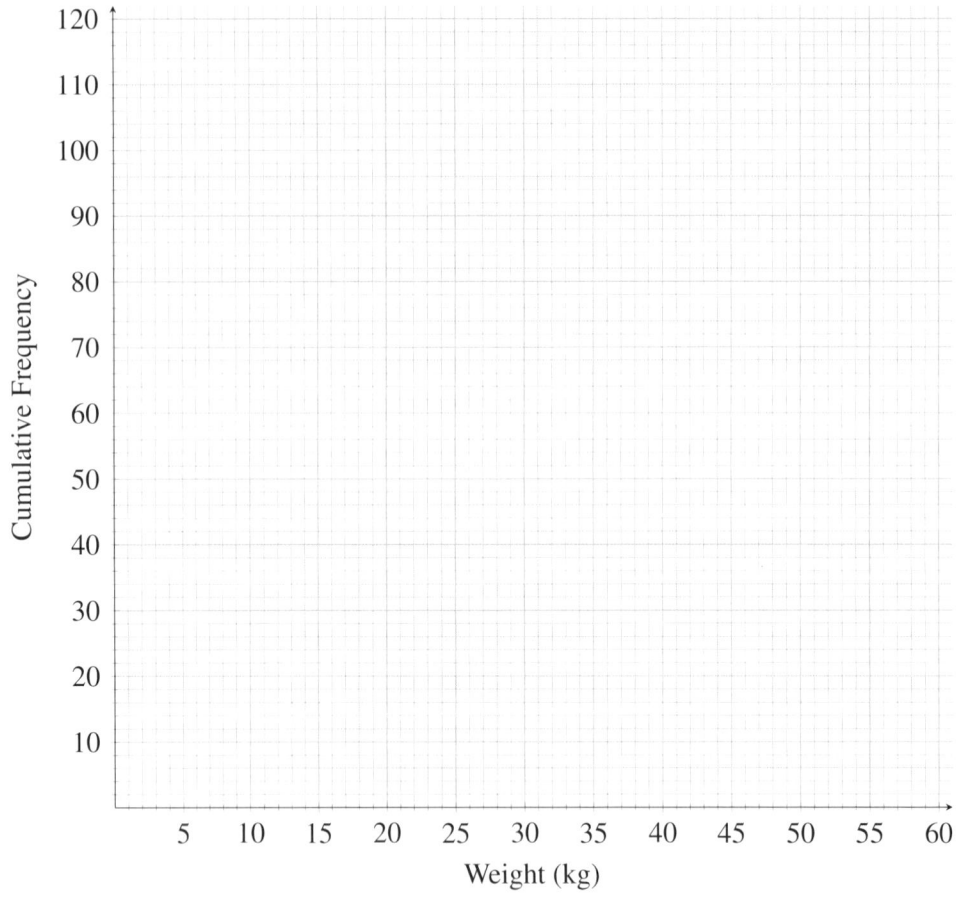

(b) Estimate the median and interquartile range.

39 Scatter Diagram

39.1 Correlation

Scatter Diagrams

Scatter diagrams are used to observe the relationship or correlation between two numerical data sets.

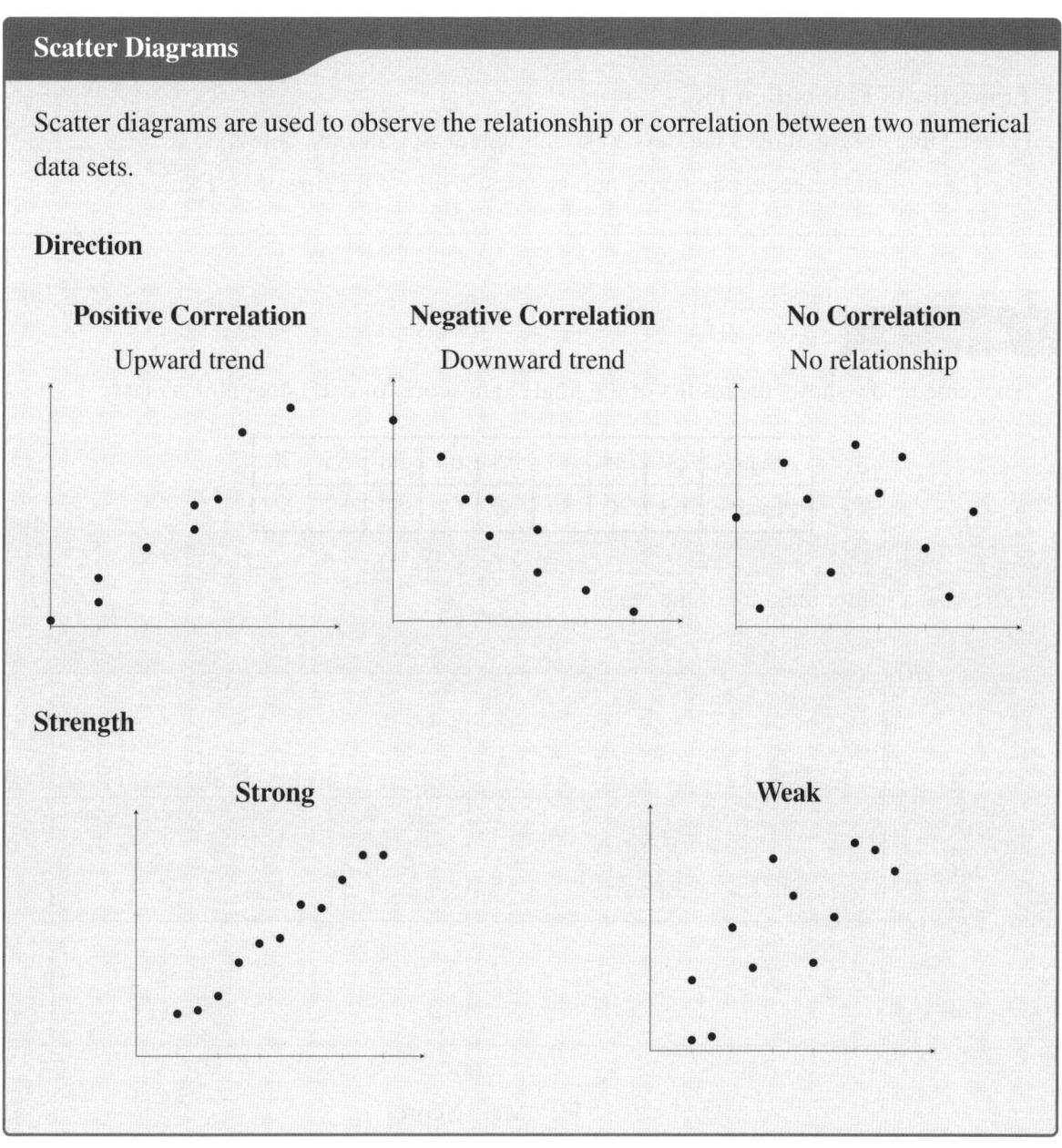

39.2 Line of Best Fit

Line of Best Fit

Line of best fit is used to estimate the trend of scatter diagrams.

Properties of Line of Best Fit

(1) The line of best fit does not have to go through any of the data points.

(2) There should be equal number of points on each side of the line of best fit.

Example 39.2.1

The table below shows the results of the final exam scores of each student in a class.

Math	60	75	48	48	65	38	55	70
Physics	63	70	56	60	61	50	57	66

(a) Draw a scatter diagram of the results.

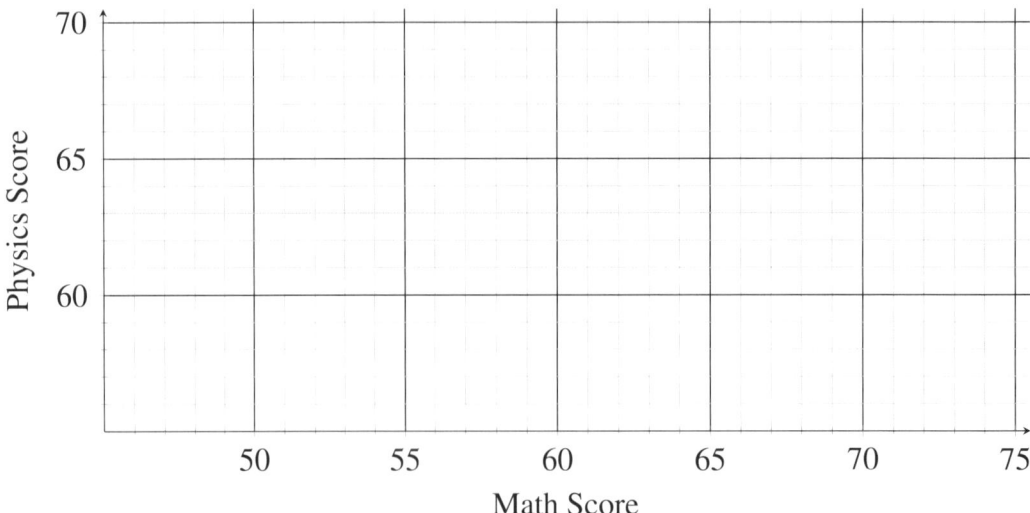

(b) State what type of correlation the diagram shows and explain the meaning of the correlation.

(c) Draw a line of best fit

(d) Estimate the physics exam score of a student who would have scored 59 on math.

(e) Estimate the math exam score of a student who would have scored 64 on physics.

1 Numbers and Operations

1.1 Numbers

Example 1.1.1

(a) $\dfrac{3\pi}{\pi}$, -5

(b) $0.4\dot{5}$, 0.67, $\dfrac{3\pi}{\pi}$, -5, $\dfrac{20}{7}$

(c) $\sqrt{3}+5$, $\dfrac{\pi}{5}$

(d) $\sqrt{3}+5$, $0.4\dot{5}$, $\dfrac{\pi}{5}$, 0.67, $\dfrac{3\pi}{\pi}$, -5, $\dfrac{20}{7}$

1.2 Directed Numbers

Example 1.2.1

(a) $25 + 55 = 80°C$

(b) $80 - 34 = 46°C$

Example 1.2.2

$-130 - (-746) = 616$

The shark is 616m below the surface.

1.3 Decimals

Example 1.3.1

(a) 25.34 (b) 2.22 (c) -5.49

Example 1.3.2

(a) 3.42 (b) 3.612

Example 1.3.3

(a) 90.3 (b) 9.35

Example 1.3.4

(a) 0.01 (b) 0.154

1.4 Fractions

Example 1.4.1

(a) $\dfrac{2}{7} + \dfrac{1}{3} = \dfrac{6}{21} + \dfrac{7}{21} = \dfrac{13}{21}$

(b) $3\dfrac{7}{8} - 1\dfrac{5}{12} = \dfrac{31}{8} - \dfrac{17}{12} = \dfrac{93}{24} - \dfrac{34}{24} = \dfrac{59}{24} = 2\dfrac{11}{24}$

Example 1.4.2

(a) $\dfrac{5}{6} \times \dfrac{3}{4} = \dfrac{5 \times 3}{6 \times 4} = \dfrac{5}{2 \times 4} = \dfrac{5}{8}$

(b) $\dfrac{8}{3} \times \dfrac{7}{2} = \dfrac{8 \times 7}{3 \times 2} = \dfrac{4 \times 7}{3} = \dfrac{28}{3}$

Example 1.4.3

(a) $\dfrac{12}{5} \times \dfrac{3}{16} = \dfrac{3 \times 3}{5 \times 4} = \dfrac{9}{20}$

(b) $\dfrac{28}{5} \div \dfrac{7}{3} = \dfrac{28}{5} \times \dfrac{3}{7} = \dfrac{4 \times 3}{5} = \dfrac{12}{5}$

Example 1.4.4

(a) $\dfrac{11}{20}$ (b) $\dfrac{28}{9}$

1.5 Conversion Between Decimals and Fractions

Example 1.5.1

(a) $8 \overline{)3.000}$ gives 0.375

$$\begin{array}{r} 0.375 \\ 8\overline{)3.000} \\ 2.4 \\ \hline 60 \\ 56 \\ \hline 40 \\ 40 \\ \hline 0 \end{array}$$

(b)
$$\begin{array}{r} 0.46 \\ 50\overline{)23.00} \\ 20.0 \\ \hline 3.00 \\ 3.00 \\ \hline 0 \end{array}$$

$7 + 0.46 = 7.46$

(c)
$$\begin{array}{r} 0.\overline{3} \\ 3\overline{)1.0} \\ 9 \\ \hline 1 \end{array}$$

Example 1.5.2

(a) $\dfrac{0.25}{1} = \dfrac{25}{100} = \dfrac{1}{4}$

(b) $13 + \dfrac{0.22}{1} = 13 + \dfrac{22}{100} = 13\dfrac{11}{50}$

Example 1.5.3

(a) $x = 0.555...$

$10x = 5.555...$

Subtract: $9x = 5$

$x = \dfrac{5}{9}$

(b) $x = 0.121212...$

$100x = 12.121212...$

Subtract: $99x = 12$

$x = \dfrac{12}{99} = \dfrac{4}{33}$

(c) $x = 2.1454545...$

$10x = 21.454545...$

$1000x = 2145.454545...$

Subtract: $990x = 2145 - 21 = 2124$

$x = \dfrac{2124}{990} = \dfrac{118}{55} = 2\dfrac{8}{55}$

1.6 Using a Calculator

No Examples

1.7 Calculations and Order

Example 1.7.1

(a) $-5.1 < -5.095$

(b) $\dfrac{3}{8} > 0.275$

(c) $\dfrac{11}{5} < 2.201$

Example 1.7.2

$$\sqrt{0.04} < 4^{-1} < 0.26 < 0.55^2 < \frac{1}{3}$$

1.8 Calculations and Order

Example 1.8.1

(a) $S = \{11, 13, 15, 17, 19\}$
(b) $A = \{0, 3, 6\}$ (c) $B = \{3, 4, 9, 15\}$

Example 1.8.2

$n(A)=4 \qquad n(B)=5$

Example 1.8.3

(a) $7 \in A$ (c) $5 \in A$
(b) $2 \in B$ (d) $0 \notin B$

Example 1.8.4

(a)

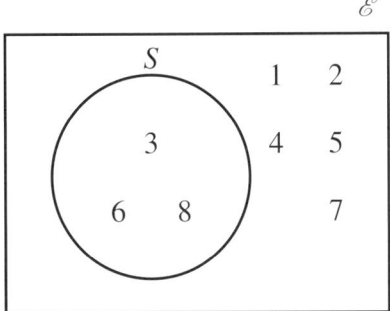

(b) $S' = \{1, 2, 4, 5, 7\}$
(c) $n(S) = 3 \qquad n(S') = 5$

Example 1.8.5

(a) $\varnothing, \{2\}, \{5\}, \{6\}, \{2,5\}, \{2,6\}, \{5,6\}, \{2,5,6\}$
(b) $\varnothing, \{2\}, \{5\}, \{6\}, \{2,5\}, \{2,6\}, \{5,6\}$

Example 1.8.6

(a) $\subset$ or $\subseteq$ (d) $\subset$ or $\subseteq$
(b) $\in$ (e) $\not\supseteq$
(c) $\subseteq$ (f) $\subseteq$

Example 1.8.7

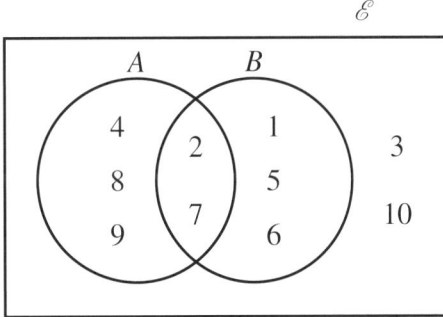

(a) $\{2, 7\}$
(b) $\{1, 2, 4, 5, 6, 7, 8, 9\}$
(c) $\{1, 5, 6\}$
(d) $\{2, 3, 4, 7, 8, 9, 10\}$
(e) 8
(f) 2

2 Powers and Roots

2.1 Powers

Example 2.1.1

(a) $5 \cdot 5 = 25$
(b) $(-6) \cdot (-6) \cdot (-6) = -216$
(c) $3 \cdot 3 \cdot 5 \cdot 5 \cdot 5 = 1125$

Example 2.1.2

(a) 5
(b) $\dfrac{1}{12}$
(c) 13
(d) $\dfrac{2}{3}$
(e) -5
(f) 7

Example 2.1.3

(a) $\dfrac{1}{3^2} = \dfrac{1}{9}$

(b) $5^3 = 125$

(c) 1

(d) $6^2 = 36$

(e) $1 \times \dfrac{1}{49} = \dfrac{1}{49}$

(f) $4 \times \left(\dfrac{1}{4}\right)^2 = 4 \times \dfrac{1}{16} = \dfrac{1}{4}$

Example 2.1.4

(a) $\dfrac{\left(2^3\right)^{\frac{1}{3}}}{2^4} = \dfrac{2^1}{2^4} = 2^{-3} = \dfrac{1}{2^3} = \dfrac{1}{8}$

(b) $5^{\left(\frac{1}{2}+\frac{1}{3}\right)} = 5^{\frac{5}{6}} = \sqrt[6]{5^5}$

(c) $\dfrac{\left(5^{\frac{1}{4}}\right) \times 5^{\frac{3}{4}}}{2^{-2}} = \dfrac{5^1}{2^{-2}} = 5^1 \times 2^2 = 20$

2.2 Roots

Example 2.2.1

(a) $\sqrt{36} = 6$
(b) $\sqrt{12} = 2\sqrt{3}$
(c) $2\sqrt{5} - 3\sqrt{5} = -\sqrt{5}$

2.3 Standard Form

Example 2.3.1

(a) 5.6×10^3
(b) 9.48×10^5
(c) 7.27×10^{-4}
(d) 1.08×10^{-2}

Example 2.3.2

(a) 982000
(b) 701
(c) 0.00000123
(d) 0.000422

Example 2.3.3

(a) $(5.1 \times 10^4) \times (6 \times 10^3) = 30.6 \times 10^7 = 3.06 \times 10^8$

(b) $(1.6 \times 10^4) \div (8 \times 10^{-3}) = 0.2 \times 10^7 = 2 \times 10^6$

3 Factors and Multiples

3.1 Prime

Example 3.1.1

(a) $24 = 2^3 \cdot 3$ (c) $60 = 2^2 \cdot 3 \cdot 5$
(b) $20 = 2^2 \cdot 5$

3.2 Factors

Example 3.2.1

(a) 1, 2, 3, 4, 6, 12   (c) 1, 2, 13, 26
(b) 1, 2, 3, 6, 9, 18

Example 3.2.2

(a) Factors of 12: 1, 2, 3, 4, 6, 12
Factors of 30: 1, 2, 3, 5, 6, 10, 15, 30
Common Factors: 1, 2, 3, 6
Highest Common Factor: 6

(b) Factors of 15: 1, 3, 5, 15
Factors of 24: 1, 2, 3, 4, 6, 8, 12, 24
Common Factors: 1, 3
Highest Common Factor: 3

(c) Factors of 28: 1, 2, 4, 7, 14, 28
Factors of 42: 1, 2, 3, 6, 7, 14, 21, 42
Common Factors: 1, 2, 7, 14
Highest Common Factor: 14

Example 3.2.3

(a) $60 = 2^2 \cdot 3 \cdot 5$
$90 = 2 \cdot 3^2 \cdot 5$
$120 = 2^3 \cdot 3 \cdot 5$
HCF $= 2 \cdot 3 \cdot 5 = 30$

(b) $56 = 2^3 \cdot 7$ $98 = 2 \cdot 7^2$
$42 = 2 \cdot 3 \cdot 7$ HCF $= 2 \cdot 7 = 14$

(c) $33 = 3 \cdot 11$ $132 = 2^2 \cdot 3 \cdot 11$
$99 = 3^2 \cdot 11$ HCF $= 3 \cdot 11 = 33$

3.3 Multiples

Example 3.3.1

(a) $12 = 2^2 \cdot 3$ $30 = 2 \cdot 3 \cdot 5$
LCM $= 2^2 \cdot 3 \cdot 5 = 60$
Common Multiples: 60, 120, 180, ...

(b) $15 = 3 \cdot 5$ $21 = 3 \cdot 7$
LCM $= 3 \cdot 5 \cdot 7 = 105$
Common Multiples: 105, 210, 315, ...

Example 3.3.2

(a) $14 = 2 \cdot 7$ $21 = 3 \cdot 7$ $28 = 2^2 \cdot 7$
LCM $= 2^2 \cdot 3 \cdot 7 = 84$
Common Multiples: 84, 168, 252...

(b) $9 = 3^2$ $13 = 13$ $26 = 2 \cdot 13$
LCM $= 2 \cdot 3^2 \cdot 13 = 234$
Common Multiples: 234, 468, 702, ...

(c) $9 = 3^2$ $20 = 2^2 \cdot 5$ $22 = 2 \cdot 11$
LCM $= 2^2 \cdot 3^2 \cdot 5 \cdot 11 = 1980$
Common Multiples: 1980, 3960, 5940, ...

4 Accuracy

4.1 Rounding

Example 4.1.1

(a) 424,000
(b) 424,000
(c) 423,990
(d) 423,991.743
(e) 423,991.74
(f) 423,991.7

Example 4.1.2

(a) 12.4
(b) 12.35
(c) 12.353
(d) 12.3530

Example 4.1.3

(a) 3 s.f: 2, 3, 5
(b) 4 s.f: 2, 0, 4, 9
(c) 6 s.f: 3, 0, 5, 8, 9, 0
(d) 3 s.f: 1, 0, 0

Example 4.1.4

(a) 8
(b) 7.6
(c) 7.65
(d) 7.650

4.2 Lower and Upper Bound

Example 4.2.1

(a) Lower bound: 175.5cm
    Upper bound: 176.5cm

(b)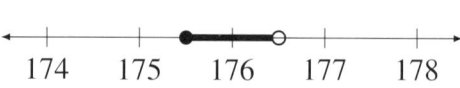

(c) $175.5 \leq$ height < 176.5

Example 4.2.2

Range of 34.2: $34.15 \leq$ Number 1 < 34.25
Range of 18.6: $18.55 \leq$ Number 2 < 18.65

(a) Lower bound: $34.15 + 18.55 = 52.7$
    Upper bound: $34.25 + 18.65 = 52.9$

(b) Lower bound: $34.15 - 18.65 = 15.5$
    Upper bound: $34.25 - 18.55 = 15.7$

(c) Lower bound:
    $34.15 \times 18.55 = 633.4825$

    Upper bound:
    $34.25 \times 18.65 = 638.7625$

(d) Lower bound: $\dfrac{34.25}{18.55} = 1.846361...$

    Upper bound: $\dfrac{34.15}{18.65} = 1.831099...$

5 Ratio and Proportion

5.1 Prime

Example 5.1.1

(a) 2:5

(b) 1:2:7

Example 5.1.2

(a) 6:18

(b) 50:100:250

Example 5.1.3

(a) $120 \times \dfrac{6}{5} = 144$

(b) $60 \times \dfrac{2}{3} = 40$

5.2 Proportion

Example 5.2.1

(a) 50cm : $20 = 300cm : $120

The ribbon costs $120.

(b) 50cm : $20 = 162.5cm : $65

You can purchase a ribbon of 162.5cm.

Example 5.2.2

5 students = 16 hours

1 student = 80 hours

4 students = 20 hours

∴ It takes 20 hours.

5.3 Exchanging Currency

Example 5.3.1

(a) $\$2.5 \times \dfrac{\text{₩}1200}{\$1} = \text{₩}3000$

(b) $\$120 \times \dfrac{£0.74}{\$1} = £88.8$

(c) $€200 \times \dfrac{\$1}{€0.86} = \$232.56$

5.4 Rates

Example 5.4.1

(a) 6 litres ÷ 2.5 min = 2.4 litres/min

(b) 2500 m ÷ 7200 s = 0.347 m/s

5.5 Distance, Speed, and Time

Example 5.5.1

$$\dfrac{16 \text{ m}}{\text{s}} \times \dfrac{1 \text{ km}}{1000 \text{ m}} \times \dfrac{60 \text{ s}}{1 \text{ min}} \times \dfrac{60 \text{ min}}{1 \text{ hr}}$$

$= 57.6$km/h

Example 5.5.2

(a) speed $= \dfrac{5 \text{ km}}{\text{h}} \times \dfrac{1000 \text{ m}}{1 \text{ km}} \times \dfrac{1 \text{ h}}{60 \text{ min}}$

$= 83.333$m/min

time $= \dfrac{3200 \text{ m}}{83.333 \text{m/min}} = 38.4$ min

(b) 0.4 min = 0.4 × 60 sec = 24 sec

If 38 minues and 24 seconds has passed since 17:34:00, the time is 18:12:24.

(c) distance $= 83.333$ m/min $\times 12$ min $= 1000$m $= 1$ km

Example 5.5.3

(a) $t_1 + t_2 = \dfrac{30 \text{ km}}{25 \text{ km/h}} + \dfrac{65 \text{ km}}{20 \text{ km/h}} =$

$1.2 + 3.25 = 4.45$ hours

$0.45 \times 60 = 27$ minutes

$\therefore 4$ hours 27 minutes

(b) average speed $= \dfrac{(30+65) \text{ km}}{4.45 \text{ h}}$

$= 21.3$ km/h

6 Percentage

6.1 Basic Percentage

Example 6.1.1

(a) 73%

(b) $\dfrac{65}{100} = \dfrac{13}{20}$

(c) 0.263

Example 6.1.2

(a) $200 \times 0.23 = 46$

(b) $45 \times 0.8 = 36$

6.2 Percent Increase and Decrease

Example 6.2.1

(a) $50 \times (1 - 0.1) = 45$ dollars

(b) $45 \times (1 + 0.25) = 56.25$ dollars

Example 6.2.2

(a) $\dfrac{24.50 - 20}{20} \times 100 = 22.5\%$

22.5% profit

(b) $\dfrac{120 - 150}{150} \times 100 = -20\%$

20% loss

Example 6.2.3

(a) $\dfrac{2400}{1 - 0.3} = 3248.57$ dollars

(b) $\dfrac{300}{1 + 0.45} = 206.90$ dollars

6.3 Simple and Compound Interest

Example 6.3.1

(a) $\dfrac{400 \times 6 \times 3.5}{100} = \$84$

(b) $400 + 84 = \$484$

Example 6.3.2

(a) $5000 \left(1 + \dfrac{4}{100}\right)^{10} = \$7401.22$

(b) $7401.22 - 5000 = \$2401.22$

7 Algebraic Expression

7.1 Substitution

Example 7.1.1

(a) $2(-2)-(-3) = -1$

(b) $\dfrac{-3((-2)^2-3(-3))}{4} = -\dfrac{39}{4}$

(c) $\sqrt{(-3)^2-4(-2)(4)} = \sqrt{41}$

7.2 Expanding

Example 7.2.1

(a) $12xy+15x$

(b) $-10p^2+16pq-6pr$

(c) $3x^3+12x^2-x$

Example 7.2.2

(a) $x^2+4x-3x-12 = x^2+x-12$

(b) $2x^2+6x-5x-15 = 2x^2+x-15$

Example 7.2.3

(a) $(x^2-x-2)(x+3) = x^3+3x^2-x^2-3x-2x-6 = x^3+2x^2-5x-6$

(b) $(2x^2+5x-12)(x+5) = 2x^3+10x^2+5x^2+25x-12x-60 = 2x^3+15x^2+13x-60$

7.3 Factoring

Example 7.3.1

(a) $-42p+49 = -7(6p-7)$

(b) $ab(a-8b)$

(c) $5xy(x^2y-4x+6y)$

Example 7.3.2

(a) $(2x+5y)(2x-5y)$

(b) $(abc+4c)(abc-4c)$

(c) $(4m^2+9n^2)(4m^2-9n^2) = (4m^2+9n^2)(2m+3n)(2m-3n)$

Example 7.3.3

(a) $(x-12)^2$ \qquad (b) $(2a+3b)^2$

Example 7.3.4

(a) $(x-4)(x+1)$ \qquad (b) $(x-2)(x-3)$

Example 7.3.5

(a) $(2x+3)(x+2)$ \qquad (b) $(4x-1)^2$

Example 7.3.6

(a) $a(b-3)-4b(b-3) = (a-4b)(b-3)$

(b) $y^2(x-6)-(x-6) = (y^2-1)(x-6) = (y+1)(y-1)(x-6)$

260 IGCSE & MYP Math

7.4 Transformation of a Formula

Example 7.4.1

(a) $x = \dfrac{3a - 5c}{b}$ (c) $x = \dfrac{b + c + ay}{3a}$

(b) $x = \dfrac{a - b}{a + b}$

Example 7.4.2

(a) $x = \dfrac{bn - a}{m}$ (c) $x = \dfrac{a + b}{c}$

(b) $x = \dfrac{b}{c - a}$

Example 7.4.3

(a) $x = -\dfrac{n + q}{m - p}$ or $\dfrac{n + q}{p - m}$

(b) $x = -\dfrac{b + ac}{2c - 3}$ or $\dfrac{b + ac}{3 - 2c}$

Example 7.4.4

(a) $x = \pm\sqrt{n^2 + m}$ (c) $x = \dfrac{ab - c^2}{3}$

(b) $x = \dfrac{n \pm \sqrt{p}}{m}$ (d) $x = \dfrac{a}{1 - b^2}$

7.5 Algebraic Fractions

Example 7.5.1

(a) $\dfrac{3}{7x}$ (b) $\dfrac{x(x - 4)}{6xy} = \dfrac{x - 4}{6y}$

Example 7.5.2

(a) $\dfrac{x(x - 2)}{(x - 2)(x - 3)} = \dfrac{x}{x - 3}$

(b) $\dfrac{(x - 4)(x + 5)}{(x - 1)(x + 5)} = \dfrac{x - 4}{x - 1}$

Example 7.5.3

(a) $\dfrac{ax}{by}$ (c) $\dfrac{4a}{5} \times \dfrac{25}{2a^2} = \dfrac{10}{a}$

(b) $\dfrac{24x^2yz^2}{3xy^2z} = \dfrac{8xz}{y}$

Example 7.5.4

(a) $\dfrac{3x}{6} + \dfrac{2(x - 5)}{6} = \dfrac{5x - 10}{6}$

(b) $\dfrac{9x}{12} - \dfrac{8(x - 7)}{12} = \dfrac{x + 56}{12}$

(c) $\dfrac{x - 4}{(x + 2)(x - 4)} - \dfrac{3(x + 2)}{(x + 2)(x - 4)}$

$= \dfrac{-2x - 10}{(x + 2)(x - 4)}$

7.6 Indices

Example 7.6.1

(a) $36x^{14}$ (b) $\dfrac{9}{25x^6}$ (c) $343x^2$

Example 7.6.2

(a) $5x^{-\frac{5}{2}} = \dfrac{5}{x^2\sqrt{x}}$

(b) $\dfrac{2}{65}x^{\frac{5}{2}} = \dfrac{2}{65}x^2\sqrt{x}$

8 Equations and Inequatlities

8.1 Linear Equations

Example 8.1.1

(a) $x = \dfrac{36}{5}$ (b) $x = 20$

Example 8.1.2

(a) $x - 3x + 6 = 6 - 2x - 2$

$-2x + 6 = -2x + 4$

$6 = 4$

No solution

(b) $x^2 + 4x + 4 = x^2 + 2x - 3 - 6$

$2x = -13 \qquad \therefore x = -\dfrac{13}{2}$

Example 8.1.3

(a) $x = \dfrac{1}{15}$ (b) $x = -\dfrac{19}{5}$ (c) $x = \dfrac{80}{11}$

Example 8.1.4

length= x width= $2x$

$2(x+2x) = 66 \qquad x = 11$

11×22 Rectangle

Example 8.1.5

$x = 5(x+3) \qquad x = 5x + 15$

$4x = -15 \qquad x = -\dfrac{15}{4}$

8.2 Linear Equations

Example 8.2.1

$y = 2x + 12 \qquad 6x + 5(-2x + 12) = 40$

$-4x = -20 \qquad x = 5$

$y = -2(5) + 12 = 2$

$\therefore x = 5$ and $y = 2$

Example 8.2.2

1. Eliminating x

   $6x + 10y = 38$

   $6x - 3y = 12$

   Subtract: $13y = 26$, thus $y = 2$

   Plug in: $2x - 2 = 4$, thus $x = 3$

   $\therefore x = 3, y = 2$

2. Eliminating y

   $3x + 5y = 19$

   $10x - 5y = 20$

   Add: $13x = 39$, thus $x = 3$

   Plug in: $2(3) - y = 4$, thus $y = 2$

   $\therefore x = 3, y = 2$

Example 8.2.3

$b + r = 20 ...(1) \qquad 1.5b + 2r = 34 ...(2)$

$(1) \times 3 \longrightarrow 3b + 3r = 60$

$(2) \times 2 \longrightarrow 3b + 4r = 68$

Subtract: $r = 8$ Plugin: $b + 8 = 20$

$\therefore$ 12 blue pens and 8 red pens

8.3 Quadratic Equations

Example 8.3.1

(a) $(3x+1)(2x-5) = 0$

$\therefore x = -\dfrac{1}{3}$ or $x = \dfrac{5}{2}$

(b) $(3x-4)(3x+4) = 0$

$\therefore x = \dfrac{4}{3}$ or $x = -\dfrac{4}{3}$

(c) $2x^2 - 5x = 0$

$x(2x-5) = 0$

$\therefore x = 0$ or $x = \dfrac{5}{2}$

Example 8.3.2

(a) $x = \dfrac{-1 \pm \sqrt{1^2 - 4(2)(-28)}}{2(2)}$

$= \dfrac{-1 \pm \sqrt{225}}{4} = \dfrac{-1 \pm 15}{4}$

$\therefore x = -4$ or $\dfrac{7}{2}$

(b) $x = \dfrac{3 \pm \sqrt{3^2 - 4(1)(1)}}{2(1)} = \dfrac{3 \pm \sqrt{5}}{2}$

Example 8.3.3

(a) $x^2 - 8x = 3$

$x^2 - 8x + 16 = 3 + 16$

$(x-4)^2 = 19$

$x - 4 = \pm\sqrt{19} \qquad \therefore x = 4 \pm \sqrt{19}$

(b) $2x^2 + 6x = 5 \longrightarrow x^2 + 3x = \dfrac{5}{2}$

$x^2 + 3x + \dfrac{9}{4} = \dfrac{5}{2} + \dfrac{9}{4} = \dfrac{19}{4}$

$(x + \dfrac{3}{2})^2 = \dfrac{19}{4}$

$x + \dfrac{3}{2} = \pm\sqrt{\dfrac{19}{4}}$

$\therefore x = -\dfrac{3}{2} \pm \dfrac{\sqrt{19}}{2}$

(c) $2x^2 - 5x = 1 \longrightarrow x^2 - \dfrac{5}{2}x = \dfrac{1}{2}$

$x^2 - \dfrac{5}{2}x + \dfrac{25}{16} = \dfrac{1}{2} + \dfrac{25}{16} = \dfrac{33}{16}$

$(x - \dfrac{5}{4})^2 = \dfrac{33}{16} \qquad x - \dfrac{5}{4} = \pm\sqrt{\dfrac{33}{16}}$

$\therefore x = \dfrac{5}{4} \pm \dfrac{\sqrt{33}}{4}$

8.4 Non-linear Simultaneous Equations

Example 8.4.1

(a) $7x + 5 = x^2 + 4x - 5$

$x^2 - 3x - 10 = 0$

$(x-5)(x+2) = 0$

$\therefore x = 5, y = 40$ or $x = -2, y = -9$

(b) $y = 3x - 1$ and $y = x^2 + 4x - 2$

$x^2 + 4x - 2 = 3x - 1$

$x^2 + x - 1 = 0$

$x = \dfrac{-1 \pm \sqrt{1^2 - 4(1)(-1)}}{2(1)}$

$= \dfrac{-1 \pm \sqrt{5}}{2}, y = \dfrac{-5 \pm 3\sqrt{5}}{2}$

8.5 Exponential Equations

Example 8.5.1

(a) $(3^2)^x = 3^3$

$3^{2x} = 3^3$

$2x = 3$

$\therefore x = \dfrac{3}{2}$

(b) $(2^6)^{2x-1} = 2^1$

$2^{6(2x-1)} = 2^1$

$6(2x - 1) = 1$

$\therefore x = \dfrac{7}{12}$

8.6 Linear Inequalities

Example 8.6.1

(a) $3x < 21$

$\therefore x < 7$

(b) $-7x \leq -35$

$\therefore x \geq 5$

Example 8.6.2

(a) $25 + 2 < 3x < 43 + 2$

$27 < 3x < 45$

$\therefore 9 < x < 15$

(b) $-8 - 12 \leq -5x < 67 - 12$

$-20 \leq -5x < 55$

$\therefore -11 < x \leq 4$

9 Sequences

9.1 Arithmetic Sequence (Linear)

Example 9.1.1

(a) Next two terms: 19, 23

n-th term: $u_n = 4n + 3$

(b) Next two terms: $-12, -19$

n-th term: $u_n = -7n + 16$

9.2 Geometric Sequence

Example 9.2.1

(a) Next two terms: 108, 324

n-th term: $u_n = 4 \times 3^{n-1}$

(b) Next two terms: $-27, 9$

n-th term: $u_n = 243 \times \left(-\dfrac{1}{3}\right)^{n-1}$

9.3 Quadratic and Cubic Sequence

Example 9.3.1

$2a = 2 \qquad \therefore a = 1$

$3a + b = 4 \qquad 3(1) + b = 4 \qquad \therefore b = 1$

$a + b + c = 2 \qquad 1 + 1 + c = 2 \qquad \therefore c = 0$

$\therefore u_n = n^2 + n$

Example 9.3.2

$6a = 24 \qquad \therefore a = 4$

$12a + 2b = 38$

$12(4) + 2b = 38 \qquad \therefore b = -5$

$7a + 3b + c = 13$

$7(4) + 3(-5) + c = 13 \qquad \therefore c = 0$

$a + b + c + d = 1$

$4 - 5 + 0 + d = 1 \qquad \therefore d = 2$

$\therefore u_n = 4n^3 - 5n^2 + 2$

10 Variation

10.1 Direct Variation

Example 10.1.1

(a) $a = k \cdot b \quad\quad 5 = 2k$

$\therefore k = \dfrac{5}{2}$

(b) $a = k \cdot b \quad\quad 9 = \dfrac{5}{2}b$

$\therefore b = 9 \times \dfrac{2}{5} = \dfrac{18}{5}$

Example 10.1.2

(a) $d = k \cdot t^2$

$20 = k \times 2^2$

$\therefore k = 5$

$125 = 5t^2$

$\therefore t = 5$ seconds

(b) $d = k \cdot t^2 = 5 \cdot 6^2 = 180$ meters

10.2 Inverse Variation

Example 10.2.1

(a) $t = \dfrac{k}{\sqrt{s}}$

$6 = \dfrac{k}{\sqrt{144}}$

$\therefore k = 72$

(b) $t = \dfrac{k}{\sqrt{s}} = \dfrac{72}{\sqrt{36}} = 12$

$\therefore t = 12$

(c) $9 = \dfrac{k}{\sqrt{s}} = \dfrac{72}{\sqrt{s}}$

$\sqrt{s} = 8$

$\therefore s = 8^2 = 64$

11 Functions

11.1 Function Notations

Example 11.1.1

(a) $f(-4) = (-4)^2 - 5 = 16 - 5 = 11$

(b) $g(13) = -2(13) + 6 = -26 + 6 = -20$

(c) $g(0) = -2(0) + 6 = 0 + 6 = 6$

(d) $f(x) = x^2 - 5 = 116$

$x^2 = 121 \qquad x = \pm 11$

11.2 Composite Functions

Example 11.2.1

(a) $f(g(x)) = (-5x + 9) - 3 = -5x + 6$

(b) $g(f(x)) = -5(x - 3) + 9$

$= -5x + 15 + 9 = -5x + 24$

(c) $f(g(15)) = -5(15) + 6 = -69$

OR

$g(15) = -5 \times 15 + 9 = -66$

$f(g(15)) = f(-66) = -66 - 3 = -69$

11.3 Inverse Functions

Example 11.3.1

(a) $y = -3x + 14 \qquad x = -3y + 14$

$3y = -x + 14$

$\therefore f^{-1}(x) = \dfrac{-x + 14}{3}$

1. Show $ff^{-1}(x) = x$

$f(f^{-1}(x)) = -3\left(\dfrac{-x+14}{3}\right) + 14 = x$

2. Show $f^{-1}f(x) = x$

$f^{-1}(f(x)) = \dfrac{-(-3x + 14) + 14}{3} = x$

(b) $y = \dfrac{6x - 5}{13} \qquad x = \dfrac{6y - 5}{13}$

$13x + 5 = 6y$

$\therefore g^{-1}(x) = \dfrac{1}{6}(13x + 5)$

1. Show $gg^{-1}(x) = x$

$g(g^{-1}(x)) = \dfrac{6(\frac{1}{6}(13x + 5)) - 5}{13} = x$

2. Show $g^{-1}g(x) = x$

$g^{-1}(g(x)) = \dfrac{1}{6}(13(\dfrac{6x - 5}{13}) + 5) = x$

12 Linear Functions

12.1 Gradient

Example 12.1.1

(a) $\dfrac{y_2 - y_1}{x_2 - x_1} = \dfrac{3-1}{3-0} = \dfrac{2}{3}$

(b) $\dfrac{y_2 - y_1}{x_2 - x_1} = \dfrac{2-(-1)}{-1-0} = -3$

12.2 Midpoint and Distance

Example 12.2.1

(1) Midpoint

$M\left(\dfrac{-2+2}{2}, \dfrac{5+(-1)}{2}\right) = (0, 2)$

(2) Distance

$\sqrt{(-2-2)^2 + (5-(-1))^2}$
$= 2\sqrt{13} \approx 7.21$

12.3 Gradient-intercept Form

Example 12.3.1

(a) Gradient: -2 \qquad y-intercept: 3

(b) Gradient: $-\dfrac{3}{2}$ \qquad y-intercept: 3

Example 12.3.2

(a) $y = 4x + c$ \qquad $3 = 4(-1) + c$

$c = 7$ \qquad $\therefore y = 4x + 7$

(b) $y = -6x + c$ \qquad $2 = -6(5) + c$

$c = 32$ \qquad $\therefore y = -6x + 32$

Example 12.3.3

(a) $m = \dfrac{6-(-4)}{5-1} = \dfrac{5}{2}$ \qquad $y = \dfrac{5}{2}x + c$

$-4 = \dfrac{5}{2} \times 1 + c$ \qquad $c = -\dfrac{13}{2}$

$\therefore y = \dfrac{5}{2}x - \dfrac{13}{2}$

(b) $m = \dfrac{-3-1}{5-3} = -2$

$y = 2x + c$ \qquad $1 = -2 \times 3 + c$

$c = 7$ \qquad $\therefore y = -2x + 7$

12.4 Parallel and Perpendicular Lines

Example 12.4.1

(a) $m = -2$ \qquad $y = -2x + c$

$3 = -2(7) + c$ \qquad $c = 17$

$\therefore y = -2x + 17$

(b) $m = -\dfrac{1}{5}$ \qquad $y = -\dfrac{1}{5}x + c$

$1 = -\dfrac{1}{5} \times (-3) + c$ \qquad $c = \dfrac{2}{5}$

$\therefore y = -\dfrac{1}{5}x + \dfrac{2}{5}$

13 More Complicated Functions

13.1 Quadratic Function Graphs

Example 13.1.1

(a)

x	−1	0	1	2	3	4	5
y	8	3	0	-1	0	3	8

(b)
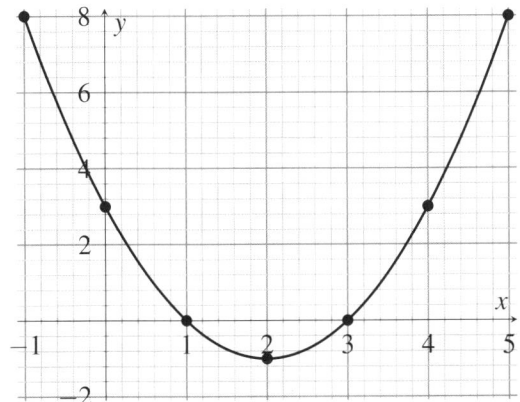

Example 13.1.2

(a) $y = 2(x^2 - \frac{3}{2}x) + 4$

$= 2(x^2 - \frac{3}{2}x + \frac{9}{16}) + 4 - \frac{9}{8}$

$= 2(x - \frac{3}{4})^2 + \frac{23}{8}$

∴ vertex $\left(\frac{3}{4}, \frac{23}{8}\right)$

(b) $y = -(x^2 - 6x) - 11$

$= -(x^2 - 6x + 9) - 11 + 9$

$= (x-3)^2 - 2$ ∴ vertex $(3, -2)$

13.2 Cubic Function Graphs

Example 13.2.1

(a)

x	-1.5	0.5	2
y	3.125	0.625	4

(b)
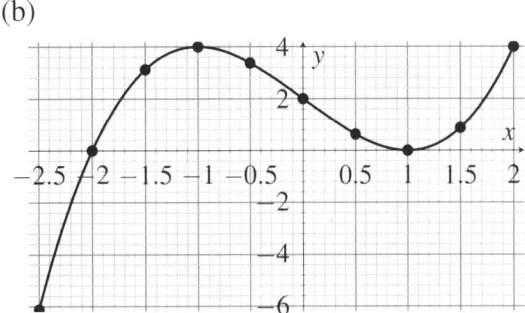

13.3 Rational Function Graphs

Example 13.3.1

(a)

x	−0.4	0.2	2
y	−2.5	5	0.5

(b)
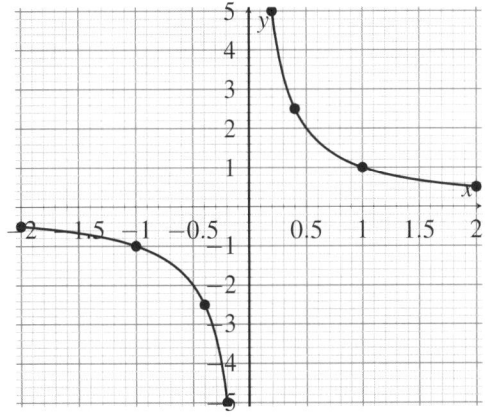

Answer   269

13.4 Exponential Function Graphs

Example 13.4.1

(a)
x	-3	-2	-1	0	1	2	3
y	0.125	0.25	0.5	1	2	4	8

(b)
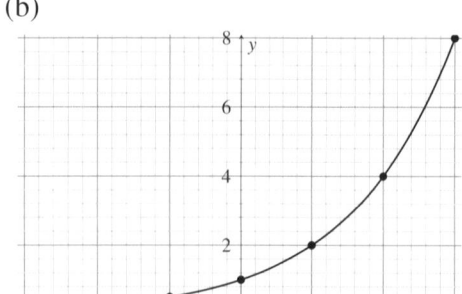

13.5 Solve Equations Graphically

Example 13.5.1

(a) $\dfrac{5}{x} + x^2 = 2x$

$5 + x^3 = 2x^2$

$\therefore x^3 - 2x^2 + 5 = 0$

(b) The x coordinate of the x-intercept is the solution.

$\therefore x \approx -1.24$

Example 13.5.2

(a) $x \approx 0.1$ or 2.4

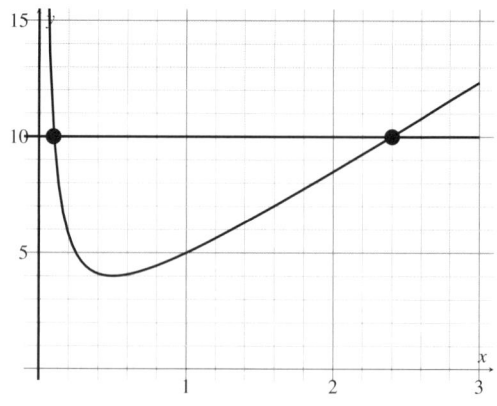

(b) 1 or 2 or 3

Example 13.5.3

(a) $x = \dfrac{1}{x}$ $2x = x + \dfrac{1}{x}$

Graph $y = 2x$ and find the intersection.

$\therefore x = 1$ or $x = -1$

(b) $x - \dfrac{1}{x} = 0$

$x^2 - 1 = 0$ $(x-1)(x+1) = 0$

$\therefore x = 1$ or $x = -1$

14 Differentiation

14.1 Derived Functions

Example 14.1.1

(a) $f'(x) = 3 \cdot 2x - 5 = 6x - 5$

(b) $f'(x) = -2 \cdot 4x^3 + 12 \cdot 2x = -8x^3 + 24x$

14.2 Gradients at a Point

Example 14.2.1

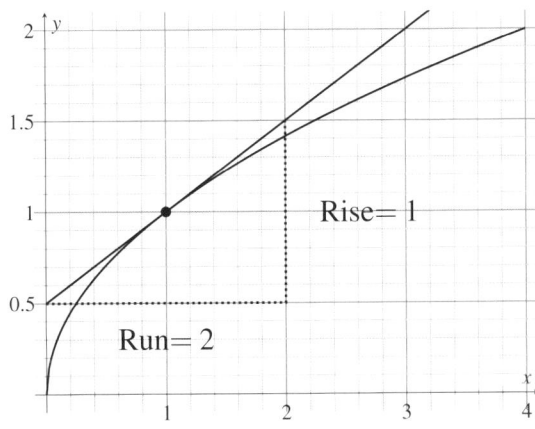

Gradient $= \dfrac{\text{Rise}}{\text{Run}} = \dfrac{1}{2}$

Example 14.2.2

(a) $y' = 6x^2 - 10x$

$y'(-3) = 6(-3)^2 - 10(-3) = 84$

(b) $y' = -2x + 4$

$y'(2) = -2 \times 2 + 4 = 0$

14.3 Equations of Tangent Lines

Example 14.3.1

$y' = 10x - 3$

Gradient: $y'(2) = 10 \times 2 - 3 = 17$

Point: $y(2) = 5 \cdot 2^2 - 3 \cdot 2 + 4 = 18$

$y = 17x + c \qquad 18 = 17 \times 2 + c$

$c = -16 \qquad \therefore y = 17x - 16$

14.4 Turning Points

Example 14.4.1

$y' = 6x^2 - 6x - 12 = 6(x^2 - x - 2)$

$ = 6(x-2)(x+1) = 0$

Turning points at $x = 2$ and $x = -1$

$y(2) = -11 \qquad y(-1) = 16$

$\therefore (2, -11)$ and $(-1, 16)$

Example 14.4.2

$f'(x) = 3x^2 - 6x - 9 = 3(x-3)(x+1) = 0$

Turning points at $x = 3$ and $x = -1$

$f''(x) = 6x - 6$

$f''(3) = 5 \times 3 - 6 > 0 \implies$ Minimum

$f''(-1) = 6(-1) - 6 < 0 \implies$ Maximum

$\therefore (3, -27)$ is a minimum and $(-1, 5)$ is a maximum.

15 Inequality Graphs

15.1 Vertical Boundary Lines

Example 15.1.1

(a) (b)

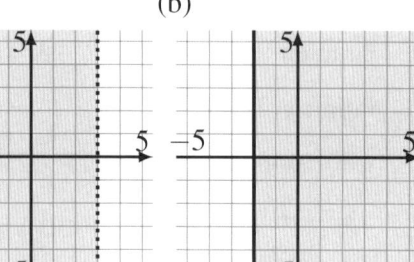

Example 15.1.2

(a) $x \leq -3.5$ (b) $x > 1$

15.2 Horizontal Boundary Lines

Example 15.2.1

(a)   (b)

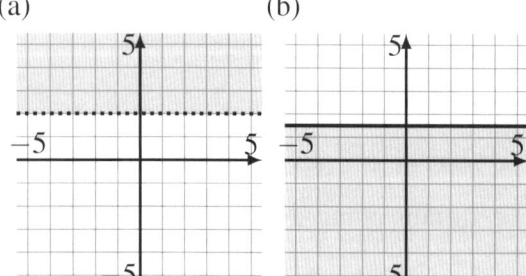

Example 15.2.2

(a) $y > -1$ (b) $y \leq 3$

15.3 Linear Boundary

Example 15.3.1

(a)   (b)

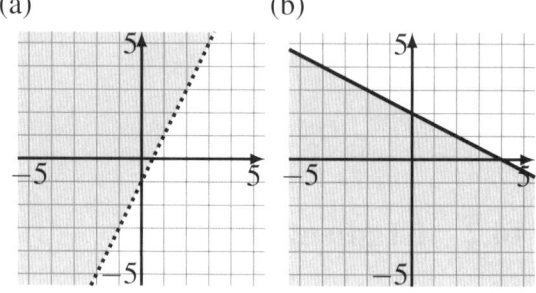

Example 15.3.2

(a) $y < \dfrac{2}{3}x - 2$ (b) $y \geq -3x - 1$

15.4 Linear Programming

Example 15.4.1

(a)

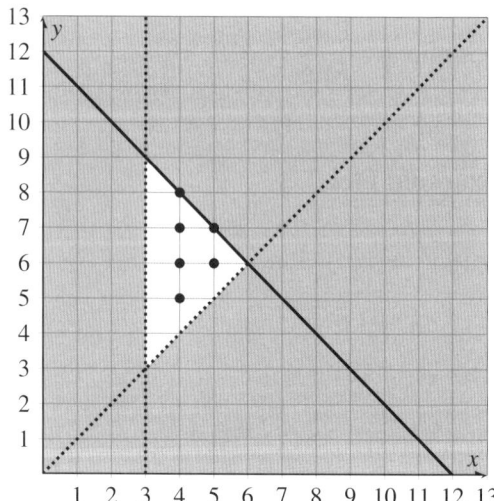

(b) (4, 5), (4, 6), (4, 7), (4, 8), (5, 6), (5, 7)

(c)

x	y	2x + 3y
4	5	2 × 4 + 3 × 5 = 23
4	6	2 × 4 + 3 × 6 = 26
4	7	2 × 4 + 3 × 7 = 29
4	8	2 × 4 + 3 × 8 = 32
5	6	2 × 5 + 3 × 6 = 28
5	7	2 × 5 + 3 × 7 = 31

$\therefore 2x+3y$ is maximum at point (4, 8).

16 Graphs in Practical Situations

16.1 Conversion Graphs

Example 16.1.1

(a) 7 meters ≈ 23 feet

(b) 20 feet ≈ 6.1 meters

16.2 Distance vs. Time Graphs

Example 16.2.1

(a) 10:05

(b) 15 minutes

(c) On the way to the post office:

$$\frac{7 \text{ km}}{20 \text{minutes}} = \frac{7 \text{ km}}{\frac{1}{3}\text{hours}} = 21 \text{ km/h}$$

On the way back home:

$$\frac{-7 \text{ km}}{15 \text{minutes}} = \frac{-7 \text{ km}}{\frac{1}{4}\text{hours}} = -28 \text{ km/h}$$

Example 16.2.2

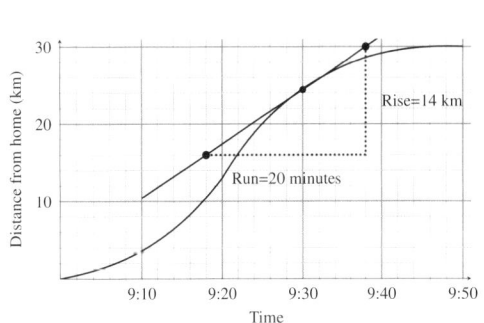

$$\text{Speed} = \frac{14 \text{ km}}{20 \text{ minutes}} = \frac{14 \text{ km}}{\frac{1}{3}\text{ h}} = 42 \text{ km/h}$$

16.3 Speed vs. Time Graphs

Example 16.3.1

(a) Gradient $= \dfrac{-20\text{m/s}}{20 \text{ s}} = -1 \text{ m/s}^2$

(b) Area $= \dfrac{1}{2}(30+60) \times 20 = 900$ meters

(c) Average Speed $= \dfrac{900 \text{ m}}{60 \text{ s}} = 15 \text{ m/s}$

17 Measures

17.1 Units of Length

Example 17.1.1

(a) $6.2 \div 10 \div 100 = 0.0062$ m

(b) $9800 \div 1000 = 9.8$ km

(c) $0.023 \times 1000 \times 100 = 2300$ cm

17.2 Units of Area

Example 17.2.1

(a) $0.047 \times 1000^2 = 47000$ m^2

(b) $18000 \div 10^2 = 180$ cm^2

17.3 Units of Volume

Example 17.3.1

(a) $930{,}000 \div 1000^3 = 0.00093$ km^3

(b) $0.034 \times 100^3 = 34000$ cm^3

17.4 Mass, Capacity, and Density

Example 17.4.1

(a) $63500 \div 1000 \div 1000 = 0.0635$ t

(b) $0.00593 \times 100 \times 10 = 5.93$ ml

Example 17.4.2

(a) $5 \text{ litres} \times \dfrac{1000 \text{ cm}^3}{1 \text{ litre}} = 5000$ cm^3

(b) $5.86 \text{ m}^3 \times \dfrac{1000 \text{ litres}}{1 \text{ m}^3} = 5860$ litres

Example 17.4.3

(a) $\dfrac{\text{Mass}}{\text{Density}} = \dfrac{48 \text{ g}}{60 \text{ g/cm}^3} = 0.8$ cm^3

(b) $\dfrac{\text{Mass}}{\text{Volume}} = \dfrac{400 \text{ g}}{80 \text{ cm}^3} = 5$ g/cm^3

18 Geometrical Terms

18.1 Points and Lines

No Examples

18.2 Angles

Example 18.2.1

(a) acute
(b) straight
(c) obtuse
(d) revolution
(e) reflex
(f) right

18.3 Polygons

Example 18.3.1

(a) Obtuse, Isosceles
(b) Acute, Equilateral
(c) Right, Scalene

Example 18.3.2

(a) square, rhombus, rectangle, parallelogram
(b) rhombus, parallelogram
(c) parallelogram

19 Two Dimensional Figures

19.1 Triangles

Example 19.1.1

(a) Perimeter: 9
Area: 3.9

(b) Perimeter: 10.7
Area: 5.18

19.2 Quadrilaterals

Example 19.2.1

(a) Perimeter: 26
Area: 32

(b) Perimeter: 12.5
Area: 7.7

19.3 Circles

Example 19.3.1

Perimeter: $18 + \frac{1}{2} \times 2\pi r = 18 + 9\pi$

Area: $\frac{1}{2} \times \pi r^2 = \frac{81}{2}\pi$

Example 19.3.2

(a) $\pi r^2 \times \frac{70}{360} = 22 \quad \therefore r = 6$ cm

(b) $2r + 2\pi r \times \frac{70}{360} = 19.3$ cm

20 Three Dimensional Figures

20.1 Prisms and Cylinders

Example 20.1.1

(a) Volume:

$$\left(\frac{1}{2} \times 1 \times 2\right) \times 3.5 = 3.5 \text{ cm}^3$$

Surface Area:

$$2\left(\frac{1}{2} \times 1 \times 2\right) + 3.5(1 + 2 + \sqrt{5})$$
$$= 20.3 \text{ cm}^2$$

(b) Volume:

$$\left(\frac{1}{2}(3+4) \times 2\right) \times 6 = 42 \text{ cm}^3$$

Surface Area:

$$2\left(\frac{1}{2}(3+4) \cdot 2\right) + 6(2 + 3 + 4 + 2.2)$$
$$= 81.2 \text{ cm}^2$$

20.2 Pyramids and Cones

Example 20.2.1

(a) Slant height: $\sqrt{4^2 + 1.5^2} = 4.272$

Volume: $\frac{1}{3}(3^2 \times 4) = 12 \text{ m}^3$

Surface Area: $3^2 + 4\left(\frac{1}{2} \cdot 3 \cdot 4.272\right)$
$= 34.6 \text{ m}^2$

(b) Slant height: $\sqrt{5^2 + 7^2} = \sqrt{74}$

Volume: $\frac{1}{3}\pi \cdot 7^2 \cdot 5 = \frac{245}{3}\pi \approx 257 \text{ cm}^3$

Surface Area: $\pi \cdot 7^2 + \pi \cdot 7 \cdot \sqrt{74}$
$= 343 \text{ cm}^2$

20.3 Spheres

Example 20.3.1

(a) $\frac{4}{3}\pi r^3 = 600$

$r^3 = 600 \times \frac{3}{4\pi} = \frac{450}{\pi}$

$r = \sqrt[3]{\frac{450}{\pi}}$

$\therefore r = 5.23 \text{ cm}$

(b) $4\pi r^2 = 4\pi \times 5.23^2 = 344 \text{ cm}^2$

21 Geometrical Constructions

21.1 Measuring & Drawing Angles

Example 21.1.1

(a) 325°   (b) 115°   (c) 55°

Example 21.1.2

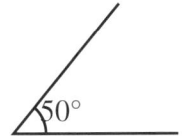

21.2 Constructing Triangles

Example 21.2.1

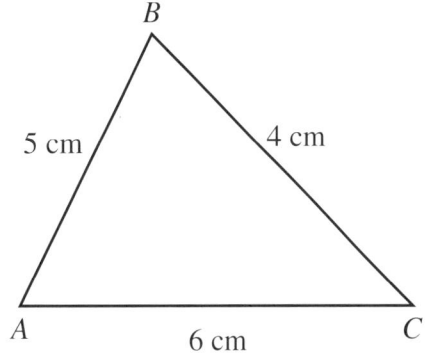

22 Similarity

22.1 Lengths of Similar Figures

Example 22.1.1

(a) Scale factor: $\dfrac{6}{4} = \dfrac{3}{2}$

$XY = 4.5 \times \dfrac{3}{2} = 6.75$ cm

(b) Scale factor: $\dfrac{4}{6} = \dfrac{2}{3}$

$AC = 7.5 \times \dfrac{2}{3} = 5$ cm

22.2 Areas of Similar Figures

Example 22.2.1

$72 \times \left(\dfrac{5}{6}\right)^2 = 50$ cm²

Example 22.2.2

$8 \times \sqrt{\dfrac{75}{12}} = 20$ cm

22.3 Volumes of Similar Figures

Example 22.3.1

$81 \times \left(\dfrac{4}{3}\right)^3 = 192$ cm³

Example 22.3.2

$6 \times \sqrt[3]{\dfrac{48}{162}} = 4$ cm

22.4 Scale Drawing

Example 22.4.1

(a) 8 km (b) 4.5 cm (c) 24 km²

23 Congruent Triangles

23.1 SSS Congruency

Example 23.1.1

(a) Not congruent (b) SSS congruent

23.2 SAS Congruency

Example 23.2.1

(a) Not congruent (b) SAS congruent

23.3 ASA Congruency

Example 23.3.1

(a) ASA congruent (b) ASA congruent

23.4 RHS Congruency

Example 23.4.1

(a) RHS congruent (b) Not congruent

24 Symmetry

24.1 Symmetry in Two Dimension

Example 24.1.1

(a) 5 lines (b) 8 lines

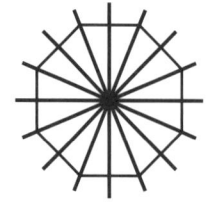

Example 24.1.2

(a) 4 lines (b) 1 line

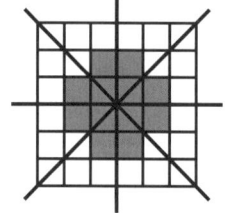 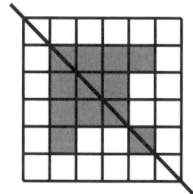

Example 24.1.3 (a) 5 (b) 3

Example 24.1.4 (a) 4 (b) 2

24.2 Symmetry in Three Dimension

Example 24.2.1 (a) 6 (b) Infinite

Example 24.2.2 (a) 2 (b) Infinite

24.3 Symmetry in Circles

Example 24.3.1

$AM = \sqrt{5^2 - 3^2} = 4, \quad AB = 4 \cdot 2 = 8$ cm

Example 24.3.2

$OM = ON = \sqrt{13^2 - 12^2} = 5$ cm

Example 24.3.3

(a) 12 cm (b) 27°

25 Basic Angle Properties

25.1 Angle Relationships

Example 25.1.1

(a) $x = 180 - 22 = 158°$

(b) $4x + x + 35 = 90 \qquad \therefore x = 11°$

Example 25.1.2

(a) $2x + 7x + 4x + 100 = 360$

$\therefore x = 20°$

(b) $x = 180 - 62 = 118°$

$y = 62°$

$z = 180 - 62 - 41 = 77°$

25.2 Angles in Parallel Lines

Example 25.2.1

$x = 58°$ (Vertical angles)

$y = 58°$ (Corresponding angles)

Example 25.2.2

$x = 51°$ (Alternate angles)

$z = 43°$ (Alternate angles)

$y = 180 - 51 - 43 = 86°$

Example 25.2.3

$98 + (y + 25) = 180°$ (Co-interior angles)

$\therefore y = 57°$

$x = 25°$ (Alternate angles)

$z = 98°$ (Alternate angles)

26 Basic Angle Properties

26.1 Angles in Triangles

Example 26.1.1

(a) $y = 65°$ (Alternate angles)

$x = 180 - 70 - 65 = 45°$

(b) $y = 180 - 62 - 20 - 27 = 71°$

$x = 180 - 62 - 71 = 47°$

26.2 Angles in Quadrilaterals

Example 26.2.1

(a) $y = 180 - 95 = 85°$

$11x + 9x + 5x + 85 = 360$

$\therefore x = 11°$

(b) $x + y + 85 + 95 + 70 = 360°$

$2x + y = 180°$

Solve systems of equations:

$x = 70°$ and $y = 40°$

26.3 Angles in Polygons

Example 26.3.1

(a) $180 \times (10 - 2) = 1440°$

(b) $1440 \div 10 = 144°$

Example 26.3.2

$180 \times (n - 2) = 2700°$

$n - 2 = 15$

$\therefore n = 17$

27 Angles in Circles

27.1 Angles in Semicircles

Example 27.1.1

(a) $x = 180 - 90 - 22 = 68°$

(b) $x = 90 - 57 = 33°$

27.2 Angle Between Tangent and Radius

Example 27.2.1

(a) $(180 - 110) \div 2 = 35°$

$\therefore x = 90 - 35 = 55°$

(b) $90 - 32 = 58°$

$\therefore x = 180 - 58 - 58 = 64°$

27.3 Angle at Center and Angle at Circumference

Example 27.3.1

(a) $360 - 130 = 230°$

$\therefore x = 230 \div 2 = 115°$

(b) $\angle AOB = 33 \times 2 = 66°$

$\angle ABO = (180 - 66) \div 2 = 57°$

$\therefore x = 90 - 57 = 33°$

27.4 Angles in the Same Segment

Example 27.4.1

(a) $85°$, vertically opposite angles are equal

(b) $75°$, angles in a triangle add up to $180°$ ($\angle ACD = 180 - 85 - 20 = 75°$) and angles in the same segment are equal ($\angle ABD = \angle ACD = 75°$)

27.5 Angles in Opposite Segment

Example 27.5.1

(a) $\angle ADC = 180 - 15 - 90 = 75°$

(b) $\angle ABC = 180 - 75 = 105°$

(c) $\angle BAC = 180 - 37 - 105 = 38°$

27.6 Alternate Angle Theorem

Example 27.6.1

(a) $\frac{1}{2}(6x - 10) = 2x + 15$

$3x - 5 = 2x + 15 \qquad \therefore x = 20$

(b) $\angle ABD = (180 - 52) \div 2 = 64°$

$\therefore x = \angle ABD = 64°$ by alternate angle theorem

28 Right Triangles

28.1 Finding Side Lengths

Example 28.1.1

(a) $10^2 + x^2 = 26^2 \qquad \therefore x = 24$

(b) $y^2 + 9^2 = 12^2 \qquad \therefore y = \sqrt{63} = 3\sqrt{7}$

$x^2 = (3\sqrt{7})^2 + 6^2$

$\therefore x = \sqrt{99} = 3\sqrt{11} \approx 9.95$

Example 28.1.2

(a) $\sin x = \dfrac{\text{Opp}}{\text{Hyp}} = \dfrac{24}{30} = \dfrac{4}{5}$

(b) $\cos y = \dfrac{\text{Adj}}{\text{Hyp}} = \dfrac{24}{30} = \dfrac{4}{5}$

(c) $\tan y = \dfrac{\text{Opp}}{\text{Adj}} = \dfrac{18}{24} = \dfrac{3}{4}$

Example 28.1.3

(a) $\cos 53° = \dfrac{x}{22}$

$\therefore x = 22\cos 53° = 13.2$

(b) $\sin 21° = \dfrac{14}{x}$

$\therefore x = \dfrac{14}{\sin 21°} = 39.1$

(c) $55 + 15 = 70°$

$\therefore x = 8\tan 70° - 8\tan 55° = 10.6$

28.2 Finding Angles

Example 28.2.1

(a) $x = \sin^{-1}\left(\dfrac{7}{25}\right) = 16.3°$

(b) $x = \cos^{-1}\left(\dfrac{10}{16}\right) = 51.3°$

(c) $x = \tan^{-1}\left(\dfrac{47}{35}\right) = 53.3°$

28.3 Elevation & Depression

Example 28.3.1 $100\tan 78° - 100\tan 70°$

$= 196 \text{ m}$

28.4 Bearings

Example 28.4.1

(a) $180 - tan^{-1}\left(\dfrac{35}{60}\right) = 120°$

(b) $360 - 60 = 300°$

(c) $BC = \sqrt{35^2 + 60^2} = 69.462$

$\dfrac{1}{2} \cdot 35 \cdot 60 = \dfrac{1}{2} \cdot 69.462 \cdot h \qquad h = 30.2$

28.5 Three-Dimensional Trig

Example 28.5.1

(a) $CH = \sqrt{8^2 + 6^2} = 10$

$CE = \sqrt{10^2 + 2^2} = 10.2 \text{ cm}$

(b) $\tan^{-1}\left(\dfrac{2}{10}\right) = 11.3°$

29 Trigonometric Functions

29.1 Sine Functions

Example 29.1.1

(a) 135°   (b) 30°   (c) 320°

Example 29.1.2

(a) 60° and 120°
(b) 194.5° and 345.5°
(c) 30°, 150°, 210°, and 330°

29.2 Cosine Functions

Example 29.2.1

(a) 300°   (b) 170°   (c) 40°

Example 29.2.2

(a) 135° and 225°
(b) 145° and 215°

29.3 Tangent Functions

Example 29.3.1

(a) 205°   (b) 280°   (c) 120°

Example 29.3.2

(a) 74.1° and 254.1°
(b) 135° and 315°

30 Non-Right Triangles

30.1 Sine Rule

Example 30.1.1

(a) $\dfrac{\sin 135°}{10.4} = \dfrac{\sin 25°}{x}$

$\therefore x = 6.22$

(b) $\dfrac{\sin 40°}{x} = \dfrac{\sin(180 - 40 - 52)°}{12.5}$

$\therefore x = 8.04$

Example 30.1.2

(a) $\dfrac{\sin x°}{9} = \dfrac{\sin 30°}{6.5}$

$\therefore x = 43.8°$

OR $x = 180 - 43.8 = 136.2°$

(b) $\dfrac{\sin y°}{4.3} = \dfrac{\sin 77°}{9}$

$y = 27.7°$ OR $y = 180 - 27.7 = 152.3°$

But $152.3°$ cannot form a triangle.

$\therefore x = 180 - 77 - 27.7 = 75.3°$

30.2 Cosine Rule

Example 30.2.1

(a) $x^2 = 15^2 + 12^2 - 2(15)(12)\cos 25°$

$\therefore x = 6.54$ cm

(b) $x^2 = 32^2 + 29^2 - 2(32)(29)\cos 125°$

$\therefore x = 54.1$ m

Example 30.2.2

(a) $9^2 = 8^2 + 12^2 - 2(8)(12)\cos x°$

$\therefore x = 48.6°$

(b) $28^2 = 20^2 + 15^2 - 2(20)(15)\cos x°$

$\therefore x = 105.4°$

30.3 Area of a Triangle

Example 30.3.1

$\dfrac{1}{2}(7)(8)\sin 45° = 19.8$ cm^2

Example 30.3.2

$\dfrac{1}{2}(7)(10)\sin x° = 33.5$

$\therefore x = 73.2°$ OR $x = 180 - 73.2 = 106.8°$

Example 30.3.3

(a) $\dfrac{1}{2}(7)(6.5)\sin 85° + \dfrac{1}{2}(5)(8)\sin 50°$

$= 38.0$ cm^2

(b) $6 \times \left(\dfrac{1}{2}(3)(3)\sin 60°\right) = 23.4$ cm^2

31 Vectors

31.1 Column Vectors

Example 31.1.1

(a) (i) $\begin{pmatrix} 1 \\ 4 \end{pmatrix}$ (iii) $\begin{pmatrix} 1 \\ 4 \end{pmatrix}$

(ii) $\begin{pmatrix} -5 \\ 2 \end{pmatrix}$ (iv) $\begin{pmatrix} 6 \\ 3 \end{pmatrix}$

(b) $\overrightarrow{GH}$

31.2 Magnitude of Vectors

Example 31.2.1

(a) $\sqrt{(-2)^2 + 1^2} = \sqrt{5} \approx 2.24$

(b) $\sqrt{4^2 + (-1)^2} = \sqrt{17} \approx 4.12$

31.3 Vector Addition & Subtraction

Example 31.3.1

(a)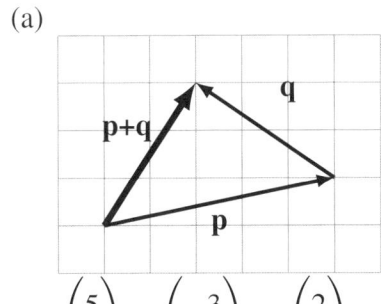

(b) $\begin{pmatrix} 5 \\ 1 \end{pmatrix} + \begin{pmatrix} -3 \\ 2 \end{pmatrix} = \begin{pmatrix} 2 \\ 3 \end{pmatrix}$

Example 31.3.2

(a)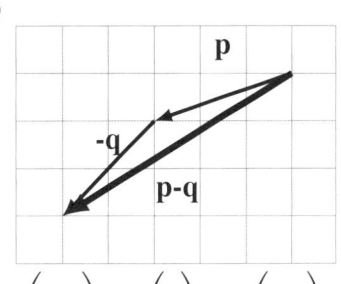

(b) $\begin{pmatrix} -3 \\ -1 \end{pmatrix} - \begin{pmatrix} 2 \\ 2 \end{pmatrix} = \begin{pmatrix} -5 \\ -3 \end{pmatrix}$

31.4 Scalar Multiplication

Example 31.4.1

(a)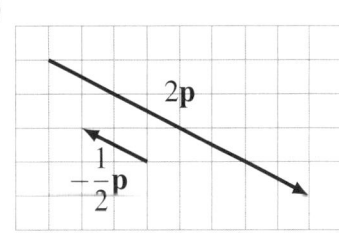

(b) $2\mathbf{p} = \begin{pmatrix} 8 \\ -4 \end{pmatrix}$ $-\frac{1}{2}\mathbf{p} = \begin{pmatrix} -2 \\ 1 \end{pmatrix}$

31.5 Vector Geometry

Example 31.5.1

(a) $\overrightarrow{DB} = \mathbf{a} - \mathbf{b}$

(b) $\overrightarrow{PC} = \overrightarrow{PB} + \overrightarrow{BC} = \frac{1}{3}(\mathbf{a} - \mathbf{b}) + \mathbf{b}$
$= \frac{1}{3}\mathbf{a} + \frac{2}{3}\mathbf{b}$

32 Transformations

32.1 Reflection

Example 32.1.1

(a) Reflection over $x = 2$

(b)
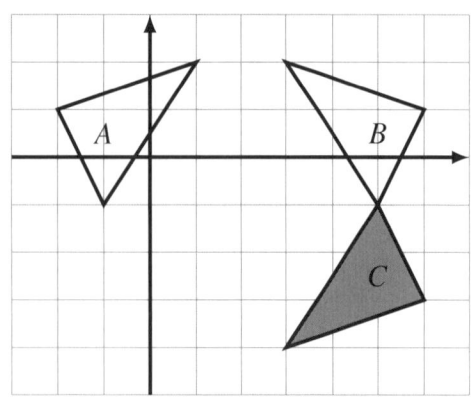

Example 32.1.2

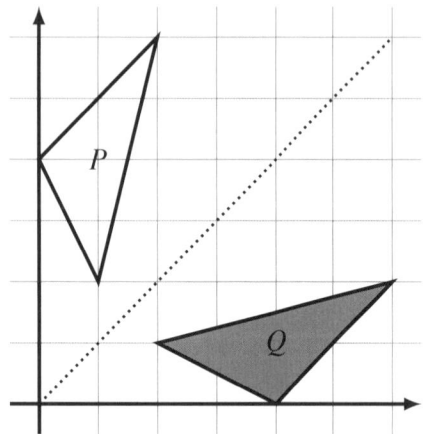

32.2 Rotation

Example 32.2.1

(a) Rotate 90° clockwise about the center (1,0)

(b)
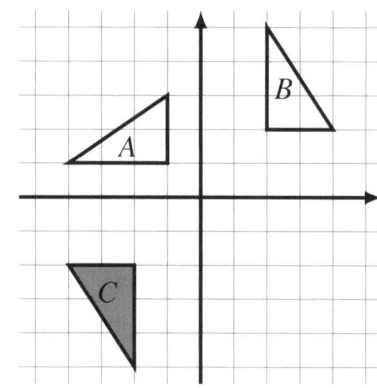

32.3 Translation

Example 32.3.1

(a) Translate by $\begin{pmatrix} -5 \\ -2 \end{pmatrix}$

(b)
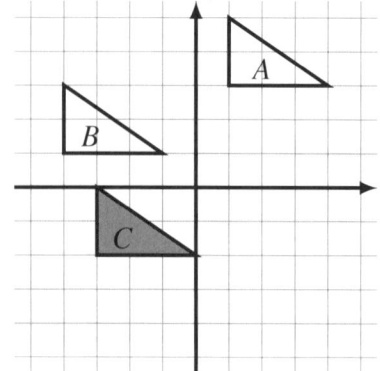

32.4 Enlargement

Example 32.4.1

(a) Enlargement by scale factor of 2 at center $(-5,0)$

(b)
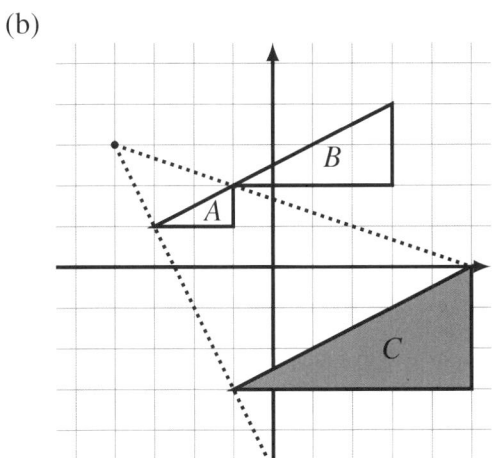

Example 32.4.2

(a) Enlargement by scale factor of -3 at center $(2,-2)$

(b)
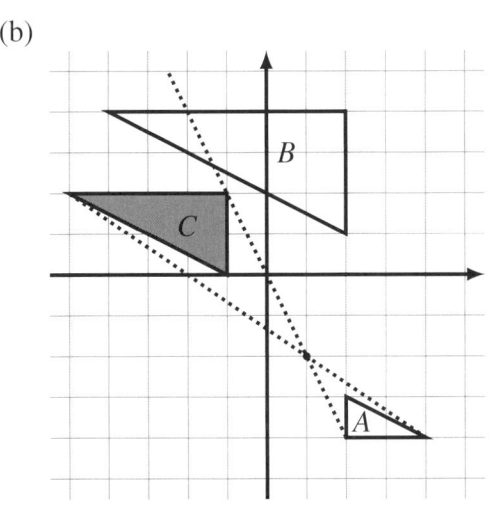

Example 32.4.3

(a)
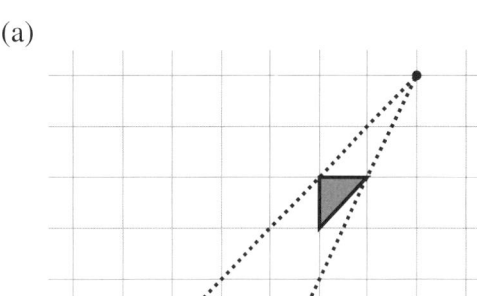

(b)
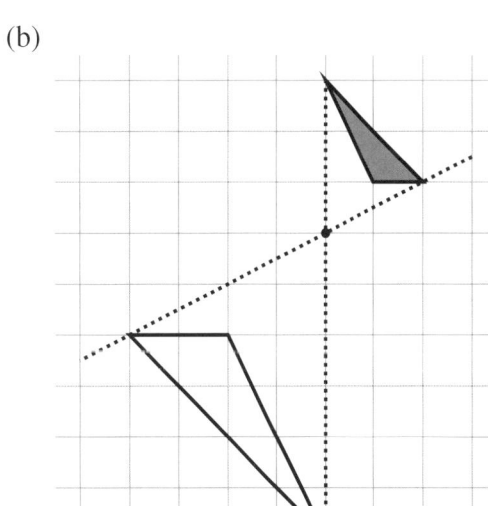

33 Simple Probability

33.1 Probability

Example 33.1.1

(a) $\dfrac{1}{2}$ (b) $\dfrac{1}{6}$ (c) 0 (d) 1

Example 33.1.2

(a) 0.2 (b) $\dfrac{1}{2}$ (c) 30%

Example 33.1.3

$3x + x = 1 - 0.1 - 0.3$

$x = 0.15$

Letter	P	Q	R	S
Probability	0.1	0.3	0.45	0.15

33.2 Complementary Event

Example 33.2.1

(a) $\dfrac{4}{52} = \dfrac{1}{13}$

(b) $1 - \dfrac{1}{13} = \dfrac{12}{13}$

33.3 Relative Frequency and Expected Frequency

Example 33.3.1

#	0	1	2	3	4 +
f	0.2	0.42	0.28	0.085	0.015

Example 33.3.2

(a) $1 - 0.35 - 0.2 = 0.45$

(b) $500 \times 0.45 = 225$

34 Further Probability

34.1 Combined Events

Example 34.1.1

(a) $\dfrac{4}{52} + \dfrac{4}{52} = \dfrac{8}{52} = \dfrac{2}{13}$

(b) $\dfrac{13}{52} + \dfrac{4}{52} - \dfrac{1}{52} = \dfrac{16}{52} = \dfrac{4}{13}$

Example 34.1.2

(a) $0.9 \times 0.8 = 0.72$

(b) $0.1 \times 0.2 = 0.02$

(c) $0.9 \times 0.2 + 0.1 \times 0.8 = 0.26$

(d) $1 - (0.1 \times 0.2) = 0.98$

34.2 Possibility Diagrams

Example 34.2.1

(a) $\dfrac{5}{36}$

(b) $\dfrac{26}{36} = \dfrac{5}{18}$

(c) $\dfrac{6}{36} = \dfrac{1}{6}$

34.3 Prob. with Tree Diagrams

Example 34.3.1

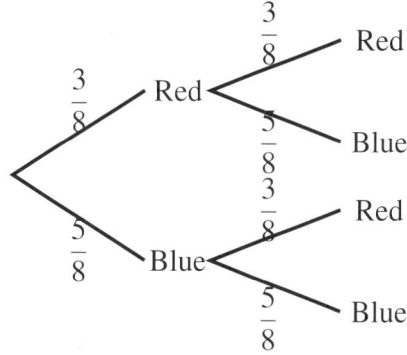

(a) $P(RR) = \dfrac{3}{8} \times \dfrac{3}{8} = \dfrac{9}{64}$

(b) $P(RB) + P(BR) = \dfrac{3}{8} \times \dfrac{5}{8} + \dfrac{5}{8} \times \dfrac{3}{8} = \dfrac{15}{32}$

34.4 Prob. with Venn Diagrams

Example 34.4.1

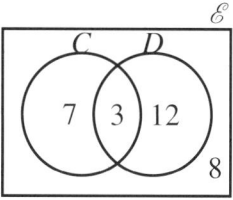

(a) $P(\text{Cat or Dog}) = P(C \cup D) = \dfrac{22}{30}$

(b) $P(\text{Cat and No Dog}) = P(C \cap D') = \dfrac{7}{30}$

(c) $P(\text{No Dog}) = P(D') = \dfrac{15}{30}$

34.5 Conditional Probability

Example 34.5.1

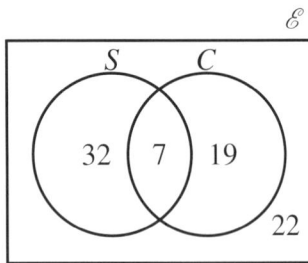

(a) $P(S \cap C \mid C) = \dfrac{7}{26}$

(b) $P(S \mid C') = \dfrac{32}{54}$

Example 34.5.2

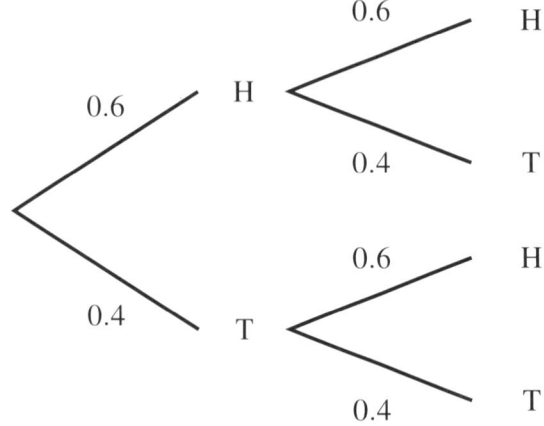

(a) $P(HT) + P(TH) = 0.6 \times 0.4 + 0.4 \times 0.6 = 0.24 + 0.24 = 0.48$

(b) $P(2\text{nd } H \mid 1\text{st } T) = \dfrac{P(2\text{nd } H \cap 1\text{st } T)}{P(1\text{st } T)}$
$= \dfrac{0.4 \times 0.6}{0.4} = 0.6$

Example 34.5.3

(a) $P(F \cap 30s) = \dfrac{42}{300}$

(b) $P(F \mid 30s) = \dfrac{n(F \cap 30s)}{n(30s)} = \dfrac{42}{78}$

35 Classifying and Organizing Data

35.1 Classifying Data

Example 35.1.1

(a) Numerical, discrete

(b) Numerical, continuous

(c) Categorical

35.2 Organizing Data

Example 35.2.1

(a)

Number	Tally	Frequency
1	︙	6
2					3
3			1
4				2
5					3

(b)

Number	Tally	Frequency
Red	|||	3
Blue	||||	4
Black	|||	3

Example 35.2.2

(a)

Score	Frequency
50-59	3
60-69	2
70-79	4
80-89	6
90-100	5

(b) 15

(c) 9

Example 35.2.3

(a)

Stem	Leaf
22	1 2 5 7 8
23	3 6 7 7 7 9
24	0 3 4 5 8 8
25	2 8 9

(b) 6 trees

(c) $\dfrac{11}{20}$

36 Displaying Data with Charts

36.1 Pictograms

Example 36.1.1

(a) Amy

(b) 5 hours and 15 minutes

(c)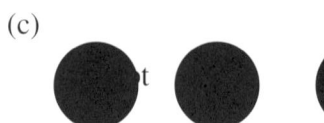

36.2 Bar Charts

Example 36.2.1

(a)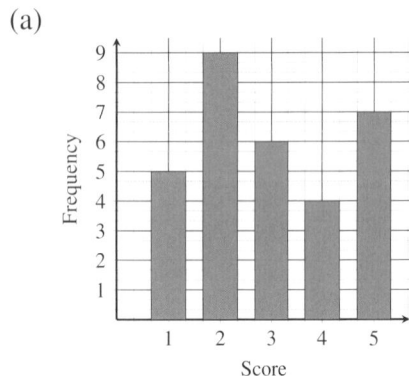

(b) $1 \times 5 + 2 \times 9 + 3 \times 6 + 4 \times 4 + 5 \times 7$
$= 92$

36.3 Pie Charts

Example 36.3.1

(a) Food

(b) $\dfrac{120}{360} = \dfrac{1}{3}$

(c) $x \times \dfrac{1}{3} = 180 \quad \therefore x = \$540$

(d) $\dfrac{97.5}{540} \times 360 = 65°$

(e) $360 - 120 - 90 - 65 = 85°$

$540 \times \dfrac{85}{360} = \$127.5$

36.4 Histograms

Example 36.4.1

Class width	Frequency density
5	$11 \div 5 = 2.2$
5	$34 \div 5 = 6.8$
10	$18 \div 10 = 1.8$
15	$48 \div 15 = 3.2$
10	$9 \div 10 = 0.9$

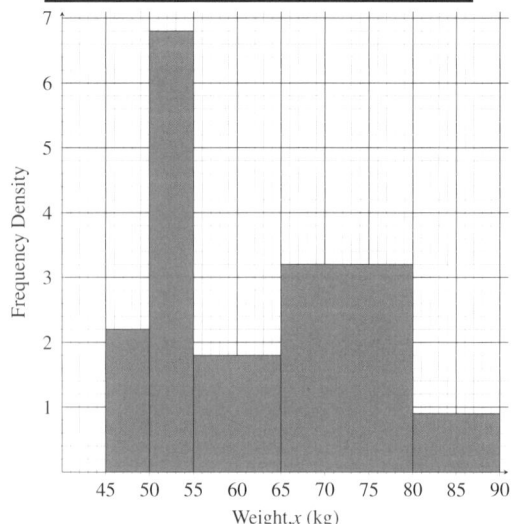

37 Central Tendency and Spread

37.1 Individual Data

Example 37.1.1

$$\frac{2+4+9+12+8+7+6+3}{8} = \frac{51}{8}$$

Example 37.1.2

(a) List: 1 2 5 5 7 8 9

$\to \left(\frac{7+1}{2}\right)$th Num. = 4th Num. = 5

(b) List: 1 2 5 5 7 8 9 11

$\to \left(\frac{8+1}{2}\right)$th Num. = 4.5th Num. =

Avg of 4th and 5th = $\frac{5+7}{2} = 6$

Example 37.1.3

(a) 3

(b) 2 and 5 (Bimodal)

(c) No mode

Example 37.1.4

(a) Range = $7 - 1 = 6$

(b) Range = $9 - (-2) = 11$

37.2 Frequency Table

Example 37.2.1

(a) $\dfrac{0 \cdot 4 + 1 \cdot 13 + 2 \cdot 9 + 3 \cdot 7 + 4 \cdot 2}{4 + 13 + 9 + 7 + 2}$

$= \dfrac{60}{35} \approx 1.71$

(b) $\left(\dfrac{35+1}{2}\right)$th = 18th $\to$ Midean = 2

(c) Mode is 1 (Greatest frequency 13)

(d) Range = $4 - 0 = 4$

37.3 Grouped Frequency Table

Example 37.3.1

(a) $\dfrac{18 \cdot 6 + 23 \cdot 12 + 28 \cdot 15 + 33 \cdot 8 + 38 \cdot 9}{6 + 12 + 15 + 8 + 9}$

≈ 28.2

(b) $\left(\dfrac{50+1}{2}\right)$th = 25.5th

$\to$ The median is in the interval 26-30.

(c) The modal class is 26-30, since it has the highest frequency.

37.4 Stem and Leaf Diagram

Example 37.4.1

(a) 59.9   (c) 70

(b) $\dfrac{58+65}{2} = 61.5$ (d) $79 - 41 = 38$

38 Continuous Data Representation

38.1 Box-and-Whisker Plots

Example 38.1.1

Minimum: 49

Lower Quartile: 59

Median: 69

Upper Quartile: 82

Maximum: 93

Example 38.1.2

(a) 225

(b) 192.5

(c) 42.5

(d) $120 \times 0.75 = 90$

38.2 Cumulative Frequency

Example 38.2.1

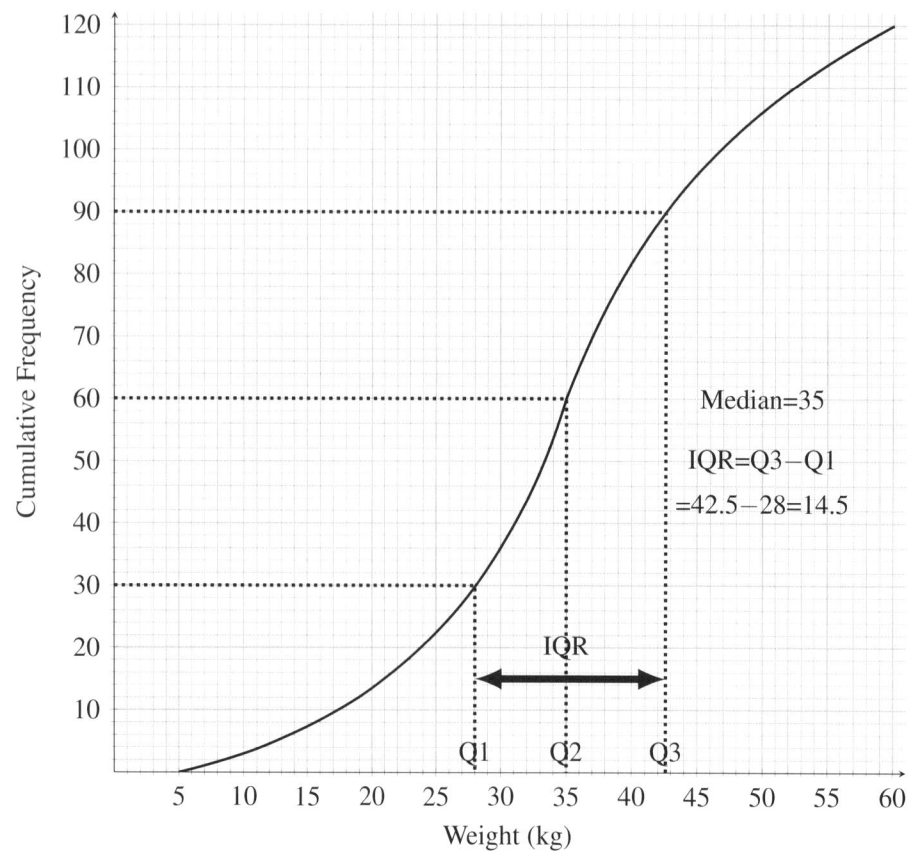

Median=35

IQR=Q3−Q1
=42.5−28=14.5

39 Continuous Data Representation

39.1 Correlation

No examples

39.2 Line of Best Fit

Example 39.2.1

(a) and (c)

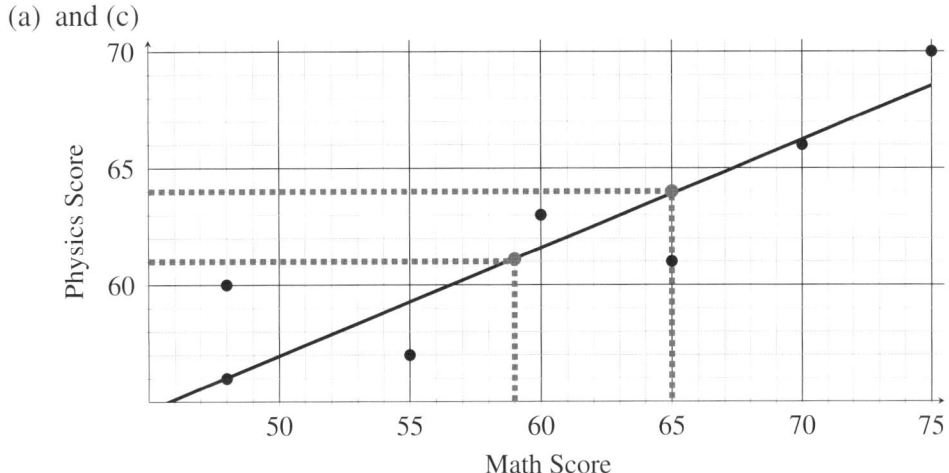

(b) There is a positive correlation between the two scores. Students with higher scores on math generally have higher scores on physics.

(d) 61

(e) 65